Counselling and Psychotherapy

Counselling and Psychotherapy after Domestic Violence

A Client View of What Helps Recovery

Jeannette K. Roddy
University of Sunderland, UK

First published 2015 by
PALGRAVE MACMILLAN

Palgrave Macmillan in the UK is an imprint of Macmillan Publishers Limited,
registered in England, company number 785998, of Houndmills, Basingstoke,
Hampshire RG21 6XS.

Palgrave Macmillan in the US is a division of St Martin's Press LLC,
175 Fifth Avenue, New York, NY 10010.

Palgrave Macmillan is the global academic imprint of the above companies
and has companies and representatives throughout the world.

Palgrave® and Macmillan® are registered trademarks in the United States,
the United Kingdom, Europe and other countries.

ISBN 978-1-349-55740-0   ISBN 978-1-137-43459-3 (eBook)
DOI 10.1057/9781137434593

This book is printed on paper suitable for recycling and made from fully
managed and sustained forest sources. Logging, pulping and manufacturing
processes are expected to conform to the environmental regulations of the
country of origin.

A catalogue record for this book is available from the British Library.

A catalog record for this book is available from the Library of Congress.

To my husband Dermot
With love

Contents

Tables

Acknowledgements

This book is based largely on the research completed as part of my PhD and I am grateful for the support I received from: York St John University, for making the funds available for a PhD studentship in domestic violence counselling, without which this project would still be an aspiration; Dr Lynne Gabriel, who encouraged me to formulate my research plan and apply for the funding and then, as my supervisor, saw the PhD through to successful completion; Dr Hazel James, my second PhD supervisor, who spent hours critiquing my written work to raise the standard of my writing to that required for a higher degree and publication; the agencies involved in the research, for their enthusiastic participation, their facilitation of the research interviews and their continued interest in the work.

The idea to publish a book at some point was a part of the research plan, although I did not know if it would come to fruition. I am thankful for meeting Nicola Jones at a research conference near the end of my PhD to talk about plans for later publication and for her guidance through the Palgrave Macmillan process to the publishing contract. Her support for, and belief in, the book helped it to come into being. I am also thankful to my colleagues Carolyn Knaggs, Becki Linley and Katerina Dogiama, who read and commented so helpfully on the script prior to its completion.

On a more personal note, writing this book immediately after concluding my PhD meant that the intensive writing process required was extended by many months. It would not have been possible to spend the many hours and days writing at the computer without the support, patience and tolerance of my family and friends. I am grateful to them all. In particular, I want to thank my husband Dermot, who has supported my transition from engineer to counsellor, encouraged me to do the research, and read and provided valuable comments on everything I have written.

Finally, I would like to thank the 20 participants involved in the research for volunteering to take part and for their courage, openness and honesty in sharing their counselling experiences in the hope that others might gain. Without their participation and commitment, none of this would have been possible.

Abbreviations

BACP	British Association for Counselling & Psychotherapy
CBT	Cognitive Behavioural Therapy
CTS	Conflict Tactics Scale
DV	Domestic Violence
EMDR	Eye Movement Desensitisation and Reprocessing
IPV	Interpersonal Violence
LGBTI	Lesbian, Gay, Bisexual, Transgender/Transsexual and Intersexed
NICE	National Institute for Health and Care Excellence
NVAWS	National Violence Against Women Survey
PhD	Doctor of Philosophy
PTGI	Posttraumatic Growth Inventory
PTSD	Posttraumatic Stress Disorder
UK	United Kingdom
USA	United States of America

Introduction

When I decided to retrain as a counsellor early in 2007, I had no idea that writing was to become such a large part of my life. At that time, even beginning a 2,000-word essay felt daunting. As I began my course, my focus was firmly on counselling practice and I felt fortunate that the counselling placements I was offered provided the opportunity to work with abused clients. However, what began as simple curiosity to find ways to improve my practice ultimately became a five-year exploration of what domestic violence (DV) counselling clients found helpful in their recovery, involving many thousands of written words.

Over time, my writing skills improved and some of my work was published, prompting a number of emails from people interested in my research. It helped to know that others were interested in finding out what worked for this client group and why. In fact, while I was training to become a counsellor, I had noticed too that there was very little counselling research available on how to work therapeutically with domestic violence clients. In addition, as I was conducting my research interviews, I was asked specifically by some of the participants if I would write a book at the end of the project, as they wanted their views to be heard by other counsellors and psychotherapists. It seemed that further publication of the research findings could be beneficial in a number of ways. Although we each recognised that the desire to write a book does not necessary result in publication, I undertook to do my best, and after five years scoping, conducting and writing up the research academically, it seemed appropriate to develop the material into something that might be useful to practitioners.

Whilst I cannot claim to have all the answers, I feel that the information generated from the study might be helpful for anyone starting to work in this field. Hence the book has been written with two objectives: to help counsellors, either beginning their training or with some experience, to understand the challenges faced by those who have experienced domestic violence; and to provide a voice to the participants who, through taking part, sought to improve the counselling offered to clients who had experienced domestic violence.

Although the book is based upon PhD research, it is not presented in the form of a thesis. Instead, it has been written to reflect the counselling process as explained by the participants during their interviews, and includes references to relevant research, theories and academic literature at each stage. However, in discussing some of the ideas that have been developed, it has become apparent that there are several differences between this book and others in the field. I want to highlight these differences from the beginning, to avoid any misunderstandings about the basis for the work and how it might be applied:

- The participants in this research had already left their relationships and/or were physically safe. Hence the issues of safety necessarily highlighted in most other domestic violence textbooks were not covered by the counsellors with these clients and are therefore not covered in any detail within this book. This is not to negate or minimise the importance of safety when working in the field of domestic violence. Any safety issues arising from domestic violence are likely to require urgent specialist support and I would urge anyone who is currently in, or counselling someone who is in, an abusive relationship to seek help and guidance from specialist agencies, such as those listed in Appendix 1.
- Although much of the domestic violence literature focuses on the female experience at the hands of a male perpetrator, this study also includes the male experience at the hands of a female perpetrator. A constructivist philosophical framework was used in interpreting the data, that is, new knowledge being constructed as a result of the interaction between the researcher and the participant. The book includes commentary from both female and male clients, and the points made in Chapters 2 and 5 are supported by both. I know from previous presentation and discussion of this material that this can receive a mixed reaction from audiences and, with this in mind, you should consider whether this is the right counselling book for you.
- There are many textbooks which will provide more detail about how and why domestic violence occurs than I have presented here. Whilst I have incorporated some of the key ideas and concepts generally known to be helpful in working with domestic violence, this is not

exhaustive. Instead, appropriate literature sources are signposted for those who wish to know more.

- I am aware that in counselling training, the beginning of therapy is generally seen as the point where the client enters the counselling room, that is, from the practitioner's perspective. However, from the client's perspective, the decision to seek counselling is complex and begins some time before that first meeting. As this study reflects on the client experience, the findings presented include this earlier part of the process and address what can be helpful or hindering from a client perspective in their search for support.
- Finally, the participants were keen to share their experiences of continued growth after counselling. As counsellors, we often end with clients and have no idea of what happens next. In addition, we may assess the efficacy of the service provided using forms that have been designed to meet the needs of the organisation or the commissioner of the service. The participants, however, shared the benefits of counselling as *they* saw them. This provided an opportunity to say how they felt they had benefited, with some commenting that they felt the forms provided at the end of their counselling had not asked the right questions.

As I reflected on how to present the information from the research study, it seemed appropriate to include an explanation about why the study was necessary, given the large amount of domestic violence research already in the public domain. Chapter 1 has been written to help to explain how support for those experiencing domestic violence has developed over the years and where the focus for that support currently lies. The reason for doing so is simple: there are a number of different academic arguments (or philosophical positions) relating to domestic violence and the development of mental illness, which have influenced current policy. It is not yet clear that one position is more appropriate than another and there are merits to each. Many of the literature sources pertinent to this area of research are referred to here and it is the most academically orientated chapter. Despite a large literature base associated with the incidence and causes of domestic violence, the characteristics of perpetrators and victims, and the difficulties of seeking assistance or leaving the relationship, the research base associated with mental health treatment for domestic violence is relatively small and written almost entirely from a professional's perspective. This study, therefore, presented an opportunity to look at the counselling clients' perspective as a way to inform future practice. At the end of Chapter 1, the participants and research process are introduced. The subsequent chapters then describe the findings from the study.

This begins in Chapter 2 by outlining one of the key steps in the process. Here, the participants describe their journey through different referral pathways to find the counselling they needed. They share the factors which were important to them in seeking mental health support and identifying help-seeking pathways. This chapter continues by exploring the idea of trust after domestic violence and how that might be affected by past and present experiences, including previous counselling. In addition, the concepts of hope and hopelessness are introduced as important aspects of help-seeking.

As the participants began counselling, the men and women then experienced different processes. Chapter 3 highlights the counselling process through the eyes of the female participants, whereas Chapter 4 describes the process for the male participants. For both groups, a key factor was the experience of being cared for by their counsellors, as well as the process that assisted in building up trust. Both of these ideas are considered in the context of the literature.

Finally, as the participants ended their counselling and went out into the world, their experiences again show some similarity. Chapter 5 explores common aspects of how the women and men responded after leaving counselling, as well as highlighting some differences in the benefits that they perceived. The research findings indicated little agreement with existing quantitative measures for domestic violence counselling outcomes, but better agreement with other qualitative research. This is discussed and an alternative measure for this client group is proposed.

Chapter 6 provides my interpretation of the findings in the context of the provision of a counselling service and the recruitment and training of counsellors. As I have previously worked as a corporate coach and am now working as a lecturer in counselling at the University of Sunderland, the emphasis in Chapter 6 on interpreting the research findings in the context of counsellor training and development and organisational issues reflects some of my personal interests. I have chosen these areas because I believe they could be helpful and important to anyone trying to provide counselling to domestic violence clients. Finally, Chapter 7 draws together the findings and relates them back to the questions posed in Chapter 1.

As you read this book, you may feel challenged by it in some way. Although I have tried to be as balanced as I can in writing it, I am aware that presenting women and men together in the same piece of work on domestic violence can provoke powerful emotions. As one academic commented, 'I had no idea I felt this strongly'. If you read the book and feel that way, I invite you to sit with both what feels appropriate and what feels challenging, and explore why this might be the case for you. Certainly in my own journey through this research, I have had to do so on many occasions.

What I have aimed to present here are the views of 20 participants who have suffered at the hands of a partner or family member. The sections in each chapter represent important steps in their counselling processes, analysed as part of my PhD. Although the presentation of the findings is very different to that in the thesis (Roddy, 2014), the underlying work is the same. The sections are therefore an accurate representation of the work completed and the views of the participants as presented.

However, the underlying processes which were identified and defined as trust, hope and compassion are my interpretation of the processes observed. Domestic violence is not yet recognised as a specialist counselling area in the UK and I believe this is partly because we have been unable to show any critical differences in the approach to working with this client group compared with others. What I am offering here is a possible explanation for the difficulties that have been observed and written about, together with a framework for good practice. If nothing else, it may spark a debate about why this is, or is not, a possible theory.

No judgements as to the merits of one client group over the other are intended in what has been written, although at times I have made observations on my perception of the relative fairness of the different support systems. Some of this book provides an explanation of how our knowledge has developed and its implications for the way we support victims/survivors of domestic violence today. If we understand the situation we are in, it may become easier to see how things might change. Equally, it shows the challenges that those of us involved in this area may face in making changes for the benefits of our clients.

Through the interviews with participants, it became clear that there was a need for mental health support which worked with not only the effects of physical domestic violence but also the effects of psychological abuse. In listening to participants, some interpretation about the counselling process was necessary to align their observations with current theory. This in turn has provided some possible insight into why this type of counselling has nuances that are different to other standard approaches, yet also endorses the view that many counsellors would be able to work effectively with this group of clients given the right training, experience and understanding of the client process.

I hope to have provided an engaging resource for practitioners who are interested in hearing what clients have to say, together with sufficient background information for those who want to put the work in context both through literature and methodology review. I would like to encourage further dialogue in the profession about the best way to work with domestic violence clients, to the benefit of those individuals. With that in mind, I hope you find the book useful and thought-provoking.

1

Differing Views in Research and Practice

What is domestic violence?

There have been references to physical harm in heterosexual relationships in religious texts for many years (Colossians 3:19; Sura 4:34) and hence the concept of violence occurring within the family between intimate partners is not new. However, the experience of domestic violence has often been hidden behind closed doors as individuals have struggled to share the difficulties they were having with their relationship. More recently, this form of abuse has become more visible in our society as a result of many years of campaigning by groups such as Women's Aid and Refuge, and more recently, ManKind and Respect. Story lines have been written over the years for television programmes such as *Casualty*, *EastEnders* and *Coronation Street* to raise awareness of the issue and to signpost organisations which may be able to help. Press articles highlight times when there is expected to be an increase in violence, such as Christmas when families can be in close contact for a period of days (Pidd, 2013) or during sporting events such as the World Cup (Duell, 2014). These are times when emotions can run high increasing the risk of family disputes and, possibly fuelled by alcohol, potentially leading to serious physical assault.

It is believed that 90% of domestic violence incidents are perpetrated by men on their female partners (Department of Health, 2005) and health guidance focuses on the physical safety of women and children with appropriate referral to advocacy support and third sector refuge organisations for those most at risk. The cost to the UK government of domestic violence was estimated as £3.1bn in 2004, primarily made up of legal costs associated with protecting victims from further harm and medical costs from treating the injuries sustained (Walby, 2004).

Statistics showing that two women per week are killed by their male partner highlight the need for women to take action to leave highly abusive relationships quickly (Women's Aid, 2007). This had been addressed through increased funding from the UK government to provide more advocates (Home Office, 2011) to support women with children in protecting themselves from their abusive partners, which in turn may reduce the cost burden on the public sector.

This view of domestic violence has been described as the public story (Donovan, 2014), that is, abuse perpetrated by men on women. Although it is generally accepted as primarily an issue for heterosexual women, domestic violence is also experienced within Lesbian, Gay, Bisexual, Transgender/Transsexual and Intersexed (LGBTI) communities and by heterosexual males. The latest definition of domestic violence in the UK (Home Office, 2012), implemented in 2013, clearly states that such abuse is not only male to female, but can include same sex relationships and female to male abuse, as well as being intergenerational. The definition includes not only physical violence but also sexual, financial, emotional and psychological abuse, introducing the concepts of controlling, threatening or coercive behaviour. Subsequently the government has indicated its intention to create a new offence for such behaviour, to allow prosecution and punishment (Home Office, 2014).

Although these actions by the government indicate an acknowledgement of the potential seriousness of psychological abuse, historical spending on mental health services for victims of DV has been relatively small. When considering Walby's (2004) study, the amount estimated as spent on mental health was just over 5% (£176m) of the total spent on DV (at £3.1bn). The updated study (Walby, 2009) omitted spending on mental health, suggesting that the expenditure was not sufficiently large to highlight. It would appear that the cost of mental health provision as a result of domestic violence is relatively small compared to other costs, supporting the continued priority for physical safety. Nevertheless, health guidance for responding to domestic violence, which was rewritten in 2014, now specifies the need to provide evidence-based treatment for any mental health conditions, either pre-existing or developed as a result of their experience, for victims (National Institute for Health and Clinical Excellence, 2014).

Although the recognition of the need for mental health services for those who have experienced domestic violence is welcomed, the requirement for evidence-based treatment may prove problematic. A government funded report (Ramsay, Rivas and Feder, 2005) concluded that the quantitative evidence base for mental health interventions with

DV was poor and, in alignment with previous reports (Chalk, King, National Research Council/Institute of Medicine et al., 1998; Wathan and MacMillan, 2003), there was little research of an appropriate quality available to make firm recommendations. Ramsay et al. (2005) suggested that, from the available data, advocacy should be preferred over counselling for women still in abusive relationships. Although the government has suggested that there would be additional support for victims available through their new mental health strategy (Department of Health, 2011) this specifically mentions family therapy as an intervention for DV, rather than individual therapy for victims. This could also preclude treatment for those not in a traditional family unit or those who have left their abusive partner. A recent briefing report for GPs does highlight the mental health impact of DV, but focuses on disclosure from women still in relationships and recommends referral to an advocacy service (Sohal, Feder and Johnson, 2012). The new health guidance for DV (National Institute for Health and Clinical Excellence, 2014) specifically asks practitioners to ensure safety assessments are included in any treatment plans and to make referrals to advocacy services and domestic violence agencies as appropriate. All of this guidance seems to indicate that most patients will be in abusive relationships at the time of seeking help and require other support.

Mental health problems after domestic violence

With the current emphasis on responding to the risk to physical safety, through assistance to leave the relationship and the provision of legal sanctions against violent spouses, life for individuals after leaving a domestically violent relationship has received much less attention. Even so, the mental health implications of living with a physically abusive partner have been recognised for many years (Walker, 1979; Dutton, 1992; Herman, 1992; Sanderson, 2008; Nicolson, 2010) and can lead to an increased risk of depression, suicidal ideation, posttraumatic stress disorder and lack of trust (termed general suspiciousness when first identified by Walker (1979)). Whilst Ramsay et al. (2005) recommended psychological intervention for those who had left their relationship and subsequently suffered depression or lack of self-esteem, they felt they could not recommend a specific form of treatment as there was insufficient evidence. Instead they suggested that further research was required to find out more about what women needed and it is hoped that this book will help with that request. The question is perhaps not only whether mental health issues develop before or from domestic violence, but also whether they continue once the relationship is over.

Depression

One of the most cited research papers involving a meta-analysis of earlier DV research (Golding, 1999), suggested that mental health problems were likely to be present after experiencing DV. For example, Golding (1999) found that the average prevalence of depression within those studies was 47.6%, compared with general population studies showing rates of depression between 10.2% and 21.3%. She also noted that on average 60.6% of women in refuges reported depression. Whilst she concluded this may be due to the recent violence they had experienced, it is also possible that fleeing to a refuge and leaving behind one's previous life had an effect. What is perhaps more striking about the data is that experiencing severe violence requiring a move to a refuge only increased the proportion of women feeling depressed by 13% on average. However, it is possible that for some women, making the decision to leave could have had a positive effect. Other factors can play a part in developing depression, including living alone, having a low income or being unemployed (Hegarty, Gunn, Chondros et al., 2004), each of which could be factors for individuals potentially relocating. Perhaps all that can be stated with certainty from the data is that a woman who has experienced domestic violence has a greater risk of developing depression.

This shows the difficulty for researchers in establishing whether the reported depression is a result only of the abuse or whether changed life circumstances play a part. It may be inappropriate to make assessments or judgements based only on the degree of violence in the relationship as past history, psychological abuse, other relational issues and current life situation may also have an impact. For example, in a study involving 403 women from Northwest USA who had had physically abusive relationships, two-thirds of the research participants had experienced domestic abuse as children and around half had suffered some form of childhood sexual assault (Walker, 2000). This description of having a history of previous abuse has been found in other research (Howard, Riger, Campbell et al., 2003; Hegarty et al., 2004; Rushlow, 2009), although the proportion measured has been as low as 25% of the participants. This still indicates a reasonable probability that some women experiencing depression after DV will have a childhood history that may, in part, be contributing to their current mental health issues.

There has been continued debate about the extent to which DV experienced as an adult, rather than previous life events, plays a part in the individual's mental health (Ehrensaft, Moffitt and Caspi, 2006). One finding from a survey of 444 Italian women found that DV does impair mental health, but that the impairment is greater for those who suffered childhood abuse (Romito, Turan and De Marchi, 2005). On the other hand, a UK meta-analysis of 41 studies from across the world could only conclude that individuals with existing mental health issues were at higher risk of experiencing interpersonal violence (IPV) (Trevillion, Oram, Feder et al., 2012). This is a complex issue which is difficult to analyse quantitatively due to an individual's continued experiences, both positive and negative, throughout life. Experiencing childhood abuse will not necessarily result in the abuse continuing through DV into adulthood. In addition, it is important to note that not all people experiencing DV will suffer from mental health problems. It is possible that other factors are present.

Learned helplessness

Another study, conducted with 101 women from eight refuges in Israel, found learned helplessness to be a statistically significant factor in developing depression whilst the total amount of violence perpetrated was not (Bargai, Ben-Shakhar and Shalev, 2007). 'Learned helplessness' is a term used to explain what happens to people when they are placed in a situation where, no matter what response they make, they are powerless to affect the outcome (Seligman, 1975). Over time, the number of attempts the individual makes to change things diminishes. The person learns that it makes no difference what they try and they begin to believe that they are powerless now and in the future. This concept was later developed in the USA to describe 'Battered Woman Syndrome' (Walker, 1977). This linked the helplessness potentially learned in childhood as a result of experienced abuse with the helplessness experienced in adulthood through DV, offering an explanation for why people who suffer childhood abuse may be more susceptible to its continuation in later life. However, learned helplessness does not specifically require the presence of physical violence but does require a means of control over the individual. This could include, for example, the threat of violence to the individual or others, or the threat to disclose shaming information to others.

The association of feelings of powerlessness with depression after DV was also noted from a longitudinal study which followed women leaving a refuge (Campbell, Sullivan and Davidson, 1995). The study assessed 83% of the women as depressed to some extent on leaving and after ten weeks this had reduced to 59% of the women. However, an assessment six months later found no further reduction, even for those who had remained free of violence during that time. Campbell et al. (1995) commented that the women who still felt powerless after leaving and had poor social support networks were more likely to remain depressed. The introduction of poor social networks as a concept is important here. Aspects of power and control which have been identified within DV models of abusive behaviour include isolation of the individual, as well as economic, emotional, sexual and psychological factors (Domestic Abuse Intervention Programs, 2012), as in the current UK definition of DV discussed earlier. Isolation from family and friends could be described as both emotional and psychological abuse.

More recent research findings suggest that experiencing psychological abuse may be a more significant factor in poor mental health after DV than previously found. In a three year longitudinal study of 2,639 women within families in the USA (Adkins and Kamp Dush, 2010) the greatest increases in depression were seen in those living in a physically and psychologically abusive environment. Perhaps surprisingly, at the end of the study, those women who had left their abusive relationship appeared on average to have the same levels of depression as those who had remained. Leaving the relationship could create physical safety but psychological aspects of the abuse, such as feelings of powerlessness, could remain unaddressed. The National Violence Against Women Survey (NVAWS) in the USA involving 6,790 women and 7,122 men, found that all forms of IPV resulted in depressive symptoms for both men and women, although those symptoms increase where psychological IPV through power and control (assessed using items from the Power and Control Scale (Johnson, 1996)) was specifically used (Coker, Davis, Arias et al., 2002).

Physical or psychological abuse

A comprehensive study investigating lifetime and recent instances of physical and emotional abuse was conducted in Valencia, Spain (Pico-Alfonso, Garcia-Linares, Celda-Navarro et al., 2006). The study recruited 182 women, 52 of whom had not been abused and 130 of whom were victims of IPV, from the local community. All of the women in the study who had been physically abused (75) had also been psychologically abused, and 25 of these women had also been sexually abused. Of the 55 women who had been psychologically but not physically abused, nine had also been sexually abused. Suicidal thoughts were experienced by

7.7% of women who had not been abused, rising to 43.6% for those who had been psychologically abused. This suggests that psychological abuse alone can have a negative impact on mental health. Where physical and psychological abuse were combined, 58.7% of the women reported suicidal thoughts. Roughly 1 in 4 of the abused women in the study reported making a suicide attempt and this rose to 1 in 2 where physical abuse was also present. This increase in suicide attempts in response to physical violence has been reported elsewhere (McLaughlin, O'Carroll and O'Connor, 2012) but it is also important to note the relatively high rates of suicide attempts without physical violence. Data from the UK suggests that there may be three completed suicides and 30 suicide attempts for women each week as a result of domestic violence in the UK (Webster, 2015), although this could be an underestimate. From a mental health perspective, this study suggests that such suicide attempts may have been prompted by psychological and/or physical abuse.

Currently, we have no robust data on the extent of psychological abuse in relationships in part because there is still no agreement on how this could be most appropriately measured (Follingstad, 2007). However, data has been collected globally to differentiate between physical and non-physical abuse (Straus, 2009). Such data is available in the UK from the National Crime Survey 2010/2011 (Smith, Osborne, Lau et al., 2012). This suggested that around 7% of women (1.2 million) and 5% of men (800,000) over the age of 16 were victims of domestic violence in the previous 12 months. Of those, 57% of female and 46% of male victims suffered non-physical abuse whilst about a quarter of men and women suffered a physical injury as a result. This suggests that there are twice as many men and women potentially suffering from forms of abuse other than physical violence. It also suggests that the number of physical attacks (excluding sexual assault) experienced by men and women are comparable, although this does not allow for the severity of the attack. Nevertheless, this presents a different situation to that given at the beginning of this chapter, where it was suggested that 90% of DV attacks were male to female (Department of Health, 2005).

The difference in these positions can be explained through different academic perspectives. Broadly, there appear to be three different views: family systems theorists (for example M. A. Straus), feminist researchers (for example M. P. Johnson) and psychologists interested in perpetrator violence (for example D.G. Dutton).

Initially, feminist researchers in the UK identified the cause of DV as male dominance within a relationship, which they believed was supported through a patriarchal society (Dobash and Dobash, 1980). Around the same time, in the USA, family violence surveys involving a cross-section of the American public, like the UK one above (Smith et al., 2012) showed that men and women perpetrated violence in roughly equal measure at home (Straus, Gelles and Steinmetz, 1980; Straus, 2009). Feminist researchers then identified specific patterns of systematic abuse as relating specifically to DV which described the tactics and strategies that men might use to dominate their partners (Pence and Paymar, 1993; Domestic Abuse Intervention Programs, 2012). The family systems group in turn produced a measurement of conflict within the relationship to identify negotiation, psychological aggression, physical assault, sexual coercion and injury within a relationship: the Conflict Tactics Scale (CTS2) (Straus, Hamby, Boney-McCoy et al., 1996).

This approach was criticised by feminist researchers, suggesting that the conclusions drawn relied too heavily on data analysis and the reported actions lacked any understanding of the motivation behind, meaning of, and context for, DV (Ross and Babcock, 2009). Measuring defined actions without linking those to a pattern of victimisation or control could simply reflect a desire to get one's own way rather than systematic abuse. Therefore behaviours which had been described as abusive in men and now measured in women could not necessarily be construed as indicative of DV. To support this view three different categories of abusive behaviour from a feminist perspective were defined: violent resistance (acknowledging that women will at times want to fight back to regain some control prior to leaving their partner), intimate (rather than patriarchal) terrorists (acknowledging that the domination of a family may not be completely about patriarchy or gender) and mutual violent control (where two intimate terrorists are fighting for control of the relationship) (Johnson and Ferraro, 2000). Although this model appeared to accept that women were capable of exerting power and control, Johnson and Ferraro (2000) indicated that the psychological effects of abuse would be felt mainly by those suffering from intimate terrorism (male or female), which equated to a very small proportion of those involved in conflict situations and, in their opinion, almost all of them women. Thus they argued that psychological harm resulting from DV occurred in a very small number of female cases.

However, linking psychological harm specifically to a combination of severe physical and psychological abuse was at odds with some of the earliest research in DV (Walker, 1979). This had clearly identified psychological and physical abuse as separate and important factors in causing emotional harm. Included within Walker's (1979) research was identification of the Cycle Theory of Violence, a cyclical pattern of abusive and reconciliatory behaviour by the man which holds or binds the female partner psychologically to the relationship. This pattern was later also confirmed by psychologists studying male perpetrator behaviour (Dutton, 1995) and the Cycle Theory of Violence is still recognised as a significant part of DV and used as part of training in DV across the world today (Agnew Davies, 2013). Walker's later research only included women who had experienced physical abuse due to the complexity of measuring the impact of psychological abuse alone (Walker, 2000). However she noted that 'the women's ratings showed that the psychological abuse created longer-lasting pain than did many of the physically induced injuries' (Walker, 2000, p. 260).

In 2006, Dutton published a book, *Rethinking Domestic Violence*, stating that perpetrators of both genders could be found (Dutton, 2006). The book was welcomed by those who supported the premise of male victims and female perpetrators in the wider context of DV and opened up discussion about whether the dominant view of a patriarchal society as the underlying reason for DV was sufficient (Straus, 2007). The subsequent discussion regarding gender and DV among academics has been heated (Johnson, 2011; Dutton, 2012) and is beyond the scope of this book. Nevertheless, the development of the arguments about the impact of physical and psychological abuse can be seen. Equally, at this point, there appears to be no agreement between the parties. Instead, what seems to be emerging is a description of DV which shows the capability for both men and women to be physically and/or psychologically abusive to their partners. Whilst both men and women may experience this abuse at the hands of their partner, it is also possible that some people may at times be both victim and abuser, that is, they may experience a co-abusive or a bi-directionally abusive relationship. This may be true for relationships irrespective of gender or sexuality, and there may be a number of different factors influencing their resultant behaviour including their culture, attachment style and individual characteristics (Langhinrichsen-Rohling, 2010).

From a therapeutic perspective, most counselling philosophies would encourage a client approach involving positive regard and non-judgement. It is much less important to determine where the blame lies for psychological distress and much more important to understand and work with the distress from a client perspective. Whilst it may be helpful to understand the range of dynamics that may be present when working with someone who has experienced domestic abuse, it can be unhelpful to arrive in the therapy room with pre-conceived ideas (Richards, 2011). Nevertheless, the different philosophical debates can have an impact on the information available to counsellors who practise in this area. Although there is growing evidence about the psychological impact of DV on both men and women (Coker et al., 2002; Hines, Brown and Dunning, 2007; Hines and Douglas, 2009; Hines and Douglas, 2011) other researchers have continued to focus the discussion on mental health as a result of the use and impact of physical violence on women (Lombard, 2013). In a recent literature review on female and male outcomes following DV, Caldwell et al. (2012) concluded that women suffer significantly more than men as a result of DV. The reasoning for this was the presence of greater injuries, fear and posttraumatic stress suffered, confirming the need to continue to focus on reducing physical violence. However, the paper presented no conclusive evidence of worse physical health outcomes for women as a result of their injuries or of an increased risk of depression, anxiety and substance abuse compared with male victims. The presence of depression and anxiety in both women and men who have experienced DV may suggest there has been psychological harm, in which case both men and women are likely to benefit from counselling (National Collaborating Centre for Mental Health, 2009; British Association for Counselling and Psychotherapy, 2013). Perhaps ironically, by focusing on the differences between men and women to build the case for female safety, rather than considering and validating the common need for psychological support, the authors are potentially undermining the case for wider funding of counselling for women.

Unfortunately, due to the research focus to date on determining the mental health effects of experiencing DV on women, there has been very little research conducted with men in this situation as most male studies have been focused on understanding perpetrator behaviour. However, one such study, which involved 57 couples who sought marital counselling for their relationship in the USA (Vivian and Langhinrichsen-Rohling, 1994) found that there were differences in the way men and women reacted psychologically to violence in the relationship, whether experiencing or perpetrating violence. Whilst women were more likely to suffer from moderate depression as a result of aggression from either partner, also found in a later study (Cascardi, O'Leary and Schlee, 1999), men reportedly suffered moderate depression only when they were being victimised, that is, the aggression was aimed at them. In this case, their depression was assessed at a slightly higher level than their female partner. However, the NVAWS found that experiencing all forms of IPV resulted in depressive symptoms for both men and women, but with higher levels where psychological IPV through power and control was specifically used (Coker et al., 2002). More recently, a study with 420 men enrolled in a health care system in Northwest USA concluded that both physical and emotional abuse can produce depressive symptoms in men over the age of 55 (Reid, Bonomi, Rivara et al., 2008) and, in keeping with the research on women, more severe symptoms related to more severe physical abuse. Although the research to date has shown a link between DV and depression for men, as with the female research, there is no consensus on whether psychological or physical abuse is more likely to be the main contributing factor although, as for women, the combination of the two has been found to be significant (Hines and Douglas, 2010b). As research teams begin to engage more with men who have experienced domestic violence, there appears to be more evidence that men, as well as women, can experience mental health difficulties (Hines and Douglas, 2015).

Suicide and suicidal ideation

In the UK in 2012, 4,590 men and 1,391 women committed suicide (Scowcroft, 2014). Perhaps surprisingly the data indicates that suicide is most prevalent in men aged 35–55, and for women aged 40–60. In addition, a research report by the Samaritans on male suicide suggested that relationship difficulties, particularly where they may feel shamed by (rather than ashamed of) their partner's behaviour, may be a particularly important aspect of their decision (Wyllie, Platt, Browlie et al., 2012). There is currently very little research about suicidal ideation resulting from domestic violence from a male perspective, although one study involving men and women indicated that physical violence in adulthood makes suicidal ideation 27 times more likely (Calder, McVean and Yang, 2010) than for non-abused individuals. On average, men complete more suicides than women by a factor of 3.5 (Scowcroft, 2014). On the figures given earlier by Smith et al. (2012) plus Calder et al.'s (2010) study, it is possible that the number of men who commit suicide in the UK as a result of domestic violence is higher than for women. This is due to the much higher suicide completion rate for men, despite the lower numbers of reported victims and slightly lower reported incidence of suicidal ideation. It has been estimated that 150 women commit suicide each year as a result of DV (Webster, 2015) which is higher than the number killed by an abusive partner, although this figure is considered to be an underestimate of the situation. That number could more than double if the number of men were also included.

There is little data relating to how many men may consider, attempt or complete suicide as a result of psychological abuse, although studies with help-seeking men have documented much higher levels of psychological abuse compared with physical abuse in the USA (Hines et al., 2007; Hines and Douglas, 2015) and in the UK (Debbonaire and Panteloudakis, 2013). In addition, men who have been in abusive relationships have raised concerns about their mental health across the world, with many studies confirming counselling as one of the preferred support routes for men (Ansara and Hindin, 2010; Douglas and Hines, 2011; Smith et al., 2012). In comparison, women in the UK are much more likely to seek help from support services and the police, rather than specifically a counsellor (Smith et al., 2012). This may reflect the system of support available in the UK for women, or it may reflect different needs. At this point it is unclear which is more likely to be the case.

The research findings of male triggers for attempting suicide suggest that the breakdown of their marriage, losing touch with their children and challenges to their masculine identities are all important factors (Wyllie et al., 2012). It is appropriate to note that these are all factors described as likely outcomes when considering female to male abuse (Cook, 2009). It is possible that the needs and experiences of male victims of DV are different to those of women. What is important, perhaps, is that there are hundreds of individuals each year who may be taking their own lives as a result of their experiences, both men and women, potentially leaving a large number of children without the opportunity to build a relationship with their parent. Whilst the headlines still highlight that on average seven women and two men are killed each month by their abusive partner (Morrison, 2014), the numbers of men and women committing suicide as a result of their experiences with their abusive partner may be three times higher. For counsellors and psychotherapists, this may make difficult reading and perhaps leads us to question how we can better help this client group.

In the UK, suicidal ideation can be regarded as part of the diagnosis for depression, showing that the depression is particularly severe. Current NICE guidance (National Collaborating Centre for Mental Health, 2009) suggests that a patient in the UK suffering from depression is likely to be treated with anti-depressants and/or referred to counselling. There is nothing within the guidance that suggests depression associated with domestic violence requires any different treatment to depression associated with other factors. However, there are practitioner views that suggest working with this client group can be quite different to normal clinical practice. It is this observation that has motivated professionals in the field to share their knowledge of working with female clients to help other counsellors (Walker, 1979; Dutton, 1992; Sanderson, 2008; Roddy, 2011a; Agnew Davies, 2013).

Posttraumatic stress

For those authors who have considered the process of DV counselling (Herman, 1992; Walker, 1994; Grigsby and Hartman, 1997; Walker, 2000; Dienemann, Campbell, Landenburger et al., 2002; Sanderson, 2008), there seems to be general agreement on the importance of a process, first identified by Herman (1992) in the context of working with trauma, that builds upon a strong therapeutic relationship and involves:

- an initial phase of supporting the client, building their resources and creating a safe environment
- a phase of working through specific issues, current and past
- re-connecting with the outside world and leaving counselling

This is not surprising as much of the literature cites and builds on Herman's clearly articulated work (Herman, 1992) and these three stages reflect the structure she outlined. These models of practice assume that there will be a need to work with the symptoms of trauma presenting within the client as a result of their experiences. This approach has been supported through research studies which identified significant levels of posttraumatic stress disorder (PTSD) within groups of women, particularly those who had accessed shelter from a refuge (Cascardi et al., 1999; Golding, 1999; Humphreys and Thiara, 2003; Araszkiewicz and Dabkowska, 2010). For example, Golding's meta-analysis reported rates of PTSD of between 31% and 84.4% in the study populations compared with rates of 1.3–12.3% measured within the general population of the USA (Golding, 1999). The few studies that have investigated male victims have also found symptoms of PTSD as a result of DV (Coker, Weston, Creson et al., 2005; Hines, 2007; Hines and Douglas, 2011; 2015). The study by Coker et al. (2005) assessed the degree of PTSD present in those who had indicated experiencing DV at moderate to severe for 24% of women and 20% of men, indicating a comparable level.

Although there have been consistent findings regarding the presence of PTSD, there appears to be no conclusive agreement about what may have been the cause. A number of potential causes have been suggested such as: high rates of re-abuse (39%) for women who had already experienced significant levels of DV (Krause, Kaltman, Goodman et al., 2008); the total amount of violence suffered in their lifetimes (Bargai et al., 2007); and the repeated victimisation of a woman through several life events rather than the continued victimisation by one person (Matlow and DePrince, 2012). These theories are based upon the assumption that physical violence is required for PTSD to develop.

More recently, theories relating to the role of shame in the development and/or maintenance of PTSD have been put forward (Harman and Lee, 2010; Beck, McNiff, Clapp et al., 2011; Herman, 2011). Other research from the USA and Spain has linked emotional turmoil and issues of trust and suspiciousness to PTSD (Morrell and Rubin, 2001; Torres, Garcia-Esteve, Navarro et al., 2010). These studies suggest that psychological abuse may therefore have an important role to play. Recent research in Baltimore, USA which compared sexual, physical and psychological violence has shown that the presence of psychological violence is most likely to result in PTSD (Norwood and Murphy, 2012). However, it appears that once PTSD has developed, symptoms may continue for over 12 months after leaving their abusive relationship (Woods, 2000; Mertin and Mohr, 2001). At the end of a three-year longitudinal study conducted in Spain with 91 women, groups containing physically/psychologically-abused and non-abused women showed similar lower levels of PTSD, whilst the levels for individuals who had been psychologically but not physically abused were higher (Blasco-Ros, Sánchez-Lorente and Martinez, 2010).

In the UK, current health treatment guidelines (due to be reviewed in March 2015) do not specifically recognise the possibility of developing PTSD due to DV (National Collaborating Centre for Mental Health, 2005). Instead the focus in the guidance is on processing the trauma caused by single traumatic events or major catastrophic events, such as those treated effectively through Eye Movement Desensitisation and Reprocessing (EMDR). It has been recognised that if the trauma has no clear root, as may be the case with DV, EMDR may not be the best available treatment (Royle and Kerr, 2013) thus presenting a potential problem for DV referrals under the current system. More recently, NICE guidance for DV (National Institute for Health and Clinical Excellence, 2014) has indicated that trauma-focused cognitive behavioural therapy may be a preferred option. However, the literature for PTSD related to shame suggests strategies which help individuals to care and feel compassion for themselves (Harman and Lee, 2010), something Herman's

(1992) model of treatment would do well. Clearly there is still work to be done before final conclusions are drawn.

Although the incidence of depression and PTSD have been discussed separately so far, both PTSD and depression can co-occur after traumatic experiences (Foa, Hembree, Riggs et al., 2001). One USA study indicated that 47% of women who were treated for marital problems and were diagnosed with either depression or PTSD actually had both (Cascardi et al., 1999), whilst another found both disorders in 49% of women from a DV service (Nixon, Resick and Nishith, 2004). Under UK guidance, where both PTSD and depression were diagnosed, the treatment of depression would take precedence which may lead to a prescription for anti-depressants (National Collaborating Centre for Mental Health, 2009). Two recent pieces of research have linked psychotropic drug intake to the continuation of depressive symptoms and PTSD, and poorer outcomes (Blasco-Ros et al., 2010; Gilbert, Morrissey and Domino, 2011), building on previous concerns expressed in the literature regarding the prescription of drugs to contain emotion when an appropriate response may be to explore those emotions (Schwecke, 2009). As research continues to develop links between PTSD and DV, it may be that where psychological abuse is a factor, the provision of a healthy, supportive therapeutic relationship to counteract this, rather than drug treatment, could be highly beneficial.

Lack of trust

Finally, it is worth considering the area of psychological harm identified by Walker (1979) which she linked to experiencing DV: becoming suspicious of or lacking trust in others. Since 1979, the term 'suspiciousness' has become more normally used in describing symptoms of paranoia and schizophrenia. This has resulted in those interested in the effects of DV acknowledging the potential for female victims to lack trust in (for example Sanderson (2008) and Nicolson (2010)), rather than be suspicious of, their partner and potentially the wider community. As therapeutic relationships rely on trust developing between counsellor and client (Cooper, 2008), a client lacking in trust may not be able to make the best use of the opportunity that counselling presents. It had been noted that some client groups, such as trauma victims, seem to need to develop more than the basic level of trust normally thought to be required, for example in cognitive behavioural therapy (CBT) (Castonguay, Constantino, McAleavey et al., 2010). Yet, with the mental health issues already presented, counselling or psychotherapy could be beneficial and it is worth considering what this might mean in the context of therapy.

In psychology, the issue of trust has been linked to attachment theory (Nicolson, 2010). It is generally accepted that individuals who did not have a sufficiently caring caregiver in early life (Winnicott, 1953) may struggle to form relationships or attachments in adult life. However, it is also possible that issues of trust and difficulties with relationships can develop at each stage of life (Erikson, 1966), which can include the period after leaving home and establishing an adult relationship. Thus in the case of DV, issues of trust could develop at any stage of life (childhood and adulthood) in response to life or relationship events and prompting changing attachment patterns.

Attachment terminology varies within the literature. Some researchers use definitions associated with infant attachment: secure, avoidant and anxious or ambivalent (Ainsworth, Blehar, Waters et al., 1978), later updated to include a disorganised pattern (Main and Solomon, 1986). Others prefer more recent adult-related terms (Bartholomew and Horowitz, 1991): secure, pre-occupied, dismissing and fearful. Both agree on the term 'secure attachment', that is, a feeling that, in a difficult situation, the individual can trust themselves to look after themselves, and failing that, they can trust others to step in. Secure individuals can therefore access counselling relatively easily by relying on themselves and/or the counsellor as appropriate. However, individuals who are insecurely attached may feel that, either:

a) They will not be able to take care of themselves and will need someone who can take care of them and they may rely on others for their self-worth (anxious, ambivalent or pre-occupied style); or
b) The only person they can really depend upon is themselves and therefore they minimise the significance of relationships (avoidant or dismissive style); or
c) No-one, including themselves, can truly be relied upon (disorganised or fearful style), yet they feel that they are dependent on others.

Attachment patterns can change over time for individuals in the light of new experiences, resulting in feelings of more or less security. This means that a securely attached individual, who becomes involved in an abusive relationship, may change their views of their own and others' abilities to assist them in difficult or frightening situations.

Studies of women and men who have suffered from DV have assessed most participants as insecurely attached, although there appears to be no agreement on how that insecurity will present. Two studies of women in the process of leaving their relationships (Henderson, Bartholomew and Dutton, 1997; Hick, 2008) each found that more than half of the participants were described as having pre-occupied attachment, although the two studies used different methods of assessing attachment. Henderson et al.'s (1997) Canadian study used a semi-structured interview based on Bartholomew and Horowitz's (1991) four category model, whilst Hick's (2008) USA PhD study used the *Adult Attachment Projective Picture System*. However, the two studies differed in their assessment of the remaining participants with a fearful attachment style identified in Henderson et al.'s (1997) study, but a dismissive attachment style in Hick's (2008) study. Adding further complexity, a USA study using *The Revised Adult Attachment Scale* and involving 32 women who had reported a history of domestic abuse found that most of the women showed a predominantly avoidant style of attachment (Walker, 2009). Interestingly, the women in Walker's (2009) study had an average age of 43, which was 12 years older than in Henderson's study. Studies involving men who were experiencing abuse also reported insecure attachment patterns, with a greater likelihood of being assessed as anxious/pre-occupied in the presence of physical violence (Henderson, Bartholomew, Trinke et al., 2005) and with avoidant attachment patterns when experiencing psychological abuse (Gormley, 2005). The small number of studies and differing methodologies preclude drawing firm conclusions, but it suggests that clients presenting for counselling after DV may exhibit some signs of insecure attachment.

The problem, therapeutically, becomes how to help such clients develop sufficient trust in the counselling relationship to allow the issues associated with DV to be discussed safely and constructively. A strong therapeutic alliance has been shown to be an indicator of successful counselling for some years (Kahn, 1996; Asay and Lambert, 1999; Paulson, Truscott and Stuart, 1999; Martin, Garske and Davis, 2000; Levitt, Butler and Hill, 2006; Cooper, 2008), irrespective of therapeutic orientation and from both a therapist and client perspective. It is also believed that counselling delivered within a strong ethical framework will create a trustworthy environment which can help the clients to make changes in their lives (British Association for Counselling and Psychotherapy, 2010). Whilst trust has been acknowledged as an essential part of good therapeutic practice, the identification of a specific need to build trust as an active part of the therapy is more unusual, less well-defined and therefore potentially more therapeutically complex.

Research into therapeutic trust is surprisingly scarce. Early studies indicated that a client's opinion was influenced more by how trustworthy the other person seemed than by the actual expertise of the individual (Strong, 1968; Rothmeier and Dixon, 1980). Strong (1968) defined a counsellor's trustworthiness through four factors: their reputation; social role or standing; sincerity and openness; and lack of motivation for personal gain. In person-centred terms, this suggested that therapist congruence and positive regard for the client may play a role in building trust. Non-verbal, empathic responses together with the therapist's interpretation of what the client said (Claiborn, 1979; Lee, Uhlemann and Haase, 1985) have also been shown to help. In other words, trust developed when therapists demonstrated openness with clients and empathically shared their thinking and reaction to the material. This suggested that a practitioner's use of Roger's core conditions (Rogers, 1957) with advanced levels of empathy (Mearns and Thorne, 1999), together with a positive reputation for the delivery of counselling could be helpful. However, societal and health care differences from 1968 in the USA to 2013 in the UK mean that many counselling clients do not know their therapist initially, as they are referred to agencies or health centres where a counsellor is allocated. This means that two of the dimensions of trustworthiness highlighted by Strong (1968), those of the reputation and social role of the individual, are not visible factors today.

This has also been the case for doctors. Previously in the UK, doctors were well-known in the community and had a professional reputation built up over many years of practice. However, with the development of larger GP practices and specialist hospital units, there is no longer a single point of contact. A study has found a change to the way that patients respond to medical practitioners: from inferred trust, based on the doctor's reputation and position, to informed trust, based on the patients' opinion of their physician and their work together (Calnan and Rowe, 2008). Patients now recognised variations in doctors' abilities and the facilities available to them and key factors in building trust were perceived to be the doctor's competence, communication ability, openness, honesty and ability to empathise. These factors were also found in a USA study specifically investigating health care for IPV survivors (Battaglia, Finley and Liebschutz, 2003), but this study also found that a caring relationship, with time to talk and share personal information, encouraged trust. Whilst the importance of trust remained unchanged in accessing and agreeing to treatment, the new organisational delivery of health care meant that a process of maintaining trust was now required. This maintenance process was found to be conditional on the positive factors that generated trust initially continuing throughout the relationship (Calnan and Rowe, 2008). In the same way, trust can be considered as a process continuing throughout therapy, also requiring ongoing attention (Herman, 1992).

As changes have been made to the way that counselling is delivered to many people, from known individuals to organisations, it is also important to recognise that trust can also be developed initially through the reputation of the organisation delivering the service (system or institutional-based trust) as well as by an individual within the organisation (personal trust) (Bachmann, 2001). Trust may need to be placed in the organisation initially to gain access to the service, prior to the development of personal trust merited by the individual delivering the service. Both personal and organisational trust can occur concurrently in an organisation, in relationships with suppliers, customers and employees (Dietz, 2011). Accessing counselling from an agency may therefore require trust in both the counsellor and the agency, for example in maintaining confidentiality, which makes the provision of a trustworthy space for delivering counselling more complex.

In these cases, it is important that the counsellor's values and chosen ethical framework align clearly with agency practices and policies on issues that may come up in therapy such as suicidal intent; harm to self or others; disclosure of past abuse; or current safety and well-being of children. This will enable any emerging issues to be handled clearly, consistently and congruently by both the organisation and the counsellor. This can be important when considering the factors found in developing organisational trust which support an individual to take a risk (Mayer, Davis and Schoorman, 1995):

1. Ability. This is the client's evaluation of the competence of the organisation in delivering the specific task or service required.
2. Benevolence. Here the client perceives the organisation as desiring, or being motivated, to help the individual in need of assistance, not simply doing a job that they have been paid to do.
3. Integrity. The client sees the organisation as having a set of principles that are adhered to and that are acceptable to the client. This can be established through the consistency of the organisation in matching action with words, in the moment and over time. Importantly, this aspect of trust is also affected by what the individual hears from other people, as they look for other evidence consistent with their own view. Hence the reputations of the organisation in the

community, and the therapist within the organisation, can both be factors in generating trust in counselling services.

A later paper suggested that the more trust that is developed, the bigger the risks that could be taken (Schoorman, Mayer and Davis, 2007). This aligns with the view that trust works best when reciprocated (Bond, 2011). The need for a therapist to have trust in both the client and the counselling process is also a vital element of the therapeutic relationship (Hazler and Barwick, 2001). Hence trust is not only developed from client to counsellor, but also from counsellor to client, and as the two work together, more trust can be developed which allows greater risks to be taken during therapy.

For clients for whom trust is not an issue, observed inconsistencies between admin and counselling staff may be forgiven as miscommunication, and a therapist failing to respond openly to a comment may be interpreted as them not hearing what was said. However, for clients who have learned that silences or misunderstandings can have serious consequences, each of these events could be an indication that they should proceed with caution or not at all. Living in an environment, often described as like walking on eggshells, where any inconsistency or guarded response may be the precursor to abuse (actual or threatened) can build hyper-sensitivity to interactions with others. Some clients may continually test their therapist to see if they can be trusted and have a number of strategies for doing so (Fong and Cox, 1983). However, as trust builds, issues can be noted, discussed and resolved with the therapist being open, honest, non-defensive and empathic (Eubanks-Carter, Muran and Safran, 2010). Ultimately, it is hoped that the client will begin to understand that any mistakes are simply mistakes, both in counselling and more generally in life, and not necessarily an indication of some greater problem about to surface.

As counsellors and psychotherapists, we may be encouraged to consider that the training we receive and our continued commitment to practise to ethical and professional standards may be sufficient for trust to develop with our clients. However, in working with DV the counsellor's personal characteristics, which might include openness, honesty, caring, advanced empathy and consistency, may also be important (Calnan and Rowe, 2008; Belcher and Jones, 2009). In addition, the perceived trustworthiness of the organisation that the counsellor works for can impact on the relationship between the therapist and client. Hence it is possible that the generation and maintenance of trust for this client group may be more complex to achieve than for other counselling clients, simply because of the experiences they have endured.

Counselling or advocacy

In contemplating domestic violence and mental health, it becomes apparent that this client group have suffered a great deal at the hands of an abusive partner, physically, psychologically or both. The focus of much of the research into DV has been related to individuals still in a relationship, where advocacy is preferred over counselling or psychotherapy in the UK. Although more recent research has indicated that individuals may still be suffering mental health issues some years after the abuse has ended, it is likely that they will be diagnosed with depression initially, resulting in medication and/or counselling with qualified counsellors who would normally expect to create an appropriate environment for the client. Hence, it might appear that mental health issues resulting from DV are being dealt with appropriately in terms of the support provided and treatment offered.

Yet there have been reports of unhelpful counselling experiences by UK participants in a European study (Farmer, Morgan, Bohne et al., 2013). There have been calls from researchers to investigate appropriate therapeutic approaches (Ramsay et al., 2005). Therapists working in the field have felt driven to derive their own models of practice as they seek to assist others in working appropriately with what can be seen as challenging clients (Dutton, 1992; Walker, 1994; Dienemann et al., 2002; Sanderson, 2008; Agnew Davies, 2013). Whilst there are broad areas of agreement about practice, such as ensuring client safety and dealing with issues of trauma, each author makes their own recommendations for primary therapeutic goals, ranging from the client being able to make their own decisions (Walker, 1994) to increasing the client's knowledge about healthy relationships (Dienemann et al., 2002). In addition, there has been no agreement so far on appropriate outcome measures for counselling this client group and each quantitative study has selected different ones (Howard et al., 2003; Kubany, Hill, Owens et al., 2004; Reed and Enright, 2006; McNamara, Tamanini and Pelletier-Walker, 2008). Whilst there seems to be a lot of activity to try to be more helpful to the clients, recognising that they face particular difficulties, there are still no firm conclusions.

In these cases where quantitative research struggles to show a clear answer, there can be value in conducting qualitative research to look in more depth at specific issues. Indeed, there has been a small amount of qualitative research conducted in the last ten years with women, from the UK, USA, Australia and Sweden who have experienced domestic violence, to try to gain an understanding of different aspects of their experiences (Davis and Taylor, 2006; Hage, 2006; Morgan and Björkert, 2006; Scheffer Lindgren and Renck, 2008; Bostock, Plumpton and Pratt, 2009; Social Policy & Research Team, 2009) and how they accessed help (Stenius and Veysey, 2005; McLeod, Hays and Chang, 2010; Keeling and van Wormer, 2012). This research has been conducted consistently from a feminist perspective (where stated) using thematic analysis, with the exception of Davis and Taylor (2006) who used a narrative analysis. The studies confirmed that access to social support whilst in their relationship was important and reportedly helped to preserve the client's sense of self, which in turn helped them to make appropriate decisions to leave.

The studies listed above also reported to some extent on accessing counselling services. They found that therapists recognising the experience of DV and being genuinely caring, empathic and non-judgemental were helpful, as was being properly diagnosed and treated, suggesting that there may have been issues with incorrect diagnosis and treatment in the past. In addition, funding issues (a particular problem within the third sector, which could mean disruption to the therapeutic process and sometimes necessitated a change of therapist) were specifically cited as unhelpful. The continuation of the therapeutic process and relationship were therefore seen to be very helpful aspects of the counselling work, suggesting that clients valued the alliance developed with their counsellor. If we specifically considered the issue of trust here, we might infer that clients who struggled to connect with a counsellor may experience the disruption more acutely than those who could more readily connect with another therapist. Nevertheless, these factors (perhaps with the exception of recognising the experience of DV) could be seen to be applicable to counselling and counselling clients more generally and aligned with common factors identified for successful psychotherapy (Castonguay and Beutler, 2006).

However, a study conducted by workers from local and regional DV networks around Melbourne, Australia collected views from clients about aspects of the counselling they had received which they considered to be negative (Seeley and Plunkett, 2002). A key finding was the difficulty found in working with a counsellor who did not understand DV and the resultant issues, or who simply ignored the DV and tried to treat the client for the symptoms rather than the cause. In addition, being asked to agree to specific pre-defined outcomes for therapy was seen as unhelpful as the clients reported that they needed to find their own solutions to their own defined problems. These issues were addressed in practice guidelines for counselling issued in Australia a few years later (Grealy, Humphreys, Milward et al., 2008). In the UK, new guidance for working with DV requires all staff to be trained in DV (National Institute for Health and Clinical Excellence, 2014) but this has still to be fully implemented.

Another study looking into the family dynamics of lesbian mothers' IPV experiences in the USA (Oswald, Fonseca and Hardesty, 2010) explored (through secondary data analysis) what motivated clients to seek counselling, what prevented or helped them to do so, and which different types of counselling were received. This confirmed that counselling was most helpful when the abuse was acknowledged and the client was guided to find her own solutions. However, the study also noted potential problems that mothers in particular may have after experiencing DV, where they may be prevented from seeking help during custody battles if their use of counselling services could be used in court against them. As a result, the participants tended to access counselling because they had reached breaking point or wanted help with apparently unrelated issues, such as concerns about their children. This is a helpful insight into some of the issues that may result from receiving counselling and may link to the perceived integrity of the organisation, as well as highlighting that initial access for therapy may not be about the client's psychological issues.

A European study, involving five countries including the UK, interviewed counsellors and clients at six different agencies and found some agreement in the outcomes described by clients and observed by counsellors (Farmer et al., 2013). These split into three categories: life functioning (problem solving, autonomy, coping strategies and confidence to get on with life); understanding their experiences; and perceiving a future again. However, it is important to note that the participants were specifically asked about problem solving, autonomy, how they now understood DV and decision making and this could account for two of the three emergent categories. The structured nature of the research interview means that there may have been other aspects of the client experience that may not have been explored. Nevertheless, the reported benefit of now seeing a future did appear unprompted, and was described as an achievement by UK clients after the despair that triggered help-seeking (Farmer et al., 2013).

Looking across the studies there are suggestions that understanding DV and naming it is a key feature of the work being done, as is developing a stronger sense of self or a feeling of empowerment to be able to decide what to do next. These themes have appeared in DV literature for many years and fit well with the advice that has been given to social and health care workers about validating the experience of the victim (Lloyd, 1998; Morgan, 1998). They also fit with the work done through the Freedom Programme (Craven and Fleming, 2008) and the many confidence and self-esteem building courses run by DV agencies within the UK for women. As such, these results are not simply within the domain of counselling, but all those working with DV. This raises the question of what domestic violence counselling may add to the recovery of the victim, beyond advocacy, outreach or group work.

The situation for men is equally complex. The embryonic nature of many male services makes substantial research projects difficult to undertake. Only one study has been identified which included a reference to counselling for male victims of DV (Sweet, 2010). Here the men said that counselling had helped them to get over their experience of abuse through talking about it and dealing emotionally and mentally with the issues they faced as a result. Although counselling was a positive experience, the men also felt that more practical help, such as advocacy and support, would have been useful. This aligns with the feedback from the women suggesting parallel objectives of problem solving in their current lives as well as working through the abuse.

As the literature has been reviewed, there are still many unknowns. It is an area of research that is still emerging as we begin to consider the relative harm of the different types of abuse that can be included under the term 'domestic violence'. Although there is strong evidence emerging about the prevalence of depression and PTSD in both women and men, there appear to be existing general treatment options that would seem to provide an appropriate referral pathway. Although there have been many commentators indicating that a particular approach is required for working with mental health issues in domestic violence, researchers so far seemed to find factors which can also be shown to be important to general counselling clients. Although there appears to be some evidence for attachment difficulties which may impact on counselling, these would not normally require a separate and individual counselling service to be set up. Indeed, however the problem is examined, there appears to be an argument that appropriate and relevant services are being offered. Yet the government's own report into mental health suggested that the third sector may be better placed to offer counselling and psychotherapy for domestic violence and recommended more attention to referral pathways (Taskforce on the Health Aspects of Violence Against Women and Children, 2010).

At this point it is appropriate to consider the significant body of work indicating the need to address trauma, which may include individuals where the threshold level for a PTSD diagnosis is not met. This sort of work could be undertaken as part of counselling, although this has not been highlighted in these studies. It could be argued that working with trauma is what has been described as understanding their experiences, of expressing the extent of the abuse (Day, 2008). Yet trauma work requires a greater depth of engagement and higher levels of therapeutic skill than this simple description suggests and would be beyond the role of advocacy workers and group facilitators. It is also worth considering the concept of understanding as not simply the counsellor explaining DV to the client, but the counsellor being seen to understand the client and their experiences (Roddy, 2011b; 2013). The levels of empathy required to 'speak for' the client and thus assist with difficult disclosures are developed through counselling skill and extensive subject knowledge. In addition, Farmer's (2013) finding that the participants now felt that they had a future suggests a deeper process than simply psycho-education. It may be that it is not simply a case of providing either advocacy or counselling, but of providing services appropriate to the needs of the client at the time.

Client-based research on counselling to date aligns with the general principles identified in DV support. However, the language used in those studies does not provide insight into the counselling process itself. It seems that a part of the problem is not fully understanding what the clients gained from the counselling process specifically and what they found helpful or unhelpful. Perhaps if we had greater understanding about these aspects, it would become easier to signpost appropriate help or develop services in a way that would support DV clients to access and gain from them. This was the basis of the PhD research that this book is based upon.

The participants and the research process

The research was conducted with the assistance of four domestic violence agencies that specialised in supporting victims of domestic violence, three working with women in the North East of England and one with men in Eire. The counselling received was independent of the research process. A summary of the research methodology is given in Appendix 2 for those interested in reading more about the research process. At the time the research was conducted (2011–2012), none of the UK agencies contacted which offered a counselling service for male victims could participate. As a result, an agency in Eire, which had been working with men for many years and had previously supported other research, was approached and agreed to take part.

Twenty individuals (14 women and 6 men) who had accessed the agencies and received counselling to support them after their experience of domestic violence volunteered to take part in the research. The participants' words have been used throughout the book, although the names attributed are pseudonyms and any personal details within any quotations have been omitted or changed to protect the identities of the individuals. At the time of the interviews 3 of the 20 participants were still in their (non-physically abusive) relationships (all women) and 5 of the 20 were in new relationships. Of the participants, 18 had experienced domestic violence as a heterosexual adult, one within a same-sex relationship and one had been abused by their child.

As a qualitative study using grounded theory, the focus of the research was on the counselling experience of the participants rather than ensuring the sample was representative of the demographics of the DV population. Nevertheless, some demographic information was collected about the participants and the way this compares with other participant groups for research in this area is described below. There was no prior assessment of the type or severity of domestic violence experienced, although during the interviews most participants did describe what had happened to them. Equally, as the research was conducted with individuals who had completed counselling at least three months prior to the research interview, there was no assessment provided of the participants' mental health before or after the counselling, although the participants did provide descriptions of how they felt at the time.

The women and men were aged between 30 and 65 and had an average age of 45 years. This average is in line with other research for male victims of domestic violence (Carrado, George, Loxam et al., 1996; Coker et al., 2002; Hines and Douglas, 2010a) but a lot older than for many other studies involving women (Henning and Klesges, 2002; Stenius and Veysey, 2005; Hage, 2006; Moe, 2007; Allen and Wozniak, 2011). Generally, domestic violence research has been conducted with women in their twenties and thirties, at the point of leaving their partner. This group may be older because the research is about resolving the experience of domestic violence. Most of the women who had suffered physical abuse had left their partner sometime before. Those who had remained in their relationship were not in physical danger from their partner, but experienced emotional and psychological abuse. This provided support for the research identified earlier regarding the longer term psychological effects of domestic violence, beyond the point of leaving. It may also highlight when counselling rather than advocacy becomes more important.

Both the men and women had a range of educational experiences, ranging from leaving school without qualifications to graduating from university with a first degree. This broadly matched other research conducted in the field (Hage, 2006; Allen and Wozniak, 2011; Douglas and Hines, 2011). Eleven of the 14 women were in employment. The men chose to disclose that at the time of their relationship breakdown they had all worked fulltime: three were employed and three self-employed. However, at the time of the research interview and after the relationship breakdown, only three of the men were still in fulltime employment. One participant was registered as disabled.

There are not many studies which provide employment figures for women, perhaps because they are mainly conducted within a refuge environment. These participants did appear to have a greater level of employment than, for example, those interviewed by Allen and Wozniak (2011). This may have been a result of being an older group with potentially fewer childcare responsibilities. Many of the women had opted for a traditionally female career choice, such as working as a carer or teacher or more generally within the public sector, but two were self-employed, a higher proportion than normal within the UK (Institute for Small Business and Entrepreneurship, 2014). The men had generally opted for traditionally male careers such as engineering and technology, which was in line with other studies of men who had experienced DV (Hines et al., 2007). Although the level of self-employment in Eire is higher than in the UK (OECD, 2011), this alone does not account for this level of self-employment. The sample size is too small to show any statistical validity, but it is an interesting observation.

This book is an abridged version of the PhD study and has been written to provide some background and information for practitioners in the field. For a more comprehensive and academic explanation of the research and evidence base, it would be better to refer to the original thesis (Roddy, 2014). The study does not answer all of the questions raised in this chapter. However, it does provide access to the voices of participants who have gained from counselling and helps them to tell their stories of therapy, both good and bad. It also provides some ideas about what might make a difference to such clients together with an outline of the processes that participants found helpful. During the interview process, many of the participants highlighted their wish that the research was ultimately published as a book to help counsellors to work better with those who had suffered from domestic violence. This book fulfils that promise to them. It is up to the practitioners who read the following chapters to determine how much, or how little, it will influence their practice in future.

Summary

As this chapter comes to a close, it is worth reflecting on some of the key messages that have emerged:

- Domestic violence support in the UK is currently aimed primarily at the safety and protection of women and children in the UK.
- There are potentially significant mental health consequences of living with DV, including depression, suicidal ideation and PTSD, although treatment for depression is most likely to be offered.
- The high levels of suicidal ideation reported suggest that there may be many more deaths as a result of domestic violence than those resulting from physical violence alone.
- There is increasing research evidence to suggest that men and women may need to seek mental health support years after leaving their abusive relationships and therefore specialist services offered at the point of leaving may not be sufficient.
- There is evidence from counsellors and clients across the world that standard counselling approaches for treating mental health symptoms, which can be accessed later on, are not always successful for this client group.
- A number of professionals have tried to establish treatment models and outcome measures based on their experience, but this has resulted in differences in approach that are not yet resolved.
- Qualitative research with victims continues to confirm that aspects of counselling valued by clients generally are also valued by people who have experienced DV.
- Adapted counselling models for working with domestic violence appear to use techniques which are not unique to counselling and can also be found in advocacy and social work services.
- There is very little research available to define what men may need from domestic violence services, although some research suggests that counselling may be a preferred service alongside advocacy support.

On the one hand, the case for providing mental health care for those who have experienced domestic violence is compelling. On the other, it seems very hard to define the specific needs of these clients for counselling or other services. Whilst many professionals have provided opinions about what they consider is in the best interests of the client, it now seems appropriate to offer counselling clients the same opportunity. The following chapters begin the process of sharing those opinions and providing a few more pieces of information for practitioners and service providers.

2
Accessing Appropriate Counselling

At the beginning of the project, the identified focus on the counselling experience might have suggested that the research would focus on what had happened in the therapy room. One of the first questions in the research interview 'Looking back at when you started counselling, what brought you to counselling?' had been intended to take the participant back to the beginning of counselling, prior to examining the detail of their counselling experience. However, what emerged from the interviews was an extensive description of their journey towards getting the support they needed.

Although these aspects of the interview could have been discounted as not specifically related to the counselling, they appeared to be such an integral part of the counselling process for the participants that they were included in the final models of practice generated (Roddy, 2014). This aspect has also been included here as it is important that counselling services not only offer therapy that would be appropriate after domestic violence experiences, but also have access and referral pathways that will support such clients to make contact with the service. The participants' stories begin with both the women and men expressing the degree of emotional pain they were experiencing which prompted them to seek help.

Recognising the need for help

Experiencing difficult emotions

As identified in the opening chapter, domestic violence in its many forms can have a detrimental effect on mental health with diagnoses of depression, anxiety, suicidal ideation and, more recently, posttraumatic stress disorder (PTSD) all possible (Walker, 1979; 1994). Whilst there were no mental health diagnoses given for any of the participants, the descriptions they gave about how they felt prior to making the decision to access counselling suggested significant levels of distress.

> Andrew: my ex-wife had moved out and she had taken the children and I was at a, at a loss, I just had so much anger with everybody
>
> Karen: I was just in bed crying. I was sort of doing what I had to do, but that was all I was doing.

The majority of the participants in this research had separated from their abuser and had been living alone, or with a new partner, prior to seeking help for their emotional difficulties. This sets the research apart from other domestic violence studies conducted with men and women who were either still in their abusive relationship or had moved out of their home and into a refuge.

Despite this difference in context, the participants' descriptions of the degree of their emotional distress fits with the research discussed in Chapter 1. Karen's response describing her very low mood and tiredness does suggest someone who is depressed, whereas Andrew's description of being at a loss is less obvious. He had been shocked when his partner had decided to end their relationship suddenly and, where this is followed by feelings of guilt and anger, it could reflect a normal process of grief (Syme, 2012) following the loss of his family and home. Feeling anger was described by the majority of the male participants in the study and men have been found to express anger in their interpersonal relationships as an expression of their depression (Cochran and Rabinowitz, 2003). Although this may not be true in all cases, this response has been suggested as more likely for men who see themselves in a traditionally male gender role (Addis, 2008). The descriptions of the participants suggested that they saw themselves providing for their family and took pride in that role, hence it is possible that the anger expressed was reflecting depression.

However, when put in the context of other DV research, the decision of the female partner to leave combined with the expressions of guilt and anger by the male partner could be interpreted as signs of male to female abuse (Abrahams, 2007). Although the literature is beginning to acknowledge that male victims may present their distress in this way (Stith, McCollum, Amanor-Boadu et al., 2012), current training on DV suggests that male perpetrators will try to control their partner through the use of anger. This immediately highlights the difficulty that the men may experience in trying to get help, as the expression of anger can be interpreted in a variety of ways, including that of evidence of perpetrating domestic violence.

Although depression is commonly measured and assessed in DV research studies, it has been suggested that externalising distress through anger and disruptive behaviour, rather than internalising it may result in lower levels of diagnosis for men (Stith et al., 2012). This research is still in its early stages, but it has been suggested that the measurement of depression and anxiety, generally used in research with women, may not be as appropriate when assessing the degree of distress in men.

Interestingly, though, some female participants also identified anger as one of the issues that prompted them to seek help and some men identified their low mood.

> Fiona: I was either angered by people or very nervous about people and I just felt everyone was judging. Because I felt such a mess emotionally, and physically, and such a low opinion of myself that you know I couldn't function
>
> Hugh: Nobody'd know, brothers, sisters, nobody, and they would say 'is there something wrong with you? Is there trouble out there?' and I'd say 'oh no, just feeling a bit down'

From the participants' perspective it would seem that gender is less of a concern than the feelings that overwhelmed them and motivated them to seek help. As counsellors and psychotherapists, it is important to note that either emotional response is possible and is not an indication of the role that the individual played in the relationship.

At this point, it is also worth highlighting the possibility of PTSD. Although, none of the participants in this study indicated that they had been diagnosed with PTSD, many of the symptoms they described (such as intrusive thoughts, flashbacks, changes in cognitive schema, difficulties with emotional control) could be linked with criteria for such a diagnosis (National Collaborating Centre for Mental Health, 2005).

> Amanda: I had still been having issues and flashbacks and just not being, not happy, just not, not getting the relationship out of my head
>
> Peter: I was in a very distressed state at the time, it's hard to remember [...] the kind of frame of mind I was in at the time, it was quite chaotic and hectic

Whilst there has been much written about the emotional impact of domestic violence and debate about whether the impact is worse for women or men, all that could be said with certainty about these participants was that the emotional impact of their feelings of anxiety, depression or anger was sufficient to interfere with their day-to-day lives. Each was aware that their behaviour was outside what they considered to be normal for them, yet they did not know what to do to control or change the way they felt or acted.

Suicidal thoughts

In addition, about a third of the participants in the study indicated the depth of their depression through identifying suicidal thoughts. This level of disclosure was not part of the interview structure, that is, the information was volunteered and not requested, and hence it is possible that other participants also had suicidal thoughts during that time, but did not mention it during the interview.

> James: Thank God I'm here, like as I said. Deepest and darkest thoughts, absolutely, I'd be lying if I said I didn't, but the counselling I got here [...] it saved my life.
> Veronica: I can't take it anymore, I've had enough and that's how I felt, I'd had enough of life and I thought I don't want to continue.

Of the women who disclosed suicidal thoughts, around half also disclosed previous suicide attempts. This level of distress is consistent with other research discussed in Chapter 1, for example, in a USA population survey, 23% of women who had experienced partner violence had at least one suicide attempt (Seedat, Stein and Forde, 2005) and the last 30 years of research has consistently confirmed a direct relationship between DV and suicidal thoughts and/or actions (McLaughlin et al., 2012).

Some of the earlier domestic violence research may have predicted that this set of participants had a lower risk of suicidal ideation and depression (Campbell et al., 1995; Golding, 1999) as not all had experienced physical violence; some were still with their partners; and those who had left their partners had done so some years before. However, as discussed in Chapter 1, more recent longitudinal studies (Adkins and Kamp Dush, 2010; Blasco-Ros et al., 2010) have reflected continuing mental health issues even after leaving the abuser as, for example, the negative comments from the abuser have been internalised. Current health guidance (National Collaborating Centre for Mental Health, 2009) is based on research which pre-dates these advances in knowledge, and the longer term risks to mental health after experiencing DV are not yet acknowledged.

The propensity of victims of DV to contemplate suicide has been noted for many years and has been considered to come from feelings of hopelessness (Dutton, 1992) and a lack of other available alternatives (Dutton, 1992; Walker, 1994). Certainly, as the participants talked during the research interview about how they had felt prior to accessing counselling, their tone, body language and demeanour all indicated a sense of hopelessness, of having run out of options. Links between DV and hopelessness (Frank, 1963) and between hopelessness and suicidal behaviour (Beck, Weissman, Lester et al., 1974) are not new, and hopelessness and suicidal ideation are seen as symptoms of depression in the UK (National Collaborating Centre for Mental Health, 2009). However, in this case, hopelessness appeared to be a trigger for the participants to seek help. As a group, they presented themselves as individuals who had tried hard to cope in a range of situations. They had tolerated abuse from their partner for many years and had tried to improve things, to find a way to be able to manage the situation. What appeared to have happened was a recognition that despite their best endeavours, which in many cases involved leaving their abuser, they no longer had any ideas about what to do next and were no longer coping.

Hopelessness, coping skills and lack of social support are aspects of DV that have been linked with suicidal thoughts (McLaughlin et al., 2012). Whilst coping skills and social support can be externally facilitated, hopelessness is something which is experienced internally (Beaulaurier, Seff and Newman, 2008) and could play a significant part in the self-efficacy and welfare of someone suffering or recovering from DV. Practitioners and academics have been aware for many years that hope was an important aspect of both life and therapeutic work which deserved more recognition (Menninger, 1959). It is, however, Frank (1963), who is generally credited with bringing hope explicitly into the therapeutic process and his concept of demoralised clients included those who had suffered DV. He suggested that such clients respond to the common elements of psychotherapy, which meant that no particular approach is preferred, a position reflected in more recent writing for DV (Sanderson, 2008; Roddy, 2013). Frank (1963) noted that such clients feel unique: they are sure that no-one has gone through their specific experience before and that no-one can understand them. This echoes the experience and feelings of others who have experienced DV (Abrahams, 2007) and will be shown later for the study participants, both women (in Chapter 3) and men (in Chapter 4). A useful quote by Bennett and Bennett (1984) (cited in Frank and Frank (1991)) describes the situation often faced within DV, when the victim finally realises that their relationship will not change (Frank and Frank, 1991):

> *In the acceptance of helplessness and hopelessness lies the hope of giving up impossible tasks and taking credit for what we endure. Paradoxically, the abandonment of hope often brings new freedom.* (p562)

The sense that a new way forward can emerge from hopelessness has also been expressed by Walker (1994) but it is equally important to recognise the tremendous loss that occurs as the hope that things might somehow work out dies. This has been described as moving from unrealistic hope, through hopelessness, towards realistic hope (O'Hara, 2011) and may form an important part of a counselling process for these clients.

Trigger points

Many of the women had described themselves as previously being able to cope, and most of the men also believed that they could cope, with their relationship. The realisation that they no longer knew what to do to try to improve their lives was significant. This has been noted as a common issue with domestic violence clients (Dutton, 1992; Walker, 1994). The emotional content of this part of the interviews suggested a sense of hopelessness, of being at the end of their known resources. Research has indicated that women often believe in their ability to control the abuse in the future, even when an incident of abuse has just occurred, and it is the loss of that belief that results in hopelessness (Clements, Sabourin and Spiby, 2004).

There was however, a divergence in the triggers for seeking help between men and women. Over half the women linked the timing of their decision to seek help with a particular incident in their lives. Something had happened recently which had tipped the balance from coping to not coping, which could be indicative of a traumatic response. However, for the men, it seemed more about recognising that they no longer felt in control of their lives, both personally and in response to the continued abuse of their partners.

The female participants described a range of different experiences each being unique to the individual. For example, it might have been the death of a family member, starting a new relationship, or a change at work, at home or in the abuser's behaviour.

Elizabeth: you know like they say it can, the loss of someone can trigger other things on, and it made me re-evaluate everything that had happened in me life, and I knew I had to, I had to sort it out.

Mary: his behaviour mimicked what was going on with his dad and different things, and so I brought him here for counselling. [...] and his counsellor basically told me that we can't sort him out until we sort you out

Reflecting on the topics discussed, it seemed to be mainly about a change to the way the woman perceived her external world. For example, beginning a new relationship triggered fears of repeating previously abusive patterns, or perceiving an increase in the degree of abuse suffered could tip the balance towards seeking additional support. This fits with recent research suggesting that the decision to seek help is related to the person's willingness to do so and may be related to a spontaneous act (Hammer and Vogel, 2013). For these women, the critical event had changed the way they viewed things, and enabled them to consider seeking help.

For the men, the link appeared to be in losing their belief in their ability to control their future as the emotional and psychological abuse continued. As well as the emotional cost of the relationship breakdown, the men continued to have problems as their ex-partners, spread rumours, told lies and affected their relationship with their children.

Mark: the fact that anybody could try and take away her innocence at [primary school age], by making that kind of allegation, for whatever kind of game or whatever, is something that I'll never understand.

Matthew: On Christmas Eve, I remember she came, there's the family all hugging and kissing and then I went out to work, came back the next day, she was gone again. The kids were all deflated, and 'ooh' then they get all angry and aggressive and take it out on me, like I was the bad guy.

There has been evidence to suggest that, in cases of female spousal abuse, the mental health of both the female abuser and their male partner could be affected (Vivian and Langhinrichsen-Rohling, 1994). It has also been suggested that some DV may result from either one or both partners being previously traumatised from childhood or sexual abuse (Bloom and Lyle, 2001; Matsakis, 2001). Almost 92% of callers to a male DV help-line indicated that their partner had a history of childhood trauma (Hines et al., 2007). Several of the male participants talked about the difficult childhood their partners had suffered and the additional pressures that brought to their relationship. It is possible that one or both partners could have benefited from access to psychological support earlier in their relationship, although the treatment focus for the two might have been different (Bloom and Lyle, 2001).

Although some of the women were no longer in contact with their abuser, as Amanda described earlier in 'Experiencing difficult emotions', acknowledging that the memories of the abuse were still there and still causing suffering was crucial. They appeared physically free from their abuser, yet they continued to experience psychological and emotional abuse. In that sense, both the women and the men continued to suffer abuse following their relationship breakdown. In recognising their inability to change their lives at that point, there appeared to be two options: to consider suicide as they no longer had sufficient internal resources to draw upon, or to try to find help from elsewhere. It seemed that there had to be a passage through this sense of hopelessness (O'Hara, 2011) to facilitate change and recognise that they needed external help.

Hopelessness has been considered an important concept in beginning recovery from domestic violence before, but attempts to measure this have failed (Clements and Sawhney, 2000; Clements et al., 2004). It is possible that this is because the assessments have taken place once the women had accessed support, and the act of accessing support could provide hope for the future. Although such an assessment could be done prior to beginning counselling, ethical considerations about gaining informed research consent during extreme emotional distress may preclude such work. This could perhaps be completed as part of a general assessment prior to the start of counselling. However, hopelessness tends to be assessed using Beck's Hopelessness Scale (Beck et al., 1974) which overlaps with the measurement for depression (Beck and Steer, 1971). The case for measuring depression is much greater, as this is more likely to be discussed and monitored in a health context.

Although some of the men contemplated suicide, this appeared to have different a motivation to that suggested by Cook (2009). He found that suicidal feelings were seen as a way out of the relationship. However, this study found that those thoughts were prompted in response to the loss of their family and/or relationship and the hopelessness of the situation, particularly where children were involved. The emotional stress of losing their family was a greater stressor than living with the abuse. The men had not taken the decision to end the relationship: that decision had been taken for them. This, combined with a social system that would not listen to their experience of abuse, left them powerless.

A combination of isolation, hopelessness and not knowing how to cope has been identified as prompting suicidal thoughts (McLaughlin et al., 2012), and therefore it is not surprising that this was the response of the participants.

For those who had considered suicide, the threat posed to them by considering taking their life appeared to overturn any previous barriers to seeking help (Beaulaurier et al., 2008) and may be indicative of why it was mentioned by so many of the participants. The existence of hope helps in prolonging life and the existential value of hope in treating mental health has also been recognised (Menninger, 1959). Therefore the consideration of suicide in response to the loss of hope is understandable. For some participants the hopelessness was triggered when recognising that, even with their partner absent, the abuse was still affecting other areas of their life. Hopelessness may be an important concept from a client perspective in seeking help and beginning the recovery process from DV. At this point in the participants' story, it seems that hopelessness was a factor in their decision to seek help, and therefore we can infer that the provision of hope in some way through the therapeutic process may be helpful.

Acknowledging past experiences

Some victims of domestic violence have also experienced abuse earlier in their lives. Women (Howard et al., 2003; Hegarty et al., 2004; Rushlow, 2009) and men (Afifi, MacMillan, Cox et al., 2009; Douglas, Hines and McCarthy, 2012) who have experienced domestic violence have disclosed abusive childhoods and the proportion of male victims experiencing childhood abuse appears to be broadly similar to that of the women. These findings were also true within this small group of research participants, with some, but not all, indicating early problematic childhood experiences.

> Mark: my father was a violent alcoholic and so he would have regularly beat up everybody in the family, including me
> Veronica: all my life I've been, I didn't really want to bother people, I used to hide away because I knew that whatever happened, I'd be punished for, I'd take the blame, it was my fault

Identifying experiences of childhood abuse within adult victims of DV is not a new finding, and was part of Lenore Walker's evidence for her term, learned helplessness (Walker, 1979). Other research has found that individuals who have endured childhood abuse may have an increased risk of experiencing DV in adulthood (Howard et al., 2003; Hegarty et al., 2004; Rushlow, 2009). In general, the assessment of childhood abuse was done to assess the increased risk of, for example, depression from domestic violence compared to what could be expected from childhood issues alone. It is beyond the scope of this study to draw any firm conclusions about this. It is simply noted that childhood abuse is a significant factor in this field and that it has the potential to cause psychological harm to both the individual and potentially his or her partner later in life (Dutton, 2006). This suggests that the simplistic model of treating individuals as either the victim or the perpetrator may be flawed. It also suggests that counsellors who wish to work with supporting victims of domestic violence may need to work with previous as well as recent abuses.

Experiencing childhood abuse can also have an effect on the support that may be available from family sources in adulthood. A continuation of the abuse from childhood may result in a lack of confidence and ability to communicate more widely outside and potentially to seek help. One of the key findings in DV research on mental health has been the psychologically protective nature of strong social networks (Campbell et al., 1995; Blasco-Ros et al., 2010; Kamimura, Parekh and Olson, 2013) and research in the UK and Canada has suggested that the majority of people will first seek help from their family and friends when suffering DV (Ansara and Hindin, 2010; Smith et al., 2012). However, if the individual does not have strong family ties, either because of childhood abuse or the isolating effects of their relationship, this becomes a risk factor not only for suffering domestic violence but also for tolerating it.

> Mary: when you've got family and friends going on at you all the time, just wears you out.
> Matthew: I had no friends, no family, it was so much less hassle not to go down to me Ma's for dinner or whatever, and before I knew it I was just on me own.

One of the common elements of the male participants' experience was finding, as their marriages broke down, that they were isolated from their family and community and as a result had no-one to turn to in their time of need. Although this was a significant factor, it is not specifically addressed by common quantitative assessment tools for domestic violence such as the conflict tactics scale (Straus et al., 1996).

Nevertheless, isolation had been identified as an issue through qualitative research (Migliaccio, 2002) as a means of power and control. In this study, the men talked about the isolation emerging as part of the pattern of life with their wives, which made it harder to recognise and address, as there were no, or few, specific requests or acts to challenge. The isolation had been a gradual process and they had been unaware that it was happening or of the potential consequences of being isolated (Bloom and Lyle, 2001).

In these cases, professional help may be required, and yet may not be accessed easily. Research relating to mental health services in the UK (Rose, Trevillion, Woodall et al., 2011), suggested that patients would need to proactively bring their experiences of DV to the attention of the mental health professional. This presents a potential problem for this client group. A USA study of a social service agency examining the communication styles of women who had been abused within the last six months (Williams and Mickelson, 2008), found that most of the women used an indirect ('show some indication something is wrong and wait to be asked') rather than a direct ('tell it as it is') approach. This indirect style of communication resulted in unsupportive responses or rejection from professionals in the organisation, and therefore potentially fewer opportunities for the women to accept help. Williams and Mickelson's research was only conducted with women, and yet one of the surprising aspects of this present study was the number of participants, male and female, who noted that they had been able to talk during the interview for the whole hour, despite being interviewed by a stranger. This was considered to be one of the benefits of undergoing counselling.

> Ailsa: I can talk to more people. Once over, I don't think I would have been able to talk to you, because I didn't know you.
> Matthew: Because I never used to talk. I never opened me mouth or I never, I'd just sit there.

This suggested that abusive experiences may also impact on the participants' ability to seek help as they can lack the confidence and ability to communicate more widely outside and may not have the more usual help-seeking options available to them. In a society that values an individual's ability to put forward their case for support clearly and succinctly, it is possible that people experiencing DV may find it difficult to articulate their needs. In addition, given their historic reliance on using their own resources, not being offered help will mean that they are most likely to continue to try to work things out for themselves, whilst they still feel this is possible.

Someone who has been constantly abused may not choose to be direct about expressing their needs as responses can be unpredictable. They may not be skilled in identifying their own needs either, as it may be unlikely that these could be met within their relationship. Nevertheless, Williams and Mickelson (2008) did indicate that the women were willing to seek and accept support when it was offered. This was something which was also found in recent research with university students in the USA which investigated help-seeking decision pathways relating to health care (Hammer and Vogel, 2013). Here it was suggested that a decision to accept help may be based primarily on the person's willingness to do so at that moment, that is, a spontaneous act in response to a perceived opportunity. This differed from the previously accepted model of decision making relating to mental health, that of relating the degree of emotional distress to the need for help, followed by a rational analysis of the costs and benefits of doing so (Greenley and Mechanic, 1976).

Although the participants clearly identified that their level of emotional discomfort was high enough for them to recognise the need for help (Greenley and Mechanic, 1976), there were differences in how the participants sought help. A few were able to look at their lives objectively, identify what help they needed and then access that help (Kessler, Brown and Broman, 1981) but most felt driven to seek help due to the emotions that they experienced and responded spontaneously to the offer or expectation of help once given (Hammer and Vogel, 2013). It is important to recognise that both types of help-seeking were present in both women and men. However, we will return to the process of help-seeking later in this chapter.

Experiences of domestic violence

The research interview did not contain a specific question about the nature of the abuse experienced, although participants shared aspects of their abuse through telling the story of their counselling. The experiences of domestic violence described by the participants below tended to focus on emotional and psychological abuse, with some highlighting physical violence and financial abuse.

Psychological

> Andrew: waking you up at night [...] hitting you, waking you up [...] to fight about it, about nothing, and then you done something wrong [...] not having her speak to you for maybe two weeks

Lucy: the way that my husband would explode, would change, become somebody that I hardly recognised in just the space of a few minutes. And that used to frighten me.

Emotional

James: like if I'd felt a row brewing I'd just shut up, I didn't talk because I was just, I suppose I went into my own little world, you know that kind of way, because it was just 'here we go again.'

Natalie: what I couldn't handle was the constant 'in my ear'. Constantly, in front of the kids and putting me down and calling me names and all the time: it just wore me out, I was exhausted.

Physical

Jackie: he literally threw his meal on top of mine and broke plates on me and it was so much easier just to toe the line and not argue

Matthew: She started becoming violent then, throwing stuff at me, giving me a broken finger, came at me with a knife

Financial

Ailsa: And we were going through the years [...] saving quite a bit. We were putting into a savings account for both of us, but it wasn't, it was just for him.

Hugh: I had my redundancy money and that also went in my wife's name so that she would have control of it

Descriptions of sexual violence were given by less than half of the women and none of the men. The experiences described in the interviews occurred before the age of 16 and the majority did not include their abusive partner or a family member. These experiences tended to be described in the context of something additional that they had gained from counselling, which went beyond the domestic violence.

For some of the participants, the experience of domestic violence was another example of the abuse that the individual had experienced during their life. For others, this had been the first time they had experienced such behaviour. All of the participants had tried to work through the issues and felt increasingly helpless to change things. They did not necessarily interpret their experiences as domestic abuse, more that this was behaviour they had come to know and expect from their partner. In addition, most of the participants were no longer in their relationships, yet they did not know what to do to relieve the pressure they felt inside and recognised they needed some help to do so. However, it was not necessarily obvious where to go for help, in part because many of them had previously tried to access help unsuccessfully.

Previous counselling experiences

Although the literature on domestic violence suggests quite strongly that help-seeking is difficult, nearly 80% of the women and two-thirds of the men had accessed counselling at an earlier point in their lives. Perhaps surprisingly, given the degree of emotional turmoil they were suffering and the potential for counselling to be helpful, over half the women and half of the men had had poor experiences of counselling previously. Whilst some of those counselling experiences had been during the relationship, others were after the relationship had ended. In some cases, the first visit to the counsellor was enough to persuade them not to come back.

> Peter: I found it extremely difficult in marriage counselling, to kind of get my mind across, and to kind of, actually to explain my emotions.
> Ruth: the first session I had was completely, phew. It just didn't work you see, it completely didn't work.

Others continued to work with the counsellor for a while in the hope that something might change, and for a few, there were multiple attempts to engage, feeling at some level that it could help. For each, there was disappointment that both they and the therapist were unable to provide what they needed from counselling.

> Mark: what I needed to a large extent were [...] tools to be able to cope with difficult stuff and counselling wasn't hugely good at providing me with that.
> Veronica: Where with other counsellors and that, I've never felt that connection, never felt that they were there, as I say, just session, right it's time, go home now, see you after. And coming home and really no different.

These experiences suggested that there was something specific that the participants required from counselling that did not seem to be generally available, and yet they continued to try.

There were some indications that the issue was sometimes related to the counsellor and client being unable to form a bond or connection, in common with many other counselling clients (Paulson, Everall and Stuart, 2001). However, underlying these issues, as described by Amanda and Mark below, was a sense that the counsellor just did not understand their situation sufficiently to be able to help or, in the case of the male counsellors, was so far away from understanding the issue and the relational dynamic as to potentially cause harm.

> Amanda: The [organisation] counsellor, she was good, that was paid for, but she still didn't get, still didn't get to the root of it. [...] I had a bad experience at a different [organisation] branch, where the counsellor there he just totally didn't know
>
> Mark: I would talk about this and sort of say [...] 'how do you cope with this?' and one of the counsellors would say 'well you have to be assertive and [...] say this is not acceptable behaviour'. I can't do that because by engaging in it at all [...] I just prolonged the whole thing

Situations like the one Mark was alluding to are often described in domestic violence, where one party has to rely on the goodwill of the other. Take, for example, picking up children for visits where the abusive party either has the power to restrict the visit by not having the children ready, where they have custody, or the power to extend the visit when the children have to be returned, when they do not. When having power and control over the other has been a central part of the relationship, trying to change that dynamic through challenge is likely to have consequences. Instead of confrontation, a more indirect approach such as one which reduces the amount of contact required with the abuser is more likely to succeed. For younger children, this might be through finding a third party such as a grandmother or neighbour who would be prepared to allow the child to be dropped off and returned at their house. For older children, arranging to meet and drop them at the end of the street may also be an option. Within counselling, however, the therapist's approach was to try to encourage Mark to assert himself more, which increased his partner's need to maintain control. Working with a knowledge of the way abusers operate and their likely motivations can help to reduce the conflict experienced even after the relationship has ended.

Whilst general counselling clients saw gaining knowledge and increasing their personal resources as being helpful to the therapeutic relationship (Paulson et al., 1999), the lack of this did not appear in the alternative study of hindering aspects of therapy (Paulson et al., 2001). However, acknowledging and naming the abuse is an area that has been highlighted in many domestic violence studies (Davis and Taylor, 2006; Hage, 2006; Day, 2008; Oswald et al., 2010) and here participants noticed when it was not present. It is possible that this is a specific requirement for working with this client group that is not generally recognised within counselling. This is perhaps not surprising, as many therapists in general practice will not have received training in domestic violence. Without such training, it may seem appropriate to focus on what the individual can do for themselves to alleviate their distress, without acknowledging or recognising the patterns of behaviour in the abuse.

Amanda: the reason it didn't help was because [...] I was in an abusive relationship, that's what was making me depressed.

As Amanda reflects above, now that she had experienced counselling specifically for domestic violence, recognising the impact of living within an abusive environment was a key factor in helping her recover from her depression. It is difficult for a GP in a short consultation to identify an abusive relationship. Words such as guilt, blame, crying and anger were used by the participants to describe how they felt and would show up positively in screening for depression (Beck and Steer, 1971). This in turn could result in a referral for counselling for depression or a prescription for anti-depressants. Yet, as Amanda described above, the specific link between the words used and the abuse present in the participants' relationship could be missed (Beck et al., 1974). As mentioned in Chapter 1, there is not a screening process for psychological abuse available currently (Follingstad, 2007), and so screening will continue to be done using signs of depression and physical violence.

It is appropriate to reflect that the main response of the participants to their negative experiences of counselling was to go back home again and try to live with their emotional difficulties. The time frame between attempts at counselling varied between participants, and in some cases it could be years before they would reach the point of trying to access help again. When this is considered in the context of the level of distress required for the participants to reach out for help, the human cost of inappropriate support is huge.

One of the differences between the male and female experiences of counselling was that none of the women, whether they had accessed general counselling for free or paid for private counselling, was referred on to specialist domestic violence support by their counsellors. However, two of the men reported being referred on quickly to the agency once the counsellor had become clear about the nature of the abuse they had experienced.

> Andrew: [counsellor] says maybe you should speak to [agency] and I asked her 'what was [agency]?' and she told me it was for men that had gone through exactly what I had gone through.

Here the therapist appeared to feel that Andrew needed more specialist support than they could offer. Previous research has indicated that counsellors may have difficulty in working with male survivors of DV (Hogan, Hegarty, Ward et al., 2012) and as there was a specialist agency available locally, it may have been easier for that therapist to provide a referral than to work with the many issues that may have been raised. However, in the UK, where there are only a few agencies in the UK offering DV counselling for men, general counselling may be the only option.

Part of the reason for the participants' desire to participate in the research was to help other people to be able to access appropriate counselling for domestic violence, given their positive experiences at their agencies after other experiences. Whilst it would be wrong to draw generalised conclusions about the counselling experience of others from such a small sample, the number of reported unsatisfactory counselling experiences is notable and in line with other published research (Farmer et al., 2013).

Other available sources of support

The ability of women suffering domestic violence to continue to try to find the right source of help, despite many disappointments, has been reported by other researchers too (Holly, 2013). Whilst it is disappointing that they so often did not get what they wanted, it is encouraging that at some level they were aware that what was offered did not meet their needs and kept trying. This, however, was slightly different for the men. Although they also had to continue to try to find the right source of help, this was primarily because they were trying to access help from a domestic violence system that was primarily set up to support women. Whereas the women could try out support before deciding it would not work for them, the men either did not receive a referral or found that the support offered was actually being directed at their partner.

> James: if the police aren't going to believe me who is going to believe me? [...] I have to say, that's the way things have panned out, like social workers and everything.
> Mark: it left a very sour taste in terms of health workers [...] where people are basically running away from you in case they become embroiled in something.

The men acknowledged during the interviews that they understood that they were physically bigger than their partners and that when their partners told a very convincing story about what had happened, they were more likely to be believed. However, there was also frustration and anger that their story was not being heard and that decisions were being made without taking into account the full story which would ultimately impact on the lives of their children. The focus of this book is on the counselling experience, rather than the experience of engaging with public sector bodies, but it seems appropriate to note that the problems for male participants reflected in their research interviews were also reported in other research (Cook, 2009).

Deciding who to trust

As discussed in Chapter 1, trust can be an issue for individuals who have experienced domestic abuse and with the difficulties experienced with counselling and potentially with other support services, there may be little trust that appropriate help is available. With ability, benevolence and integrity required to generate trust (Mayer et al., 1995), we can perhaps see why trust has become an issue. Finding people in their lives who wanted the best for them and had both the ability to be helpful and the integrity to do so can be difficult. Family and friends, where available, may want to help but may not have the experience to understand domestic violence or the objectivity required to support the individual. Previous experiences of counselling may have shown a counsellor with integrity and benevolence, but not the ability to understand their situation.

Deciding where to go to seek help is therefore highly complex and what seemed to happen then, from the participants' descriptions, was that they sought help from a source that they felt they could trust. This was an individual who, in the past, had provided them with helpful, useful and appropriate information regarding their relationship, showing ability, benevolence and integrity, or who was in a position to help and showed some understanding when told of their situation. Over half of the participants had followed a recommendation from a professional who had previously been helpful to them, whilst a few had recommendations from colleagues who had previously accessed the agency and could share a positive experience. Only two had used their own resources in finding and making contact, relying on their own assessment of the agency.

The most common way of accessing the agency was through taking the advice of professionals that they had previously been in contact with over legal or health issues. Over half of the participants found their counselling in this way.

> Matthew: I didn't know about them until the [police] told me, but as soon as I become more aware of it, like I saw on the back of buses, posters saying [agency]
>
> Samantha: I was really very strongly advised by the police to come here for quite a long time [...] Pushed me is the wrong word, but encouraged me strongly, so, having had fabulous advice and support, the counselling side of things was, it felt fine, it felt like the next step.

For those accessing help for domestic violence, it was most often the police who noted the distress of the individual and recommended the agency. This fits with other research literature on help-seeking which shows the influence of professional referral in taking the step to begin counselling (Hampton-Robb, Qualls and Compton, 2003). However, Hampton-Robb et al. (2003) concluded that it may not simply be about the source of the referral, hypothesising that it may also be a function of the quality and credibility of the source. One of the features identified by Samantha above was that of accepting the recommendation from a professional who had been helpful or understanding and was already seen to be trustworthy in the context of domestic violence, and so she was prepared to give counselling a try. The next most frequent source of information was medical professionals.

> Jenny: My doctor said you know, I'd, I told him what I've told you about counselling when he mentioned it to me, he said 'There is

good counselling out there' and he said 'Leave it with me and they'll get in touch with you.

Peter: I was referred, my GP referred me and said 'you know, because there was physical and a lot of emotional abuse'

For Jenny and Peter, their GP was both trusted and able to provide a referral straight away. This was different to the experience of Samantha and Matthew as they were advised about the agency with a recommendation, rather than referred, by the police and they had to act upon the advice themselves. This period of reflection prior to accessing counselling was mentioned by a few of the participants, indicating the difficulty of taking that final step to access support, even when it seemed appropriate. However, the confidence of the referrer in the service, as Jenny's doctor alluded to, also built hope for the participant that this service might be able to help them.

Although the concept of hope has previously been identified as having some existential qualities, hope has also been defined in a slightly different way by cognitive-behavioural psychologists. The earliest theory of hope from a cognitive behavioural stance (Stotland, 1969) comprised seven different aspects, primarily related to the achievement of success and the importance of goals. This perspective later informed the development of a new definition of hope (Snyder, Harris, Anderson et al., 1991) which had two distinct cognitive aspects:

a) Agency: a sense of successfully meeting goals in the past, present and future
b) Pathways: the perceived availability of successful pathways relating to goals.

Snyder's hypothesis suggested that both agency and pathways needed to exist to experience hope. In the context of the participants' interactions with professionals, they were able to hear that the agency that they were being referred to had successfully worked with people like them, and that they now had a pathway to achieving those goals too. Hence, in a small way, the referral process generated hope.

It is appropriate to mention that Snyder et al. (1991) differentiated hope from optimism (Scheier and Carver, 1985), which was considered to have too much agency and too few pathways, and self-efficacy (Bandura, 1982), which was focussed mainly on the individual's ability to take action. Whilst Snyder's (1991) definition of hope fits with expecting and desiring a specific outcome, and can also be seen to encompass trust in the professional (Oxforddictionaries.com, 2012), the additional element of faith or trust that is required to take part in things beyond one's control is somehow missed. Snyder (1995) acknowledged that his definition had the benefit of being measurable rather than comprehensive, and a later paper (Snyder, Michael and Cheavens, 1999) stated that

> *stress, negative emotions, and difficulties in coping are considered the result of being unable to envision a pathway or make movement toward a desired goal.* (p. 181)

and formed a basis for Snyder's later work in positive psychology (Snyder and Lopez, 2005) which included optimism, self-efficacy and compassion. Although the definition can be seen to be limited, this may be because the concept of hope has many different dimensions, as we will see later in the book. For now, however, this definition provides a useful model for showing the psychological impact of the referral process.

Although there were many positive reports of professional referrals, this was not always the case. Two of the domestic violence agencies supporting female participants also offered counselling for sexual violence and it is notable that only the women who disclosed sexual abuse were referred for specialist counselling through their GP. Women with no past history of sexual violence were more likely to come through a recommendation from the police or other sources, even when they had been to see their GP, as in Fiona's case.

> Fiona: A complete lack of appreciation of the impact that [domestic violence] has on that person's personality [...] I wasn't well, physically well at all, it took its toll physically on me and I got no, I was just sent away by my doctor, and I felt absolutely lousy

As James and Mark highlighted earlier in the chapter, not all connections with professionals were positive experiences. It is possible under current screening processes that the root cause of Fiona's physical symptoms would be missed. It is also possible that women presenting for medical help may not articulate their needs well (Williams and Mickelson, 2008) and therefore be offered medication to control their symptoms rather than addressing the underlying issues. This raises an important question about whether clients presenting with severe depression are, or should be, assessed for psychologically abusive relational issues, past and present, to allow appropriate intervention to take place immediately. This could be an area for further research and development.

The last main source of recommendation came through friends or colleagues who had had previous positive personal experiences of the agency, although this was only for the women.

> Ailsa: And my, one of my [colleagues], she mentioned [agency], she said 'Ailsa, give it a try', she said 'I used to go myself'. She said 'They're very good.'
>
> Karen: I think if I hadn't been pushed by my friend to come here the panic attacks would have got worse and I think I would've been where I couldn't get out of the house

Here Karen talks, as Samantha did earlier, about being pushed into counselling, of someone else having a very clear view of what might help. Although they were aware of their own distress, hearing that acknowledged by others seemed to help them to take action. External factors can be significant in achieving a shift or change for the individual. Whilst words like pushed were used, as Samantha says it was more about encouragement and perhaps feeling that someone else was concerned about them. In both cases, the previous personal experience of the person making the recommendation was important. The participant was aware that they had to trust the recommendation of that individual, as they had no personal knowledge of the agency.

> Lucy: I didn't know any of the people here and I was only going on the say so of a friend that these people could be trusted.

It is interesting that the care and concern came from friends and colleagues and not family members, as noted previously. From a counselling perspective, it indicates very clearly the need to have strong links with other professionals as well as welcoming referrals from previous clients. Although none of the men indicated that they had received recommendations from friends or colleagues, one of the participants did indicate making such a recommendation to one of his friends later on, which was acted upon.

> Andrew: I have a friend who is in a similar situation, and he went for counselling with a different crowd

It would seem that both the male and female participants in this study identified and used very similar pathways into counselling.

Finally, a small number of female participants, who had previously had poor or mixed experiences of counselling and/or referrals and knew it was important to find the right support, used their own resources to find the agency rather than rely on a recommendation.

> Fiona: I saw [agency]'s number advertised on the back of a, a door [...] and it was like a list of bullet points [...]. And it was like, ah yes, yes, ah, yes and I put the number in my phone

Here Fiona was checking quite carefully that the agency would have the ability to help her before moving to the next stage of contacting them. Once again there was a period of reflection after obtaining the agency details before making the telephone call. However, where this was the case, the participant then asked for further information or material that they could access. It is important to note that at this stage there was not sufficient trust in the organisation's ability to support them personally, but the credentials of the organisation suggested that information might be accessible.

> Ruth: I think I may have asked them if they had any material I could look at, books or anything like that [...] and then they basically said 'come and meet you and you know, and go through it'.

Asking for literature was a good way for them to assess how well the agency understood their situation. When offered the opportunity to come and have a chat, both responded positively based on the telephone call. However, it is important to note that they saw this as responding to an opportunity presented to them. Even although they had been instrumental in setting up the telephone call, both indicated an initial need for material to support self-help rather than a formal request for counselling. They saw the next step of accessing counselling as taking the opportunity offered (Hammer and Vogel, 2013) rather than something they had planned. Perhaps they felt after the telephone call that the agency might be interested in helping them, thus moving them towards trust. This way of approaching professionals, of using an indirect method to open the dialogue, has also been reported in the literature (Williams and Mickelson, 2008) and has been linked to the individual failing to receive the support they need from services as they have been unable to clearly state what they needed. In this case, however, the agencies were able to be appropriately responsive and help the client to take the next step.

For participants who had mixed experiences of counselling and already knew something of what was involved, a positive recommendation from someone they trusted or respected was helpful. However, this generation of hope and trust through referral or recommendation could only take the participants so far. As discussed below, those thoughts and feelings needed to be supported and endorsed during the first meeting at the agency.

Initial experience with the agency

Although the research interview specifically asked about the first counselling session, more than half the participants chose to talk about the first assessment meeting at the agency instead. This suggests that the first face to face interaction with the agency was also quite important in the resulting decision to engage further with the organisation. What became clear during the descriptions of these sessions was the importance of that first physical contact with the agency, particularly for those who had had no prior agency contact through the domestic violence outreach or advocacy services.

> Hugh: she made an appointment with [agency worker] and I met her at the [building] and she was also so, so helpful and she says, 'won't you come down' she says 'you look like you've been carrying cares around'
>
> Natalie: I came here and spoke to one of the girls [...] I believed it was all my fault and I was getting manipulated and twisted round in my head and, the, the lady who I saw just made it clear[er].

These positive experiences during their initial contact with the agency were helpful in overcoming reservations that the participants might have had about beginning the counselling process (Vogel, Wester and Larson, 2007). As Natalie and Hugh indicate above, the assessment session introduced someone who seemed to really understand and care about their experiences. It also began the process of helping them to see that their situation may not be quite as they perceived things. As the conversation continued, the participants were able to see that the agency staff not only understood domestic violence, but also wanted to help. In addition, the agency had an organisational framework to rely on, which was used to dealing successfully with issues coming from domestic violence. For those who had had unsuccessful counselling before, beginning to feel some trust and confidence in the agency gave them hope that this time might be different, and that the counselling might be helpful.

> Jenny: I went away thinking there might be light at the end of the tunnel, I'll give it a go

This was slightly different for the men, however. They were aware of a range of services available to women in a similar situation which they could not access. Finding a service that was specifically for them was a relief and some travelled a reasonable distance to access the service. The fact that the service was for them seemed to give them confidence that they could be helped.

> James: I suppose when your car's [broken] you go to a mechanic, if you're [broken] you go to [agency] because they know what they're doing!

Here James indicates his confidence in the specialist nature of the organisation, which was backed up on his first meeting. The importance of the referral for the men was not only about the professional referral source, but also about being referred to a service which specialised in helping men with their specific problems, that is, a degree of ability that they had not encountered elsewhere. Although it could be argued that the same model of hope and trust applies here, the participants indicated that there were no alternative services if this one had not met their needs, suggesting that the process of deciding to access was simplified.

There were a number of differences in this research compared with other published studies involving men. One of the most noteworthy was the speed at which an appropriate referral appeared to be made. Research in the USA (Douglas and Hines, 2011) suggested that many of the agencies the men identified were only for women, or that the agency made a further referral for them into a perpetrator's program. Only 25% received an appropriate referral first time. In this study, where there was the possibility of a suitable referral, the participants felt that they had been referred to the agency appropriately and that the prior supporting services had been helpful. However, this study only interviewed individuals who had used agency services and therefore would not include men who had been inappropriately referred. It is possible that the length of time the agency has been established, the regular radio, poster and newspaper advertising and the reputation of the agency may all have helped to provide quick and appropriate pathways. However, any agencies starting to provide such a service to male victims in the UK may need to specifically address referral pathways through existing services for women as well as through police and health services.

Another difference was the participants' approach to the agency. In line with other reported incidents, many of them had negative experiences with court systems and social services indicating that sympathy for the family breakdown was firmly with the mother (Cook, 2009). Although the participants had previously had negative experiences with other agencies, they seemed able to accept that this was because they were the wrong clients for that service. The agency referral was the first time they had encountered a service that was specifically for them and they accessed with a view that this was their service. The team were sympathetic, knowledgeable and interested in helping as much as they could, all dynamics which would increase trust (Mayer et al., 1995) in the organisation. However, the participants did not appear to need the endorsement of the referring professional to engage with the agency. It seemed to be sufficient that the person indicated that agency might be able to help because of their experiences, and the men then accessed the service and made their own judgements about whether the service would be helpful to them (Kessler et al., 1981).

This part of the client process, making the decision to access counselling, appears to be important in moving forwards and yet is quite complex and not fully addressed in the existing counselling literature. Whilst much of the literature talks about the difficulties of disclosing domestic violence (McLeod et al., 2010) and the barriers to doing so (Beaulaurier et al., 2008), the participants in this study had already disclosed their levels of distress to someone else. The difficulty with family relationships meant that many of the referrals to counselling came through professional sources and colleagues, rather than the more normal route of family and friends. Any stigma attached to domestic violence (Overstreet and Quinn, 2013) had already been challenged, as the people chosen for disclosure already had a personal or professional experience of their situation and had been supportive. In addition, the stigma attached to accessing mental health services (Judd, Komiti and Jackson, 2008) did not seem to hold for this group, as many had previously accessed counselling services. Those who had not accessed counselling before did not necessarily attend the agency with the intention of doing so, but did accept the agency's recommendation. What appeared to hold the participants back was a personal view of counselling as unproven and a general feeling that they could recognise poor counselling, but did not feel confident in their ability to identify a good counsellor or counselling service. Hence this underlines the importance of the initial meeting at the agency, as participants gained trust in the agency to deliver a service that would be of help to them.

Although it seems very obvious that participants valued their first contact with the agency, there is surprisingly little written about the impact of this on the therapeutic process. It has been suggested that the predominant emotion prior to beginning counselling was uncertainty (Lambert, 2007) and in that study only 7% of the sample suggested any wariness. However, a study looking at why clients avoid counselling suggested that this could be related to low expectations of the outcome (Vogel et al., 2007). Although Vogel et al. (2007) make a number of suggestions about how to deal with this, these are mainly around educating people about counselling so that they know what to expect. Although trust is mentioned, this is specifically with respect to the therapist rather than the process leading up to counselling. In this case, expectations were raised about counselling by the competence of the interviewing staff in understanding their situation, as many of the participants had already experienced counselling and had some idea of what to expect.

The importance of the agency experience prior to beginning counselling has been raised before in the context of reception services and pre-counselling literature (Quintana, 1974) but this does not appear to have been developed within counselling research. It has been shown that viewing a video-tape of a good counselling session has a much more positive impact than being given leaflets to read (Stewart and Jessell, 1986). It is possible that the initial interview was seen in this way, as a taste of what counselling might be like. This could indicate a preference for active rather than passive processes. In the context of feeling emotionally overwhelmed, it may be easier to respond and form a view in an assessment session than to concentrate on and process literature.

As the participants engaged with the agency, the personal or organisational trust that they had in the person recommending the agency and the hope that the agency could help, had the potential to be built upon or undermined. It is worth comparing these positive experiences with that from a different agency which also offered a service in domestic violence counselling, although this was not its primary activity.

> Fiona: I didn't realise the person I was seeing wasn't going to be a counsellor, but during that session [...] it was just like 'whoosh' [...] she explained that it would be about three or four months before I would hear because they had a waiting list [...] the following day I had a phone call, inviting me in the following week, we've fitted you in.

Fiona's description suggested that she would not have responded in the same way during the meeting had she known that the person was not a counsellor and that there was a three to four month waiting list. Ultimately, this particular piece of counselling ended badly. During the research interview Fiona linked this beginning of the process with her feelings of upset later in the process, when she felt the counselling was being dictated by the therapist and once again out of her control. She ended the work abruptly feeling very uncomfortable.

She made her next approach for help through her own endeavours, as she no longer trusted her previous referrer to make an appropriate recommendation and she did not know who else to ask. This shows how important it is for the referral organisation or individual to have confidence in the agency's ability to deliver appropriate support, as the failure to do so can have a negative impact on their own relationship with the client (Mayer et al., 1995). Trust appears to be a very complex process, being transferred from the particular individual who had referred them to the agency and then to the agency and staff working there (Bachmann, 2001). Building trust relies upon the individual's knowledge of their topic, being seen to have the person's best interests at heart, and having integrity (Mayer et al., 1995) and this will be true for each individual at each stage of the referral process. Factors relating to building trust in organisations have been developed through business research (Mayer et al., 1995) and suggest that inconsistent processes, lack of knowledge and not hearing what the client wants can undermine this. Hence the assessment interview can play an important part in nurturing or undermining the trust and hope for the process developed from the first referral.

As discussed above, having a positive experience during the first meeting at the agency helped to build up trust in the organisation and hope that they would be able to deliver an appropriate service. There is a fairly significant research base suggesting that in general, positive client expectations of therapy brings a higher likelihood of success (Cooper, 2008) and it has been estimated that about 15% of the improvement in therapy can be accounted for by this as a factor (Asay and Lambert, 1999). In addition, research indicates that positive, realistic expectations of counselling can help to establish the therapeutic alliance more quickly, leading to better outcomes (Cooper, 2008; Messer and Wolitzky, 2010). Whilst a positive experience of the agency in the beginning will not guarantee successful counselling, it does help to create an environment more likely to do so.

This client group have been seen as having particular difficulties with forming a therapeutic alliance, in the literature (Barber, Khalsa

and Sharpless, 2010; Breger, 2012) and from the accounts of previous counselling given by the participants. There is evidence that for
clients with trauma or abuse histories, it is the growth of the alliance
over time that is more important than the strength of initial therapeutic interactions (Stiles and Goldsmith, 2010). It seems appropriate
then that the relational base for the client as they come into therapy is already developing and provides a positive base on which to
build.

Issues of trust can be seen to play a part in leading up to accessing
support. However, different forms of trust play a part here: personal, professional and organisational. Referral sources need to be proficient and
credible, and equally need to understand what is required and have confidence in the agency to provide it. Reception workers have to deal with
enquiries and encourage engagement with the service. Support workers interviewing the client for the first time need to be able to recognise
and understand the person's experience, to help to build confidence and
trust that the agency will be able to provide appropriate and beneficial
counselling support. This is particularly important given the previous
counselling experiences of many of the participants.

Patients' are changing the way that they assess their trust in their
doctor (Calnan and Rowe, 2008). Whilst this research did not set out to
explore that particular aspect in third sector service provision, this did
appear to be important and potentially has significance for the way that
counselling services design their service provision in the future. It is also
an interesting perspective when considered in the context of the health
service in the UK and would benefit from further, more in-depth work
across a range of public, private and third sector providers.

Summary

The work described in this chapter was not initially envisaged at the
start of the PhD research process, but seemed to provide a wealth
of useful information about the process of accessing counselling after
domestic violence. Both women and men showed a desire to access
counselling after suffering many different forms of domestic abuse, not
only physical violence. A number of key points came out of the study
such as the:

- level of distress required to prompt access of an external source of
  help
- idea of hopelessness and hope, and the role in prompting change

- problems in help-seeking resulting from past experiences or social isolation, which have particular relevance to mental health services
- importance of previously known and trusted contacts in creating a referral pathway when trigger points occurred leading to difficulties in coping
- poor experiences that many of the participants had of previous counselling
- importance of the first contact with the agency in establishing hope that the counselling could be helpful and trust in the agency to deliver appropriate counselling

These are important findings from the research in two ways. First of all it suggests that it is not sufficient to simply provide a counselling service for this client group. It is also important that the service is visible to potential clients and to trustworthy professionals in the area. In turn, those professionals must be able to recognise the signs of domestic abuse and emotional distress, and have confidence in the counselling service, so that appropriate referrals can be made. Finding ways to reach prospective clients through new, rather than existing, pathways may be a challenge. However, secondly, and perhaps more importantly, it shows that this client group is responsive to assistance and acts on recommendations, where the right conditions are present.

3
The Female Experience of Counselling

Up until now, we have followed both the male and female participants on their journey to seek support. However, after their decision to access counselling, their paths separate and in this chapter we look specifically at the experiences of the female participants. To recap: we have seen the participants identify their need for help and have seen them progress through a referral system and into the domestic violence agency. For the women specifically, this apparent deference to the referrer in agreeing to come to counselling may previously have been identified in the literature as a lack of self-confidence in making decisions or a sign of helplessness brought on by the experience of DV (Walker, 1977). In this present study, however, it appeared to be a considered decision based on their assessment of the referring individuals concerned, using a process that was perhaps designed to protect themselves from more disappointment.

Now the female participants, having had a positive experience at their assessment interview (where that occurred) decided to take up the agency offer of counselling, believing that it may be helpful to them. As noted earlier, having positive expectations on entering counselling has been shown, in general, to lead to a higher likelihood of a successful outcome (Cooper, 2008) and these participants were entering counselling having had a positive first experience of the agency and a helpful referral process. Feeling understood and supported may have helped the participants to make the decision to begin counselling and perhaps to feel some hope that it might be helpful this time. It may seem reasonable to assume that this would facilitate an easier beginning to counselling, but this did not necessarily seem to be the case.

Although the participants were prepared to engage with the process to some extent, they still lacked confidence in their ability to recognise good counselling and they still needed to establish trust in the counsellor. Hence they had, for good reason, some reservations as they began therapy, yet they did engage with the process. As they described the first few sessions, it became apparent that the ability of the counsellor to create an appropriate environment in counselling to meet their needs was an important factor in them continuing with counselling beyond the initial stages. Their description of the work done during that period suggested testing the counsellor through a process of gradual disclosure over a period of time.

The first session

Beginning counselling is a difficult time for any client. Whereas up until now their feelings and knowledge about what had happened in their relationship had been contained to some extent, there is now an expectation that this would be shared in some way. For a small number of the participants, this led to an outpouring of emotion as they had at last been given an opportunity to talk.

> Mary: And it was like it just all rushed out of me, like where's all this coming from? [...] you've just held it all back for years and years and years.

However, this level of disclosure at the beginning was not always helpful to the participant going forward. As they reflected on their initial sessions, it could seem like a power imbalance.

> Lucy: I used to come still feeling nervous, and still feeling, I felt as if the counsellor knew everything and I didn't know everything.

For these participants, there was a sense that they had disclosed many details about their lives to the counsellor, without really knowing what reaction or response would be given. For someone suffering domestic violence, not knowing what the others response might be or how the information may be used could have repercussions. Hence it is understandable that clients may have anxiety about returning for counselling after engaging at this level initially. It may be the therapist's response to this that is a factor in whether or not the client returns. This can be illustrated through the previous experience of one of the participants who was offered a structured counselling approach within a domestic violence programme.

> Fiona: initially I was just grateful for the opportunity to sort of share what had happened and [...] I didn't really need to be reminded about it [...] I found it was very upsetting so I stopped going.

She felt that her initial outpouring of feeling was being used in subsequent counselling sessions, which she found difficult. It is possible that the particular therapist was working on the assumption that, as Fiona had talked about particular issues in the first session, it was appropriate to structure the counselling to ensure each of those had been dealt with subsequently. However, Fiona felt some of those issues were of a deeply personal and private nature and she did not want to discuss those in depth when they were later referred to by her counsellor. Her reaction has been described before as possibly trusting her therapist too quickly (Sanderson, 2008) and highlights a difficulty for therapists working in this area. Whilst it can be valuable to note, during an intense period of sharing, areas that a client may want to explore at a later stage, it is important to remember that a counsellor directing the client into specific areas of exploration against their wishes contravenes ethical guidelines for most therapists in the UK (British Association for Counselling and Psychotherapy, 2010). It is important that clients can retain control of the process, even after disclosure.

By setting the topic for each session, the counsellor was potentially expressing power in and control of the environment and this could be experienced by a client as secondary abuse (Hattendorf and Tollerud, 1997), that is, the therapist increasing the client's pain through their intervention rather than relieving it. For someone having little confidence in herself and now also suspicious of and lacking confidence in her therapist, further disclosure was likely to lead to unpleasant feelings (Saypol and Farber, 2010) increasing client distress. Whilst the counsellor may have attempted to provide boundaries and structure, which can be appropriate for some clients, this must be done as a means to facilitate rather than control the client. Appropriate boundaries as part of the counselling service were welcomed by participants, but the personal relationship that developed with the counsellor was both important and beneficial (Muller, 2009) as can be seen in the section below on creating the right environment. It is important that counsellors recognise and work with both.

However, for the majority of the participants in this study, the expectation that they may need to share their experiences prompted quite a different response. As Karen shares below, life experiences may have shown that it is not always helpful to be open with someone that you have not yet got to know.

Karen: when you are telling people things that have happened, you do tend to watch people, and watch what they say [. . .] Do I trust you? [. . .] can I tell you these sorts of things?

The development of wariness or lack of trust as a result of DV experiences has been noted before in the literature (Dutton, 1992; Herman, 1992; Sanderson, 2008; Nicolson, 2010) and therefore this response is not in itself surprising. There are hypotheses about why a lack of trust develops which include: the realisation that their life partner cannot be trusted, and they do not know who can be (Dutton, 1992); the psychological impact of a traumatic experience (Herman, 1992); specific actions taken by the abuser to undermine the victim's trust in others to increase their isolation (Sanderson, 2008); and attachment issues which have recurred through the lifetime of the victim (Nicolson, 2010). The participants together told of life experiences which could fit each of these.

This sense of wariness, of being careful initially or subsequently about what to disclose to the counsellor, is different to general counselling research (Lambert, 2007). Lambert (ibid.) found that the predominant emotion prior to beginning counselling was uncertainty about what to expect in counselling and whether it might be helpful. However, most of the participants in this study were already aware of the counselling process, through previous experiences of therapy. In fact the reaction of the participants here are perhaps better aligned with why clients avoid counselling (Vogel et al., 2007), that is, low expectations of the outcome.

Domestic violence clients have been recognised in the literature as having particular difficulties in forming a therapeutic alliance (Barber et al., 2010; Breger, 2012). For these participants, working at a pace that suited them and allowed them to get to know their counsellor helped in gradually building their confidence in disclosing more and more of their experience. Having a therapist that was able to work with the limited amount of material that they were prepared to disclose was helpful and allowed the participant to develop the relationship.

Natalie: I think maybe's it's because we built a relationship as well, so I become, I got more confident with her.

It has been suggested that it is the therapist's ability to work with levels of disclosure and exploration that the client can tolerate that is a factor in building trust (Crits-Christoph, Crits-Christoph and Gibbons, 2010). For these participants, there appeared to be two very different levels of disclosure initially and counsellors will need strategies to deal with either.

Managing levels of exploration appeared to be common to these two groups and hence the counsellor's ability to work with the participant to disclose at an appropriate rate was important. Further disclosure also required the participant to have confidence that the counsellor would be able to cope with the material in the disclosure and respond appropriately, which had not always happened in previous counselling.

> Ailsa: I really don't know what it was, but I just didn't feel right, I didn't feel comfortable.
> Elizabeth: I saw a person from [organisation] and she was just, oh god, I just couldn't relate to her at all and just didn't carry on.

When participants described previous unhelpful or short-lived counselling, it appeared to be related to being unable to form a bond or connection with the counsellor and this factor has also been reported by general counselling clients (Paulson et al., 2001). However, participants in this study, as with others (Seeley and Plunkett, 2002), noticed when the counsellors did not have sufficient knowledge to understand their situation. Whilst a lack of specific knowledge of the clients' presenting issues did not appear to hinder general counselling (Paulson et al., 2001), it appeared to have an effect on counselling for this client group. Whether the participant was very open or closed initially, it was the way that the therapist responded during that and subsequent sessions that appeared to be key as to whether or not the counselling would be successful.

Creating the right environment

Although counsellors are trained from the outset in how to create the right environment for counselling, it is interesting to reflect on how clients might see this and consider how this might compare to the reality of practice. Perhaps surprisingly, given the level of wariness reported, one of the first messages from the participants in this regard was how 'comfortable' they felt.

> Natalie: I felt really comfortable with her, she made me feel completely at ease, but I don't think I said a great deal about anything. I think I was just too, a part of me was relieved that I got to that point, but I was still struggling with the whole, talking to somebody else about it I think.

Here Natalie highlights the issue for many of the participants, feeling that the counsellor was someone who was quite easy to be around and yet, despite that, not being able to talk about her experiences initially. This also highlighted the difficulty of not only admitting what had happened to the counsellor, but in doing so also admitting it to herself.

Advanced empathy

Being comfortable with the counsellor seemed to have a number of different aspects to it.

> Jackie: I was comfortable with her, for the fact that I didn't have to spell out every little thing but she still knew.

In humanistic counselling, this could be described as advanced empathy (Mearns and Thorne, 1999), where the therapist is able to sense what it is that the client wants to say and say it for them, or to respond in a way that allows the client to see that they have been understood. The degree of therapist engagement described by participants appeared to go beyond the relational model assumed within CBT, that is, a collaborative relationship which is strong enough to engage with counselling (Castonguay et al., 2010), due to the participants reluctance to fully engage. For clients to respond reflexively in counselling, the therapists actions need to match what the client wants and can respond to safely (Rennie, 2001). Here Jackie's therapist's action fitted Rennie's criteria, although his initial findings did not include the need for counsellor subject knowledge to match the client needs (Rennie, 2011).

The need for a counsellor to have knowledge of the types of situation the participant may have been in and responses they may have made is not a new finding. Acknowledging and naming the abuse is an area that has been highlighted as helpful in many DV research studies (Davis and Taylor, 2006; Hage, 2006; Day, 2008; Oswald et al., 2010). Walker (1994) felt the abuse needed to be identified, assessed and labelled to help the client, whilst Dutton (1992) believed educating the client about the abuse and their normal reactions to it had therapeutic value. Meanwhile Sanderson (2008) talked about affirming and validating the client experience. All of these principles were mentioned by the participants. However, the focus that emerged from this present study was slightly different. It was not just about educating the participant and confirming the impact of DV. Rather, it was the counsellor's ability to understand the participant and her situation and to be able to reflect what she was feeling through observation or empathy that was the most important aspect mentioned by participants. This is in keeping with other client research in this area where the therapist's ability to offer different perspectives about the abuse was seen as particularly helpful (Stenius and Veysey, 2005; Day, 2009; Social Policy & Research team, 2009; Oswald et al., 2010), as was feeling understood by the therapist (Stenius and Veysey, 2005; Social Policy & Research team, 2009; Oswald et al., 2010). Although building the counselling relationship and providing information on DV often appear as two distinct aspects of the work, it seems the two may be intertwined.

Non-judgement

As discussed in Chapter 2, experiencing domestic violence may result in developing an indirect communication style (Williams and Mickelson, 2008). Offering possible scenarios could provide an opportunity for clients to talk about something they may have been withholding or unable to mention. Sometimes the client will have experienced situations which they find deeply shaming after the event, and they struggle to articulate exactly what happened, fearing judgement from the other party. In this situation, working with a counsellor who not only understands that these things can happen but also empathises with the client's situation, can be very helpful.

> Paula: you just think everybody's out to judge you. You know when you come here you're not being judged and that made me feel really good.

Non-judgement was an important aspect of the counselling work and supported the development of a therapeutic relationship. Participants in the study valued the explanation of how domestic violence plays out, what the impact of that would be on the individual, and how the individual's reaction was perfectly normal in the context of the situation. This fitted with other research on PTSD (Keller, Zoellner and Feeny, 2010) which found that those who felt judged by others as being at fault or to blame for what happened, as can be the case with DV, found it harder to form a therapeutic alliance. Keller et al. (2010) found that showing and reiterating that the individual was not at fault or to blame was helpful. This is also a technique that appears in recommendations for DV work more generally and was found in this study. Importantly, non-judgement by the counsellor could also be seen as an expression of congruence. Consistent views being given by the therapist were helpful to the participants and over time, they came to accept that they would not be judged, which allowed more to be shared.

> Elizabeth: I'd say something and she'd make me understand why whatever had happened or, why I was seeing it such a way, and kind of turned things around and put a reason on it for me.

In terms of being comfortable with the counsellor, this had the added dimension of the counsellor being able to deal with the material being brought, and not being shocked or upset by it, but being able to discuss it appropriately and help the participant to gain new insight. In addition, a counsellor inviting the participant into a discussion about their experiences, but without insisting, suggested a readiness to explore whatever had happened.

> Samantha: it was more that she had seen things and noticed things I think.

This comfort with the material could be shown by the therapist noticing aspects of speech, behaviour or body-language and helped with exploring different aspects of their experience, previously hidden.

The expression of non-judgement by counsellors is sometimes described as unconditional positive regard, one of Rogers' (1957) core conditions. However, unconditional positive regard can also be described as acceptance, caring, warmth or affirmation (Cooper, 2008). Here, the participants were clearly differentiating between the non-judgement of their experiences, actions and responses, and the valuing of them as people. This is also an important distinction therapeutically for a counsellor in working with DV. Whilst the participants became more comfortable with the counsellor at this stage of the therapy, the descriptions of feeling cared for by the counsellor were more important in the next stage as they settled down to more in-depth work.

Freedom to speak

In keeping with many other counselling clients, the participants valued not only the confidentiality offered within counselling but also the freedom from other people's agendas.

> Amanda: They're coming at it from a completely separate stand point, an uninvolved stand point [...] any kind of decisions that might arrive, there's nothing affecting those, they're not gaining anything in any way from making it.

Counselling provided the opportunity for participants to begin to make their own decisions about their lives. For individuals who had often been controlled by their partners, this was particularly important. Here they were able to look at situations and explore them, knowing that the other person was there to help them, as they had nothing to gain from the outcome. The ability of the counsellor to understand their situation; their care and attention to meeting the participants' needs and managing an appropriate level of disclosure; an environment that provided confidentiality and non-judgement; all ensured that the levels of trust in the organisation were maintained and that trust in the counsellor and the therapeutic process was established.

Hope for the future

Finally, the participants valued the space and time they were given in counselling to work at their own pace.

> Jackie: she allowed me to speak freely, and allowed me to realise that those things I'd gone through before, I don't have to go through again.

As Jackie notes above, it was not simply about being able to share her experiences with someone who understood and helped her to realise what was going on in her life. It was also realising that she now had a lot of knowledge about abusive relationships and could recognise the signs of abuse quickly, which would help her to assess any future relationships appropriately. This change in her perception, from feeling unable to take action to being able to identify and carry out actions, is known to provide hope for the future (Stotland, 1969). The past was no longer an indicator of the future as those conditions were unique to that time. This new insight signified a change from feeling the hopelessness of having no control over future abuse (Clements et al., 2004) to the hope of having some control, based on realistic actions and outcomes (O'Hara, 2011).

Hope has previously been identified as important to victims of DV (Davis and Taylor, 2006; Social Policy & Research team, 2009; Allen and Wozniak, 2011). Yet the need for hope is not unique to DV clients and has been identified as part of the process of treating depression (National Collaborating Centre for Mental Health, 2009). These guidelines specifically identify the need to share hope that the counselling will work at the outset of therapy. However, given that many of these participants had previously accessed counselling, the therapist's assertion that the counselling will work without providing any additional evidence may not be heard. In addition, concerns have been raised by practitioners about the explicit discussion of hope early on in counselling as potentially undermining the client experience and appearing to set a therapeutic agenda (Larsen, Edey and Lemay, 2007). Instead, what appeared to be helpful was the creation of hope through the therapy process and the changes that the participant had become aware of as they began to have a different view of previous events.

For Amanda, there was an additional benefit. As she noted in Chapter 2 in 'Previous experiences of counselling', counselling which helped her to explore the dynamics of the abuse she had suffered helped her to understand what had happened and why she felt the way she did. Now she understood that it was the environment that her partner had created that had impacted on her mental health, rather than her inability to cope with and repair relationships. Once an individual realises that previous decisions had been made to the best of their ability and that poor outcomes were dependent on factors beyond their control or knowledge, hope can be created (Larsen et al., 2007). Now that Amanda had a different perspective, she began to feel that she could deal with things more appropriately in the future.

As well as providing some insight for the participants at this stage of the counselling, almost all of the participants talked about using counselling to deal with current issues in their lives. Almost half of the participants valued the tools and models that they had learned as these were useful at the time and also in the future.

> Karen: And now I just have a moment on my own if I really need to. [...] I could never deal with that before, because I never knew what to do.

For a few of the participants, there were some specific behaviours or thoughts that the counsellor was now able to help them to resolve, some of which had been troubling them for years.

> Paula: I had OCD, I used to brush my teeth about 20, 25 times a day. I would wash my hands until they were nearly gone, my nails were bitten to nothing.

The participants' descriptions of counselling interventions relating to these issues appeared to be similar to those currently recommended for depression (Gilbert, 2006) or anxiety (Donohoe and Ricketts, 2006). This suggests that cognitive behavioural or psychodynamic approaches are appropriate for working in these areas with clients. Initially focusing on smaller things that could be resolved relatively easily in counselling sessions enabled the client to feel more positive and more in control (Snyder et al., 1991). Succeeding in those areas created the possibility that bigger things might be possible. In other words, dealing with things of immediate concern also helped to build hope, but providing tools and understanding for the future led to longer term resilience (Stotland, 1969).

These changes in perceptions also helped the participants to see themselves in a more positive light for the future (Larsen and Stege, 2012). Valuing the strengths of the individual in coping with the abuse and helping to reframe experiences can be seen as ways of building hope implicitly (Larsen and Stege, 2010). Not only was hope generated from changes in cognition about the past and the achievement of goals now, but it was also reinforced by the realistic possibility of freedom in the future. In addition, these successes helped to increase the levels of trust in the therapist and the counselling process, with participants being prepared to accept the views of their experiences offered by the therapist rather than those previously given by the abuser.

The views of the participants indicated that they saw value in the depth of the therapeutic relationship, the development of insight and the specific actions being undertaken to improve their current situation. This suggests that a combination of therapy approaches may be effective. This is not a new conclusion, as Gilbert (2006) has also noted the need for a 'mixture of treatments' (p. 392) for depression, although in this case he was referring only to cognitive behavioural and psychodynamic therapy. Here there are signs of the value of a humanistic approach too. Other research with women who had experienced DV has also found that a single, focused approach may be less effective than an integrated approach (Morrissey, Jackson, Ellis et al., 2005).

Deciding to continue

For most of the participants, forming a close, trusting therapeutic relationship and beginning to feel more positive or hopeful about being able to improve their lives led to continuing counselling. As will be seen in the next section, having these foundations in place with the counsellor allowed them greater freedom to explore other issues, some of which had been of concern for many years.

Lucy: Because we were settled with discussing what was going on in the present, that section of the counselling then started bringing up memories of the past, some memories from childhood and times that had made me really unhappy.

For these participants, the continuation was a natural process and one that was to help them to understand more about how their life had unfolded as they felt more comfortable exploring their memories, emotions and responses.

However, a few of the participants did talk about having to make a specific decision to continue with counselling. This seemed to be linked to leaving a counselling session in the early stages of therapy feeling upset at some of the memories brought back as a result of counsellor facilitation, that is, exploration at a deeper level than they had prepared for or expected, rather than high levels of distress. In these cases the participants continued because they felt that, despite their reservations, at some level the counselling was helpful and presented an opportunity to get over their experiences.

Ailsa: I just knew when I was coming [here], even though I didn't want to know these things, it was helping.

A few of the participants took responsibility for the impact that the counselling had on them, as they had specifically requested short term counselling. They felt that the counsellor had been right to push them to explore material quickly and they had been willing collaborators.

Ruth: I think if you want to be counselled quite fast [...] I was like trying to think about things [...] I think I pushed myself a bit fast through it, actually.

With hindsight, Ruth believed that going a little more slowly might have been beneficial. However, the counsellor had worked quickly at her request and therefore she felt she was responsible for any difficulties.

From a counselling perspective, there are three aspects to note.

1. Almost all of the participants who experienced this distress did not bring this to the attention of their therapist, choosing instead to make a judgement about the benefits of continuing counselling outside the therapy session (as Ailsa described above) or discussing their

experience with their friends. Just as it was hard for the participants to share their experiences, so it was also difficult for them to
raise problems or issues that they might have with the counselling
(Eubanks-Carter et al., 2010). This suggests that if a therapist feels
a client has explored some material in a session that may have dis-
turbed or upset them, it may be helpful to check out how the client
feels and, if required, what coping mechanisms the client might have
available for the week ahead.

2. The distress was more manageable for the participant where the
   counsellor had indicated at the start of the therapy that this could
   sometimes happen and, if it did, it was a normal part of the process and should be brought to the next counselling session. Knowing
   it was a normal part of the process, and having tools to cope with
   those emotions, meant that the participant was less worried by the
   experience. It also indicated that the counsellor was experienced and
   knowledgeable about client work in this area and was open to discussion about any difficulties (Muran, Safran and Eubanks-Carter, 2010).
   These are all factors known to support the repair of any ruptures in
   the therapeutic relationship.

3. The third area of potential difficulty is the use of high levels of
   empathy by the counsellor. Whilst this was clearly valued by the participants, the therapist has to balance the woman's right to choose
   what and when to disclose, with a process of exploration. In helping
   the client to decide what to share, the counsellor helps the client to
   build trust in themselves and the therapist (Stenius and Veysey, 2005)
   and also to build confidence that any disclosure could be handled
   without harming the therapeutic relationship (Sanderson, 2008). It is
   possible that by focussing on the need for rapid exploration, the
   counsellor missed the choice of exploration route by the client.

However skilled the therapist, there is always the possibility of triggering memories or thoughts within a client which are distressing or
problematic for them at the time. For the participants in this study,
resolving these memories was seen to be productive and helpful given
the right supportive conditions, and therefore was something to be
worked through. A process of checking in with the client about how
they experience the counselling, providing literature about the risks
of counselling and what can be done to help if thoughts begin to
intrude between sessions, and working at the client's pace will all help
to alleviate any problems early on in the relationship.

Taking time to work together

The participants entered counselling after their relationships had ended or were in non-physically abusive relationships. Each of the participants were at different points in their lives, from caring for young children to adjusting to retirement. Nevertheless, it took time to develop a new kind of relationship with the therapist which allowed an honest exchange. This part of the process, of settling down and beginning to trust the counsellor and to have hope that counselling could create a positive difference in their lives was estimated by participants to take between four and eight sessions.

Whilst there were few direct quotations from the participants that specifically defined the timescale, the concept was endorsed through participants' descriptions of several sessions of work before finally disclosing an important issue and was confirmed as part of the research review process, as outlined in Appendix 2.

> Elizabeth: then after a while, the trust comes [...] and then the real nitty-gritty of it came out.
> Natalie: You've got to be able to trust that person [...] you're saying things and you think 'oh god I can't believe I've done that' or 'I can't believe that happened to me' or 'I can't believe I allowed that to happen to me'.

Other authors have suggested that this process of testing the therapist and settling down occurs over a relatively short period of time (one or two sessions) (Walker, 1994; Sanderson, 2008). Previous research has suggested that some changes in attachment pattern between client and therapist are possible during the first six sessions of counselling (Strauss, Mestel and Kirchmann, 2011) and perhaps this is what is reflected here. The participant descriptions suggested a change in the way they related to their therapists over that time period, which was important in continuing the counselling. Once the relationship was established, the focus changed for the next part of the counselling, which is consistent with other counselling research (Stiles, 2006). It would seem that building the foundation for this work cannot be rushed and yet strong foundations create an environment that brings positive change relatively quickly (generally 11–20 sessions in total, although clients with significant childhood abuse needed up to two years).

The need for trust

Natalie also describes some of the issues that may have held her back from disclosing earlier. There is a sense that at times she responded to or pre-empted the abuse, or went along with her partner's behaviour in the heat of the moment. As she reflected on what had happened, she acknowledged that this was outside what she considered to be her normal standards of behaviour, resulting in feelings of shame. However, there were two different aspects of shame: shame related to the abuse that was happening behind closed doors; and shame related to her own behaviour as a result of the abuse. In order for Natalie to be able to share the detail of the experiences, she had to feel that the counsellor would be able to understand her situation and would be able to help her to understand what had happened and why she had reacted as she had. The earlier work of the counsellor, in identifying and explaining other aspects of her experience that she had been able to share, was important now. As Natalie says, the trust that had been built was necessary for her to be able to go a little further and talk about those aspects that she found difficult to bear due to her own involvement.

Although trust has been noted previously in Chapter 1 as an issue for DV clients, it is not usually specifically addressed in standard coun-selling text books and rarely appears in the subject index. Generally trust is believed to be formed through the provision of empathy, uncon-ditional positive regard and congruence within therapeutic practice and appears to be assumed as an implicit requirement for all coun-selling. As such, it is generally not highlighted for particular attention. Indeed, these elements relating to counselling were, perhaps unsur-prisingly, highlighted as important by the participants. Whilst this study did not set out to explore the development of trust as part of the therapeutic relationship, elements of building trust appeared to be important throughout this stage of the process. The three contributing factors of ability, benevolence and integrity (Schoorman et al., 2007) can be seen in developing trust with these participants: the ability and knowledge of the counsellor to work at the participant's pace; their interest in exploring and interpreting the client situation and expe-riences; and the integrity of the counselling environment all helped. However, each of these factors needed time to become established with the participant.

Whilst many therapists may consider that they already work with clients in this way, other research findings have also suggested that a significant number of DV clients drop out of counselling within a few sessions (Howard et al., 2003; McNamara et al., 2008). It is possible that managing the complexity of this dynamic without understanding the factors contributing to client anxiety or distress is particularly challenging. Perhaps working with a six-session model adds additional pressure for both the client and therapist to make progress at a rate that can be difficult. It is also possible that it is not just about taking time to work together, but about making or creating time for the work, from both a client and therapist perspective.

Establishing firm foundations

As the participants began to accept and trust their counsellor, they began to relax more and share more of their experiences. As they talked about the counselling at this point, there was a difference in the way they described it. There seemed to be a deepening of the therapeutic relationship, of increased feelings of safety. This change or shift in the way they talked about the relationship is described below as a new phase of the counselling, that of the participant and the counsellor settling down together to address issues that had more significance for them. This provided the opportunity to talk about the more difficult events in their lives, related to their abusive relationship and/or their past lives. They had the opportunity to explore things that they had been concerned about but had not been able to share up until now. The counselling sometimes also prompted memories that they had forgotten about, but which now seemed relevant to their current situation. For some, those memories were of traumatic experiences and the exploration, understanding and resolution of those formed an important part of the counselling they received. Hence, taking the time to establish the therapeutic relationship, or the working alliance, or the necessary trust and hope to allow further disclosure, was a vital part of the work.

From a counsellor's perspective, the next few sections of the chapter appear to follow much of the literature previously published about domestic violence counselling with its roots in earlier work published by Dutton (1992), Herman (1992) and Walker (1994). However, not all of the women who participated in the research had undergone trauma work as part of their counselling, although more than half of them had. Instead, counselling was seen to have wider benefits than just the opportunity to process trauma: that of beginning to see themselves differently; to feel differently about themselves (sometimes as a result of the trauma work); and make changes in their lives. Having time to establish the relationship opened up the opportunity for further exploration. As this chapter shares the participants' descriptions of what counselling was like for them and what was important in the way that the counselling was delivered, it provides a slightly different focus. Here, existing theory and practice are seen to come together to meet client needs. In the following sections these three aspects, of settling down, working through past experiences and changing perspectives, are described in more detail.

Settling down

Now that the relationship with the counsellor had been established, the participants found that there were many different aspects of their experiences that emerged in sessions. The new found freedom to share what had happened in truthful detail provided the participants with a sense of relief. This in turn led to more and more being shared with the counsellor.

> Jackie: I felt really comfortable with [counsellor] and she could just say a couple of words and it brought things flooding out of me and I felt so relieved at times to walk out, even though I had cried for an hour solid.

This shows quite a change in relationship. At the start of counselling, the participants described a process of letting the counsellor see a little of their life story to see how they responded, to see if they could cope with and understand their situation. Now they described being able to share whatever they felt was important and needed to be discussed. The process of filtering material prior to bringing it to the session appeared to have stopped. Indeed, some of the participants described waiting for counselling so that they could explore new material. However, the impact of this change was not just in relation to the work done within counselling sessions.

> Lucy: the sense to be able to trust somebody again, because in trusting the counsellor and informing that relationship where everything that was said there was just between the pair of us, I actually began to trust other people more.

The experience of having someone to talk to who could be trusted implicitly had an additional impact outside counselling. The participants talked about how they recognised an increasing ability to talk with others outside counselling, to be able to share a little more of their lives, to ask for and accept support or help. Previous research has shown that those women who had a stronger social network were more likely to recover from the impact of domestic violence (Campbell et al., 1995). Here one of the noted benefits of domestic violence counselling was being able to start building those social networks again. In doing so, the foundations for leaving counselling and being independent once more, which is discussed in Chapter 5, were being laid.

Establishing trust, through the ability of the counsellor to understand the construct of domestic violence, the benevolence shown through wanting the very best for the client, and the integrity of a safe and confidential space away from others involved in the family, ultimately allowed the sharing and healing of the participants experiences. However, the deepening of the trust at this stage in the relationship appeared to be a strengthening of the participants' experience of benevolence. At this stage, it was not just the counsellor's experience of domestic violence that was important, it was also the quality of the relationship, as experienced by the participant.

> Karen: I've never felt loved. I have now but, I'm not saying that she, she loved me, but I thought she was bothered about me, and she showed me some signs of, like, motherly, sort of in comfortable and warmth, and I thought this is nice to have this.
>
> Veronica: I know there's somebody there that's been there for me and cared, and I know she's doing her job, but at the end of the day, I think she give me more than 100% of her job.

From a counsellor's perspective, this could be described as unconditional positive regard from a person-centred perspective, or as providing a secure relationship from a psychodynamic perspective. However, both Karen and Veronica indicate a quality to the relationship which seems to go beyond basic counselling theory.

The value of compassion

Clients who have experienced abuse (Barber et al., 2010; Breger, 2012) or trauma (Keller et al., 2010) have been identified as having particular difficulties in forming a therapeutic alliance and the growth of the alliance over time that may be more important than initial therapeutic interactions (Stiles and Goldsmith, 2010). In trauma work, the benefits of a deep therapeutic relationship showing tolerance and compassion for the client have been noted (Allen, 2005) and supported in more recent work (Briere, 2012). Although there are difficulties, not least with agreeing an appropriate definition of compassion (Gilbert, 2005b; 2009; Ricard, Kerzin and Hangartner, 2011; Siegel and Germer, 2012), this area of research has shown some promise as there are signs that this may have a physiological basis.

It has been suggested that experiencing cruelty can shut off the individual's ability to be compassionate, as their attention is focussed on self-protection (Gilbert, 2005a). A physiological hypothesis is that the experience of harm prompts the use of the right side of the brain for protection rather than for emotion regulation, thus resulting in hypervigilance in the pursuit of safety (Kirouac and McBride, 2009). This, in turn, may reduce the activity on the left side of the brain identified with compassion and social connection (Herrington, Mohanty, Koven et al., 2005). Interestingly, a reduction in the amount of left brain activity has also been found in work on patients experiencing depression (Grimm, Beck, Schuepbach et al., 2008). Therefore, trauma treatments which focus on improving only the emotional regulation capability of the individual may improve the emotional distress associated with trauma, but potentially miss the opportunity to also address the reduced stimulation of the left side of the brain associated with positive experience and affect, social connection and compassionate thoughts for others (Wang, 2005). Herman (1992) specifically addressed this issue by focusing on social reconnection as the third phase of her model for trauma. More recent work on brain activity suggests that feeling compassion for others can stimulate the left side of the brain and that this can also be developed and accessed more effectively (creating new brain pathways) through practising compassion based meditation (Lutz, Brefczynski-Lewis, Johnstone et al., 2008). The inclusion of compassion as a factor within therapy for treatment in cases of abuse may therefore have a physiological as well as an observed practice basis and has gained researchers' interest (Gilbert, 2009; Briere, 2012).

Experiencing compassion from the counsellor can result in positive feelings and promote well-being in the client. However, it is important to note that compassion can also be seen as something to fear by individuals who are insecurely attached and experiencing depression, anxiety and stress (Gilbert, McEwan, Matos et al., 2011). In those cases, compassion could be perceived as manipulation or dishonesty, or it could generate an expectancy of inconsistency based on the client's previous experiences. In the context of this study, it is interesting to note that the participants specifically commented on this aspect of the work after they had been working with the counsellor for a period of time and that the relationship had been considered to be consistent and honest.

Both Gilbert (2009) and Briere (2012) recognised a strong overlap with person-centred theory (Rogers, 1957). However, Briere (2012) positioned compassion as specifically different to empathy due to the additional need for caring, kindness and warmth, although those aspects had also been highlighted as being part of a helping relationship in person-centred therapy (Rogers, 1958). Perhaps Briere's description of compassion is not simply about technique, as empathy might imply, but about a way of being (Rogers, 1958). Briere (2012) and Gilbert et al. (2011) have also written widely about the need for compassion, yet the way they describe compassion is different: Gilbert et al. talk about a motivation to care, whilst Briere speaks of unconditional caring; Gilbert et al. encourage therapists to have the capacity for sympathy and empathy, whilst being non-judging or non-condemning, whereas Briere believes compassion requires attunement to, and acceptance of, the client. They appear to be discussing the same issues, yet the required degree of therapeutic engagement is quite different. This may be because Gilbert's (2009) view of compassionate therapy is positioned to be widely applicable, whereas Briere (2002) has based his views on his work with adult victims of childhood trauma. From this study, the participants' views would appear to align more closely with Briere, with a need for empathy rather than sympathy and an appreciation of the counsellor's acceptance for, and attunement to, them.

Research with practitioners in the USA considered to be compassionate showed a closer alignment with Briere's (2012) views, through identifying with being engaged, attuned and fully present with the client, whilst also being connected to the client's suffering (Vivino, Thompson, Hill et al., 2009). These practitioners also noted that although compassion can be present from birth, it can also be developed through sensing it from others or feeling the pain of others. This suggests that a client, working with a compassionate therapist, may have the potential to develop their own compassion for themselves and others. Research on the development of self-compassion suggested that it could reduce depression and anxiety (Barnard and Curry, 2011) and create a more stable sense of self-worth than focusing on self-esteem (Neff and Vonk, 2009). These are all outcomes that would seem to be particularly relevant to domestic violence counselling given the research findings discussed in Chapter 1.

During the research process, I was struck by the level of compassion offered by the participants involved in the study. They had been motivated to take part in the study for a variety of reasons: to help others, as they hoped the research would help to inform other counselling;

to support the agency by taking part in the research; and to acknowledge the very positive shifts that they had made in their own lives. In addition, after the interview had concluded a number of the participants asked me about my experiences during the research process, suggesting that it could not be pleasant listening to all the stories of abuse. What struck me was the caring, empathy and engagement of the participants in the process, all factors described above within compassion. Indeed, this observation ultimately led to a conference paper (Roddy, 2012) exploring the interaction of agency staff, participants and the researcher in the development, offering and receipt of compassion during the research process. If developing compassion within the therapeutic relationship was a significant building block for successful counselling with this client group, this may provide an explanation for research findings in a study with third sector volunteer counsellors, showing that counselling could be provided successfully without using specific trauma techniques (Humphreys and Joseph, 2004).

Given this fairly recent and ongoing research, it is perhaps not surprising that earlier studies of the therapeutic relationship for victims of trauma had also suggested that sensing an empathic connection (Payne, Liebling-Kalifani and Joseph, 2007) or developing a strong therapeutic relationship (Paivio and Patterson, 1999; Cloitre, Stovall-McClough, Miranda et al., 2004; Follette, Palm and Pearson, 2006) within therapy was particularly beneficial, whatever the modality of the therapist. It is also interesting to note that a compassionate approach to therapy could deliver a strong and caring therapeutic relationship, part of the foundation of a trusting relationship (Battaglia et al., 2003). The strength of the therapeutic relationship has been identified as an important aspect of successful therapy in counselling generally (Cooper, 2008) but, as implied in Herman's (1992) model, with trauma can come withdrawal from human connection and it may require a strong therapeutic relationship to reconnect.

Defining compassion

Although there are difficulties, not least with agreeing on an appropriate definition of compassion (Gilbert, 2005b; 2009; Siegel and Germer, 2012), this may be a potentially interesting area of exploration for future research, as cognitive behavioural, person-centred and neurological research interests meet. In this study, the participants' descriptions of what they felt was important to them in the relationship appear closer to the description of compassion given by the Dalai Lama (Bstan dzin rgya, 2010), rather than those highlighted above. The definition was derived from the writings of the major religions in the world and, interpreted from the counsellor's perspective within the context of DV counselling, includes the safety of both therapist and client, the ability to empathise, and the willingness to go beyond what is expected from a counselling relationship.

This definition seems particularly appropriate in this instance as it includes the safety of the therapist and client. Certainly the client needs to feel safe to be able to work effectively with the counsellor, and the participants indicated that they needed to feel that their therapist could cope with the disclosures they wanted to make, that is, feel safe to do so. However, a key topic for research from a therapist perspective is that of compassion fatigue which can prevent counsellors from working effectively with a client and cause them psychological harm if not properly addressed (Figley, 1995; Sexton, 1999; Baird and Kracen, 2006). In that sense, both the therapist and the client have to be able to work safely together. There is research to suggest that there are risks to the mental health of the counsellor of empathic engagement (Bush, 2009). These risks have been noted to increase where the therapist has a high case load of trauma work (Baird and Kracen, 2006) or lacks experience and training (Canfield, 2005). It is appropriate to note that the preferred characteristics of the therapists as noted by the participants indicated both training and experience, which would help to create safety for the counsellor and the client.

The important role of empathy both in this research and in other definitions of compassion is supported. It could perhaps be argued that to some extent all of the therapists working with these clients addressed the first two aspects, of safety and empathy, but it was the third aspect, the concept of going beyond what was expected by the client, that seemed to separate the participants who made progress from those who appeared transformed by the experience (see Chapter 5).

The perception that the counselling had gone beyond their expectations of therapy is shown by the responses of Karen and Veronica earlier in this section and was added to by other participants. Examples that were given included: providing comfort in bereavement; having belief in their potential; of feeling loved in some way by the counsellor; and feeling that the counsellor was prepared to go beyond the client's perception of the scope of the job. Although this can be linked to aspects of the valuing process (Rogers, 1964), the description from the participants related to connection to, rather than separation from, the counsellor. Whilst it may be questionable whether this level of relationship could be sustainable with every client, particularly given the potentially high personal cost for counsellors, it did indicate a high level of commitment by the therapists.

It is possible that this deeper change in the participant, as they not only thought differently but also felt differently about themselves, did have a physiological basis. It is possible that the depth of feeling experienced with the therapist was successful in stimulating the right brain's positive experience and affect function, resulting in the participant feeling differently as well as thinking differently. Perhaps working with a compassionate therapist allowed them to connect more clearly with this part of the brain and at the same time the positive feeling function. This would support the participants' identified valuing of a close therapeutic relationship. Clearly this is a hypothesis, but perhaps one worthy of further investigation, whilst recognising that there may also be other mechanisms involved.

Given the needs identified in this research study for DV clients, it appears that the challenges for general practice counsellors to provide the right conditions when seeing clients are great. The need for an empathic knowledge of DV, showing competence to be able to cope with what may be traumatic disclosures to ensure safety for client and counsellor, plus extending the scope of the counselling to meet the new and emerging challenges faced by the client, all suggest this might be difficult to achieve without specific training. Whilst this is a small study and cannot be generalised, the drop-out rate of counselling research studies within domestic violence has been high (Howard et al., 2003; McNamara et al., 2008). In addition, there have been no quantitative studies which specifically address the domestic violence client's perception of the therapeutic relationship. In effect, if this is a critical aspect of therapeutic work in domestic violence, it is one that could, and perhaps should, be included in future research.

Changing perspectives

As the participants became more open about their experiences and how they thought and felt about them, so their counsellor was afforded more opportunities to discuss the experiences and challenge some of their views.

> Mary: And also realising that it wasn't your fault [...] it's always been put on you that you're the one to blame [...] and suddenly you realise [...] It's not what you're doing, it's what's being done to you that's creating it.

The value of working with someone who could understand the dynamics of domestic violence and could link what is known about DV to the client experience is not a new finding (Stenius and Veysey, 2005; Day, 2009; Social Policy & Research team, 2009; Oswald et al., 2010), but this provides a good reminder of the value of that sort of support. Here Mary expressed her frustration at finally understanding that she had been accepting the blame for events in her relationship which had been orchestrated by her partner. This provided the motivation for her to be clearer and firmer with boundaries when dealing with her ex-partner.

However, it was not only changing the client perspective of their abusive partner that was important.

> Fiona: I wasn't judged or undermined. You know it wasn't 'are you being an absolute…?', the only person that was judging or undermining me was myself.

As Fiona worked with her counsellor, she began to realise that a lot of her ideas about how the world may see her were coming from herself, the product of years of feedback undermining her confidence and feelings of self-worth. Here the counsellor was able to help Fiona see herself in a different light, leading to increases in her self-confidence and self-esteem. There seemed to be value for participants like Fiona in examining their own beliefs about themselves and being encouraged to think more positively about themselves, partly through their counsellor's belief in their capability.

However, there was some evidence that this aspect of counselling was not always successful, particularly when the counsellor urged a particular philosophical view which was at odds with the clients own values.

> Ailsa: I'm sort of letting people tell me what to do, I think that's how we put it. Going along with people […] and please people. I used to get upset over that, thinking 'how am I going to change that?'

Ailsa had spent much of her life in service to others and gained a great deal through being able to help when she could. The presentation in counselling of an alternative view which suggested that she should spend less time helping others and more time putting herself first, led to further internal conflict. As she tried to be less helpful to others to make time for herself (which she did appreciate) she felt guilty for letting them down. Although undoubtedly well-meaning, it is a pertinent reminder to us, as counsellors, that the client knows best and that any challenges to perception of self or others must be aligned with their own system of values.

> Elizabeth: I just tell myself what [counsellor] has told me and try and try and believe it, which is easier said than done.

Here the counsellor had been trying to raise Elizabeth's self-esteem and help her to see herself in a more positive light. Whilst she felt she needed to try, there was something that had not quite connected. As a result, she felt that she was somehow not able to do something she should be able to do: have a good opinion of herself.

These are the difficult areas of research, as these are instances that could occur in any counselling practice. However, the concept of empowerment seems to play a part here. Empowerment has been identified as an important therapeutic goal by leading researchers in the field (Dutton, 1992; Walker, 1994; Sanderson, 2008) although their definitions have varied. Dutton (1992, p. 115) defined it as 'choice making', whereas Sanderson (2008, p. 167) talked about 'restoration of control' (Sanderson, 2008, p. 167) and Walker (1994) discussed empowerment in the context of understanding the dynamics of abuse. Different definitions of the word suggest it could mean to invest with a power, to equip with an ability or to enable, that is, an externally applied intervention. In this case, it seemed that for successful change, the power had to develop internally in the participant through their own understanding and insight, rather than by adopting views presented externally by the counsellor, however well-meaning or constructive the intention.

A third aspect of changing perspectives was around their own self-concept.

> Jenny: she said 'How have you been?' [...] 'Oh I've been really depressed for a couple of days this week', she said 'You know it's all right to have a down day.' I don't put it down to depression anymore, it's just a day where I don't particularly feel good or something like that.

Here, Jenny had suffered with depression for many years. Although she had made good progress in counselling, she continued to see any dip in her new, brighter outlook on life as a return of the depression. Hearing that having the odd 'down day' was a normal experience and not something to be unduly worried about provided a reassurance that down days could be managed and were not necessarily indicative of the beginning of a longer spell of depression. This change in perspective was life changing for Jenny.

Finally, changing perspectives also provided the impetus to make physical changes in their lives. Paula had spent many years unable to go out on her own as a result of her earlier experiences. Her family had been very supportive in ensuring that there was always someone available to accompany her.

> Paula: I just went along with what everybody else wanted, and she made me realise that I could go out on my own. The first time I went out on my own [...] when I got home [...] I just sat down and cried my eyes out: I can do things.

Each of these participants had benefited from a change in their perspective: of themselves, others, their own capability. Participants who were able to see that there was a different way to view things, and that their previous view was in some way flawed, were able to make substantial changes to their lives.

These are not new findings. Beneficial change to the way that individuals, who have experienced DV, think about themselves and others has been noted as a therapeutic goal in the literature for many years (Dutton, 1992; Walker, 1994; Dienemann et al., 2002; Lee, 2007; Sanderson, 2008). This research serves to show that the identified need for the work by psychologists and psychotherapists has also been reflected in what the participants themselves have found helpful.

Working through past experiences

For more than half of the participants, counselling led to discussion of significant events in their past, which benefited from resolution. Although most of the participants were already conscious of the events that they needed to share, some found that things came into their consciousness as a result of the counselling.

> Amanda: it's more just the [...] talking about things that you've never told anybody ever and that triggers other memories, and other things that I haven't even admitted to myself

Where there appeared to be some differences in the counselling received was the therapist's response to the need for trauma work. For some, the process of remembering the trauma was facilitated by the counsellor, using imagery of the event in keeping with Herman's (1992) recommendations. Where it appeared that a single, significant childhood event had taken place, and the therapist had been trained in Eye Movement Desensitisation and Reprocessing (EMDR), this was offered.

> Lucy: the counsellor asked 'can we try a few different ways of exploring them?' [...] and I asked loads and loads and loads of questions, but then I thought 'well this could be the way forward to explain the thoughts that I'd had for years and years that I couldn't explain'.

Most participants seemed to have a similar experience to Lucy, where the counsellor had discussed the options and risks surrounding trauma work with the participant and there was clear consent to do the work. Whilst there was understandable anxiety going into the process, there was also a great sense of achievement and relief when they could finally understand their forgotten experience.

> Jenny: I couldn't believe it. Wheewww! I just can't describe the immense relief it felt to confront it [...] and once I did the difference it made.

One of the reported physical effects of working through trauma, reported by three of the participants, was a sense of relief or energy release during the process. This aspect of trauma work is not often mentioned in the literature, but it has been noted before (Kepner, 1996). The concept of storing trauma in the body, and the impact of that on physical health has also received attention (Rothschild, 2000; Etherington, 2003). However, here the release appeared to happen without any focus on bodywork, simply as a consequence of reprocessing the trauma. There is no clear explanation of the reasons or mechanisms for this occurring, but it was perceived positively by the participants.

Although most of the participants reported positive experiences of their trauma work, there were other examples where the experience was described as more challenging. Here, the decision to explore the past seemed to have been directed by the therapist.

> Samantha: all my brushing away of things and minimising of things didn't quite work with her. She still stuck at it and [...] it was a few sessions before we really got down to what was really at the heart of it.

Whilst ultimately Samantha felt she had benefited from confronting the issues identified in her counselling, the process of uncovering these, without her conscious consent and despite her best endeavours to stop the explorations, left her at times with out-of-body experiences and so shaken she struggled to walk out of the counselling room. Ruth also described feeling out of control as a result of uncovering traumatic memories.

> Ruth: it just unlocked loads of stuff in me mind. I kept on dreaming it, it was just unlocking all this stuff, I mean I felt like I was going bonkers. I was just a massive roller-coaster of emotion for like two months.

Although Ruth also felt that she had ultimately benefited from her experience, this sense of feeling out of control for an extended period was one that only she and Samantha appeared to share. Briere (2002) highlighted that there is a balance to be struck in counselling between working with client avoidance and triggering re-traumatisation. It is important for counsellors to understand the experiences of people reliving trauma (Herman, 1992) to ensure that they can take appropriate action to support a client in difficulty.

Working safely with trauma

Ruth and Samantha's stories were also different from the other participants in that their counsellors appeared to have directed them into examining their past. In trauma work, it is usually considered appropriate for the client to choose which areas to explore at any given time (Herman, 1992) with the counsellor constantly monitoring the client during the session to ensure they can tolerate the emotional intensity. Sessions should be structured to allow exploration of new material at the beginning and allow for a period of reorientation and calming for the client in the last third of the session (Herman, 1992) enabling them to leave the session safely. This did not appear to be the case here, and may explain some of the difficulties that these two participants described. Clearly, it is important for counsellors working with this client group to have appropriate training in working with trauma.

Concerns could be raised about Samantha's experience under the BACP ethical framework values of autonomy, beneficence and non-maleficence (British Association for Counselling and Psychotherapy, 2010). These values identify the need for practitioners to act in accordance with the trust placed in them, to seek freely given and adequately informed consent and to act in the client's best interests particularly when their capacity is diminished through extreme distress or lack of understanding. It is important to remember that the client's decision to seek counselling is not equivalent to consenting to any counselling process. Although to suggest working with previous trauma could be in line with acting in the client's best interests, carrying this out needs the informed consent of the client. The counsellor also has a responsibility to help the client to manage the level of distress prompted both at the time and during the following week. This can be achieved, for example, by explaining the process to the client and providing leaflets for them to read, so that they know the potential impact of the work, as well as teaching mindfulness and relaxation techniques prior to beginning.

Summary

Although the elements discussed in this section could be considered part of the wider knowledge base regarding good counselling practice and good DV practice, it is important to recognise that these are two different things. At first sight, the elements of counselling described by participants could each be covered technically by a general counselling practitioner. However, what has been described is closer to integrated practice and suggests counsellors are working with very high skill levels in creating a highly empathic and non-judgemental environment. Helping the client to understand DV was not simply helpful to the client, but appeared to be essential to building the relationship. Whilst this is widely recognised within the DV community, this is still not taught as a standard part of counselling training. At the same time, the DV community is being focussed through government funding on giving priority to advocacy. Whilst this does provide support to understand the DV situation and consequences, it does not provide the time and focus to facilitate the deeper relationship which provides the foundation for the next, very important, stage of recovering from the experience by being able to understand it in the context of their own thoughts and feelings.

The therapeutic process outlined here introduced a number of factors which are important for this client group. The development of trust through the competence of the counsellor and the integrity and desire to help from both the counsellor and the organisation, and of hope, through understanding, achieving small improvements in their lives and gaining a sense of being able to control their future, were both important aspects. Yet it took time for the participants to be able to settle down into the relationship properly. In addition, trust was deepened as the participants sensed the counsellor to truly have their best interests at heart. The deepening of the relationship may have been linked to compassion from the therapist. It is possible that, in working compassionately, counsellors also facilitate changes in the participants' view of themselves and the world.

In keeping with previous literature, the participants valued taking more control of their lives, of being able to work through and process past experiences which until now had been hidden, and in gaining a change in their perspective on their experiences, themselves and their capability to make changes in their lives. However, there were some pertinent reminders about the difficulties in working with trauma, and the need to ensure fully informed consent for work in this area. In addition, the concept of empowerment which is readily accepted as an appropriate outcome in DV work is questioned in the context of change coming from within the individual, rather than absorbed from others.

In summary, these are the main points coming from the therapeutic process described by female participants:

- DV clients are likely to have problems initially with disclosing the extent of their experiences and may require support to disclose at a rate appropriate for them.
- Facilitating disclosure requires high levels of empathy and extensive knowledge of how DV happens and its impact on the individual from the outset.
- Trust is developed through the ability of the therapist to work with DV, their genuine interest in the client and their story and the integrity of both the counsellor and their environment – confidentiality is important.
- Hope is developed by helping the client to: understand their experiences in the context of the abuse rather than any failure on their part; resolve current issues that are troubling for them; value their strengths; and see a future that can be different from the past.
- Understanding the potential for counselling to trigger distressing memories for clients and ensuring appropriate support for clients may help to resolve early difficulties in counselling.
- Therapist training in counselling models which employ techniques of therapeutic depth, facilitating client insight and problem solving is likely to be beneficial and may encourage an integrative practice approach.

- This client group requires time to settle into counselling and this may require a different model of service provision than generally available, that is, more than six sessions.
- Compassion appeared to be valued by the participants, particularly during the second phase of the counselling where more in-depth disclosure occurred. This included acceptance of, caring about and attunement to the participant, as well as a sense of safety for the participant and counsellor and a belief that the counsellor would go beyond the normal scope of counselling work to support and help the participant.
- Trauma work will not be required for all clients, but where it is, properly informed consent and a process that can be guided by the client fits with ethical guidelines for counselling and psychotherapy. Appropriate training in trauma is also a prerequisite.

In all of this, it is important to note some of the economic challenges being faced by counsellors today. As services come under increased pressure, not all third sector agencies can offer up to 20 sessions of counselling to all clients. From a private sector perspective, not all clients can afford to commit to up to 20 sessions. From a public sector perspective, 20-session therapy may be an option, but may require more than one referral and early disclosure from the client to access appropriate support. Any of these factors may preclude this client group from getting the support they need. In our current systems of counselling provision, it would appear that this type of specialist service is not available to this client group easily. Although this may be a new area to consider and requires more research, perhaps aspects of this study could be taken into account when designing and funding counselling services for DV in the future.

4
The Male Experience of Counselling

As we leave the women in Chapter 3 coming to the end of their counselling, so we re-join the men at the beginning of theirs. As outlined in Chapter 2, the process for deciding to seek help had many similarities in the descriptions of both men and women, although the response to those requests had, at times, been different. Whereas the women were able to access a local agency, the men had to travel some distance as there was only one available to them. In addition, the women had generally received a sympathetic response to their experiences, whereas the men had struggled to find someone that believed their story.

Initially, when the decision was taken to include men as part of the research study, it was assumed that third sector agencies within the UK would be available and able to take part in the research. Unfortunately, in 2011, this was not possible. Although there were agencies that worked with male victims, they were not in a position to contribute to the research. Some were in their infancy, and their clients were still going through the process, yet to complete. Those who had worked with men had only a few who had accessed counselling and were uncertain about how many clients, if any, would be prepared to participate in the research. In addition, the levels of funding provided for the services were small, and the need for the participating agencies to offer additional counselling to research participants if required, precluded their inclusion. Ultimately, an agency in Eire was identified and agreed to become part of the research process, allowing this part of the research to be followed through.

Initially, the assumption regarding counselling was that the male process would be similar to the female one, to the extent that the two processes could be integrated to produce a combined DV counselling approach. However, that proved to be impossible for a variety of reasons, including political, economic and social factors. Nevertheless, some of the challenges presented by men in Ireland as a result of their experiences are very likely to be experienced by men in the UK. On occasions where this research on the male experience of counselling has been presented in the UK, men have come up at the end of the session to disclose that they too have suffered from domestic violence. Each of them indicated that the representation given had resonated for them. Each of them also felt that it would be useful to have a similar piece of work conducted in the UK, something that is now being considered as part of future research plans.

At the time of writing, no literature expressing a model for counselling men who had experienced domestic violence had been found. As a result, the information contained in this chapter is, in some ways, unique. Whilst it has not been possible to link the research data back to existing literature for this reason, the research process outlined in Appendix 2 included review processes with both participants and agency staff. Hence, this model is seen as representative of the participants' experiences and the described process was recognised by staff who work on a daily basis with other male victims of domestic violence.

As a result of funding differences with agencies that support women who have experienced DV, the men were not usually offered long term counselling as the agency could not afford to do so. Instead, the men were offered a variety of support including one-to-one support from agency staff as needed, up to six sessions of counselling (extended only in extenuating circumstances) and participation in ten sessions of group work led by a counsellor. In addition, some of the men accessed their own counselling privately although, as found with the women, their experience was mixed. When the agency was recruiting participants for the research, the men identified each of these services as being counselling. During the interviews, the men talked in depth about each of the services, switching between them to show specific helpful aspects of each. What became apparent was that there were different strengths to each approach, and it was more appropriate to look at the way the men had experienced one-to-one intervention compared with a group intervention. Hence this chapter is structured differently to the previous one, where all of the participants had undergone a recognisable counselling process, and describes the two intervention approaches separately. Nevertheless, there are a number of points which come from this work which are helpful for anyone working therapeutically with this client group.

The other factor to note was that the men who accessed short-term interventions, tended to re-access the services at the agency, whereas the women did not. However, the two men who had been able to access counselling on a similar basis to the women had not had any need to re-access the services since then. There is therefore an apparent difference in outcome between counselling and short-term support and group work. However, there was insufficient time and funding for this research project to investigate this further and it remains an area for future development.

The remainder of this chapter will discuss the two main forms of counselling described by the men, namely one-to-one support and group work.

Working one-to-one

Five of the six participants had experienced one-to-one support for their experiences. Two had positive experiences of support at the agency, two had positive experiences of counselling at the agency and one had a variety of experiences of counselling which he felt had not yet resolved his issues. The small number of participants means that the views represented here may not be representative of all men in this situation, but they do start to provide a perspective on how men viewed counselling and support and what was important to them.

The value of talking to the right person

One of the key benefits the men identified in working one-to-one with someone was the benefit of talking to someone independent of their normal social circle. They felt relief at being able to offload to someone they felt was able to hear the things they needed to say.

> Mark: I suppose the most important thing is that it was very useful to offload painful and difficult things that I couldn't necessarily expect my friends to be able to cope with

Many of the men talked about how difficult it was to find someone to confide in. The sort of relationships they had with individuals outside of their relationship did not support a discussion about the difficulties they had with their partner. They also felt it was easier to talk to someone who was not involved in their lives.

> Matthew: The family are great, but I just found it easier talking to a stranger you know, I'd be embarrassed talking to my mam or me brothers or sisters, about certain things or issues.

This is an important theme in the work, as the men seemed to make judgements about what they could discuss with different people. In the context of their relationship, they felt they could not talk to anyone who knew their partner in case the details shared might reflect badly on her, or the conversation might get back to her and have a negative impact on the relationship. It is important to note that these men had already identified that part of their problem in seeking help was the isolation they had experienced as a result of the abuse. Hence, for some of the men, this was not simply about finding the right environment in which to talk about their relationship, but also about learning how to talk about themselves and how they felt.

> Hugh: he'd ask me a question and he'd let me carry on, and there was no shutting me up then, because I felt I was free of this burden.

For Hugh, being allowed to carry on with his answer was a different experience. The importance of this step in the process is also highlighted when considering the outcomes that were valued, which included now being able to talk to people about a range of issues (see Chapters 2 and 5). Whereas some of the women talked about making a judgement relating to the level of disclosure, some of the men talked about not really understanding what was required of them, and it taking a while to get used to talking about things.

The difficulties that men can have in talking about their emotions and feelings has been documented in the literature (Betz and Fitzgerald, 1993), yet the experiences of the participants suggested that this was only a problem initially. Working with someone who was interested in what they had to say, facilitated the discussion and indicated that it was appropriate to discuss their difficulties, meant that it became very easy to talk.

As well as having the freedom to talk, the participants found that talking through the many issues they were facing helped them to clarify issues.

> James: Things are put into their right boxes.

Feelings of being overwhelmed before accessing the agency meant that they had found it difficult to decide what to do. Being helped with sorting out priorities enabled them to take back some control in their lives. As they began to achieve small successes with the goals they set, the hope they felt on arrival at the agency began to grow (Stotland, 1969).

The men were offered the opportunity to work with both male and female staff. Men who worked with both noted that they chose to discuss different aspects of their situation with the different staff members. For example, many of the participants had children and wanted to find someone to share any incidents that had happened and seek ideas on what to do next. Here they valued the female members of staff.

> Matthew: I can ring up the girls there saying 'Oh, I had a bad night with the young guy' or 'they're giving me a lot of stick because they hate me' [...] I get upset, you know, and I just ring up the girls.

On the other hand, there were issues, sometimes of a very personal nature, where they felt it was much easier to talk to a man.

> Hugh: Now, the fact that he's a man and he'd have certain understandings of life, what way life, the role as a man, the man's role and as I say, that's where the comfortability come into it, whereas with [female counsellor] as I said, I held back on a lot of stuff.

Previously research has indicated that gendered pairing of counsellor and client can produce better results (Betz and Fitzgerald, 1993) and this research suggests that the men did gain a great deal from being able to share their experiences with another man. The possible impact of gender within counselling relationships prompted by experiencing DV has been raised previously (Hogan et al., 2012). Hogan et al. (2012) suggested that men may be reluctant to work with a woman given their experiences with a female perpetrator, or that they may be scared to disclose to a male therapist if they felt they had to present a manly image to him. This study suggested a different dynamic. Hugh had previously worked with a female counsellor and whilst he found her personally very pleasant and helpful, it took him quite a long time in counselling to disclose his situation. He explained this as his feelings about being a man and the difficulty of sharing his perceived weakness of being abused by his spouse with a woman. This particular aspect could be related to Gender Role Conflict (O'Neil, 2008), which describes the tension felt by men when not living up to their perceptions of masculinity, and this may have been a factor for other participants.

If we consider this also in the context of the need for trust highlighted in Chapter 1, it is possible that for men, the component around competence in the area to be explored is significant (Mayer et al.,

1995). There was certainly recognition of the need for all of the staff to understand the experience of DV, but it seemed that there was also a need in counselling for that understanding to extend to their feelings as a man abused by a woman. Whilst the female members of staff worked successfully with many male clients, particularly in areas of advocacy where their level of expertise was clear, it may be the perception of some male clients that someone who is not male would not fully understand their situation.

When considering UK provision for male victims, much of this has been developed by encouraging existing DV agencies, who worked exclusively with women, to extend their service to men. Such female DV services in the UK were outside equality legislation as the case had been made for female only services (Exempt under the Equality Act 2010 pursuant to Schedule 9, Part 1). From the limited data in this study, it appears that there are aspects of this service which would be acceptable to men in some circumstances, as the participants saw female agency workers as very professional and capable of dealing with a range of issues that could emerge.

Whilst there appeared to be no problems for the men in this study of talking to women and accepting help from them, the participants clearly valued the opportunity to discuss their situation with other men, someone that they believed could understand their situation from their perspective. This could be a gender issue relating to assumptions that the men might make about the different areas of expertise being offered by male and female staff members. This study may highlight the need for agencies working with male clients to make it easy for them to access male counsellors or staff members, which may need to go beyond offering male support workers on request. Given the difficulty the participants identified initially in talking about and articulating their feelings and needs, it may require a facilitative approach to determine their preferences. It is also worth considering whether female or male assessors should conduct the initial interview, and if women do so, how they could approach the question of any gender preference in a counsellor.

It would be wrong to draw firm conclusions from such a small study and the discussion here shows that gender issues in the context of talking to someone who may be able to help are not yet fully understood and would benefit from further research. However, there is some evidence to suggest that simply extending the existing female only services may not fully meet the needs of male victims.

Finding someone who cared

This was perhaps one of the most poignant of findings from the whole of the research project. It was difficult to listen to the participants talk about their experiences prior to contacting the agency, of not being believed, of their actions being misinterpreted, of assumptions being made about their part in the breakdown of the relationship.

> James: the very first thing, the most important thing was to be believed. That was essential as far as I was concerned ... and not to be judged.

The stories the men told were reminiscent of those told by women in the 1980s and 1990s, when there was an assumption that she must have done something to provoke the abuse that she had suffered (Frost, 1999). Now there appeared to be a similar assumption that the man must have contributed in some way to the abuse. His denial was not believed and his frustration and anger at not being believed were an indication of his guilt. Identification with being a victim during an abusive relationship can continue even when the abuse has ended, leading to feelings of low self-worth and depression (Matsakis, 2001). It is possible that the institutional response to these men compounded these feelings. Just as they had not been able to get their wives to see how hurt they had been, so this continued as they tried to get help from external sources.

The men described the disbelief and lack of support they encountered from the public sector generally and, more specifically, the advice they had received from the police.

> Matthew: she advised me certain things, no matter how much anger, never, ever raise me hand. If it got that heavy just go out and walk around the block until things had calmed down

The police did ask if he wanted to press charges, which he did not want to do. There was no advice for Matthew about how to deal with his partner, who was attacking and physically harming him, other than to walk away. Their advice was designed to keep his partner safe and him from facing court charges relating to domestic violence.

For these men, the agency represented the first organisation they had contact with where they felt someone did care about them.

Peter: somebody who is genuine and somebody who genuinely cares about what you have to say and who's genuinely, you know, cares about your welfare, which is strange coming from a stranger.

It is hard to describe in a few words the emotional context of these particular disclosures in the interviews. Having been faced with a variety of people who did not understand the gravity of the situation they were in, to find someone who recognised their difficulties and cared about how they were, made a tremendous difference to them and to their ability to get on with their lives.

Equally, as Mark identified, where this was not present, it made it very difficult to make progress.

Mark: Do you know the whole idea of compassion fatigue, that's kind of what it felt like with him. He was there and he was going through the motions and waiting for a thirty second pause, and then he'd say 'go on'.

There were two important aspects to this. First of all, Mark needed to know that the person he was talking to was responding genuinely (or congruently in person-centred terms) and secondly that he was listening to and cared about what he was saying. Having had a variety of people claiming to want to help them but with little assistance given, it became much more important to the participants that the response to them was genuine. Once they knew at least one person did support and want to help them, that provided a beginning. Interestingly here, whilst the concept of compassion fatigue was raised in Chapter 3 as a risk to the counsellor, Mark correctly identifies this as a risk to the client too, as it may prevent them from sharing their experiences.

Defining compassion

Matsakis (2001) identified that men who have been abused can feel that they do not deserve to be cared for, and so finding someone who could help them to see they were worthy of care could be a significant factor in recovery. This concept is very much in line with the basis of person centred counselling (Rogers, 1957) and both the therapist and support workers at this agency had been trained in person centred support. This also fits with more general recommendations for counselling male victims which specifically highlighted the need to work with someone who was warm, caring and compassionate (Cook, 2009). Indeed, this also fits with the concept of working with a compassionate therapist introduced in Chapter 3, one who could be attuned to the client and accepting of them.

However, it is possible that the compassion valued by the male participants was slightly different to that described by the females. Whilst the women valued a relationship that allowed their own and the counsellors' safety, where they could experience empathy and sense commitment from their counsellor (Bstan dzin rgya, 2010), the men valued feeling cared for (positive regard) and understood (empathy) by their counsellor and helped, both emotionally and practically. This suggested an alternative definition of compassion as:

> (1) 'I feel for you' (affective), (2) 'I understand you' (cognitive), and (3) 'I want to help you' (motivational).
>
> (Hangartner, 2011)[1] (Siegel and Germer, 2012, p. 12)

What is not clear, because of the limited nature of this research, is whether this appreciation of help in a more practical sense is a difference in the needs of men and women, or reflects that the service was delivered at an earlier stage of the support process, where gaining help to resolve issues may have been a greater priority.

As the agency has been active for over 15 years, it is possible that the way the service was delivered has been developed to meet the needs of the men it supports. There is some evidence to suggest that men value help given or received (Addis and Mahalik, 2003) and even for those engaging in longer term counselling it was the helpfulness in supporting them to make changes that was emphasised by participants. In addition, research at a male DV agency in Northern Ireland suggested that practical as well as emotional help was required (Sweet, 2010). The participants wanted to become independent and resolve issues on their own, and therefore wanted support which helped them to do so. As a small study, this is not a conclusive finding, but it does show an area of work where further research at different agencies and with other counsellors could be beneficial. Nevertheless, it is reasonable to hypothesise that, as with the women, the need for caring and/or compassion appears to be central to the work required with this client group.

Learning about his partner

In keeping with other research about DV, the participants all valued learning more about the behaviour of their partner. One of main aspects that the participants seemed to find helpful was the knowledge that, despite everything they had tried to do to support and help their partner, she was not going to change.

> Mark: I got out of my DV situation [x] years ago, and since then the DV has continued with its perpetrator through [daughter]. So you have [daughter] is being used as the stick

This description of the abuse not ending even after the relationship was over was commented on by most of the participants, and is something that has been confirmed subsequently in discussions with other men in the same situation. Although the relationship was over, keeping in touch with their ex-partner over the children was often fraught with difficulty. In addition, abusive texts, e-mails and telephone calls were common. Here, one of the helpful things they learned was how to change their response to their abuser to make life a little easier for them.

> Hugh: I was feeding into things like [...] my 'phone might ring maybe 20 times a day, and it would be [partner swearing] so [counsellor] says 'look, you don't, you just don't answer the "phone"'

As the participants changed their behaviour, so it changed the relationship they had with their ex-partner.

> Matthew: she used to call into the house and she'd stand at the door, and she'd shout and roar [...] I used to give it back then but after coming here for a few weeks, then I would just say something like 'Calm down, you'll give yourself an aneurysm or a heart attack. Do you want a cup of tea or something?'

It seemed as though the models of DV that had been developed for women were just as applicable to the situations the participants found themselves in.

> Peter: So there's a pattern and I didn't realise it and it was only by answering questions that I made the link.

Just as for the women, having a counsellor who understood what happened in DV situations and how it had impacted them, and who also had a knowledge of different patterns of abusive behaviours, helped the participants to believe that they would recognise and avoid an abusive relationship in the future (Snyder, 1994). This helped them to begin to plan a future again.

Perhaps surprisingly, Cook (2009) discussed counselling support with two leading experts in the field and suggested that there was no point in trying to understand the dynamics of the situation, as this would ultimately lead to victim blaming. On the other hand, agency research in the UK has recommended counselling for coming to terms with the abuse, which may include this aspect (Sweet, 2010; Debbonaire and Panteloudakis, 2013). The participants above suggest that an understanding of the two people involved and how the situations evolve can be very helpful.

It is possible that the difference in approach is simply context. Cook's (2009) writing on counselling seemed to suggest that counselling would only be accessed while the men were still in their relationships. Where this is ongoing abuse, strategies focused on minimising harm rather than understanding the dynamics of previous abuse, are likely to be appropriate. The participants in this study had already separated and had either ended or were in the process of ending their relationship. Once the relationship is over, it may be more helpful to focus constructively on the relational dynamics, to identify strengths in the client's coping behaviours and to facilitate understanding and insight rather than allocation of blame. In this way, the men could feel more confident that if they embarked on a relationship again, they would know how to recognise signs of abuse and know how to respond, creating hope for the future (Snyder et al., 1991).

It is concerning that Cook (2009) indicated that attending counselling could result in victim blaming. In this study, the participants talked about how helpful it was to discuss the ongoing difficulties they were experiencing with their partners, and to recognise patterns of behaviour between the two of them which could be changed. Taking small steps to address issues, and seeing positive change as a result, led to more confidence that they would be able to deal constructively with their partners in the future. This provided a sense of freedom and control of their lives that they had not felt before. Importantly, the outcomes from the participants at this agency aligned well with the study from MAPNI (Sweet, 2010) which reported:

> *counselling was a very important source of help to those men who accessed it in coming to terms with the abuse and moving on from the relationship, as well as in being emotionally and mentally able to deal with the issues they face as a result.* (p. 85)

Whilst it is clear that this can be helpful, it is also worth remembering that individual counsellors may not have had training in DV, and therefore may not understand enough about the dynamics of DV to be able to support that discussion constructively. Once again, specific counsellor training in DV seems to be important.

Beginning to live again

As the men engaged with the support offered and began to sort out and action their priorities, have more control over the relationship with their ex-partner, and feel valued and cared for again, so they also began to take steps towards creating a new life for themselves. However there were differences in the way those steps were taken depending on whether participants had one-to-one support or counselling. For those who had counselling, there appeared to be support to make greater changes in their lives.

> Hugh: I met this lady walking the dog [...] and we both just felt so comfortable with one another and I just said it to [counsellor], he says 'did you never ask her out?' I says 'no' and it was actually him put that into me head.

For these participants, who had come to the agency overwhelmed by their feelings and at a loss of how to cope with the continued abuse they were suffering, the future was now brighter. They had been given an opportunity to explore their experiences more deeply and personally, leading to greater understanding about how they had reached this point in their lives. This appeared to support their independence and facilitate moving to a life beyond the agency.

> Peter: I got to understand the kind of person I am and why I kind of, what attracted me to my wife [...] I wanted to know why I was drawn to somebody who would make me feel less about myself

On the other hand, the participants who had received one-to-one support talked more about getting back to the way they had been prior to the abuse.

> James: I think I'm the me that I was when I was [age], I got married at [age] and he was gone. I've got me back.

For these participants, finding a new course of action for problems that had arisen seemed to be sufficient and they were happy to come back for further support when they had identified another problem that required help. Whilst this approach lent itself to short-term support work, it also meant that the participants took longer to become self-supporting as it seemed that they continued to re-access support, sometimes for years. On checking with both the agency and the participants, this was confirmed as an appropriate interpretation of what the agency staff observed and the participants had described.

> Matthew: Yes, I was just saying to [support worker] it does feel like going round in circles [...] going round in circles but spiralling up

It is worth remembering that at this time, the agency had very limited counselling resources and so only those men who were seen to be in a very distressed state were referred for counselling. Other clients were supported to move on with their lives, but did not have access to additional resources, that is, the option to look at other past experiences which may have contributed to their situation with a view to resolving things. It is possible that this was not required for this client group, although some of the men also indicated abusive childhood experiences.

> Mark: I'm pretty certain that most kind of men, including me would have had these issues and [...] I'm not sure whether going back and digging it all up again would be useful

Mark in particular had had a number of earlier counselling experiences which had not been helpful to him, although as indicated above, he did not necessarily see the benefit of counselling to resolve issues that had happened so long ago. However, as he listened to the research findings for female participants, he could see that they had found exploration of the past to be a useful process. When he was asked in the light of this new information whether he thought this would be a helpful extension to counselling for male victims and if he would want to access such a service, he said 'I'd bite your hand off'.

Counselling at this agency dealt mainly with relationship issues and how those had contributed to the abuse, alleviating feelings of guilt and inadequacy. Ultimately it supported the individual to form new relationships, whilst working towards self-sufficiency. On the other hand, support work addressed specific practical or relationship issues as they emerged, providing relief for the individual at that time. Any underlying problems or beliefs that emerged as a result of the particular issue were also addressed, hence the sense of making progress but still needing further support.

Both models of support are valuable and have delivered benefits to the participants. However it is important to note that there was no indication of trauma work for men. The counselling that was offered by the agency was relationship based, and the counsellor maintained boundaries by focusing on that area of counselling. This may have been due to time constraints which affected the counselling that could be offered or it may have reflected the expertise of the particular counsellor. However, this meant that the opportunity to explore past experiences, should the participants have wanted to, was not available.

Although both participants indicated that time to explore those issues could have been helpful during the review, it was unlikely with current funding that this could be provided at the agency. Since this research was conducted, the agency has changed the way that counselling is delivered, and has increased the number of counsellors and sessions available to clients. It would be interesting to review these changes with the agency in the future, to see whether or how this has affected the delivery of its service. It does, however, reflect that the way support is delivered is an important area to consider both in terms of agency service development and future research.

Working within a group

This was quite an ambitious project for the agency, as group work with men in DV is generally associated with perpetrator programmes (Day, Chung, O'Leary et al., 2010). Nevertheless the idea of group support as a positive experience for victims has been around for a while, although developed primarily for women, initially, in the context of rape and sexual abuse experiences or bereavement (Coates and Winston, 1983). Male involvement in victim group support has been mainly as the partner of a female victim (Coates and Winston, 1983; Barcus, 1997) to be able to provide better support to her. However, Heppner (1981) proposed group therapy as particularly appropriate for men who would benefit from trying out new behaviours and could learn from others in the process, without having to articulate their needs. In fact this was seen as one of the benefits of group working described by the participants: that of listening to the other men's stories and learning from them.

The group work within the agency was structured as a ten week programme. Although most of the men who attended the group accessed only group support, the agency also offered one-to-one support for attendees where things cropped up that they needed assistance with, such as an unexpected court appearance in a child custody case. In addition, the group leader would occasionally recommend that one or two of the men should think about accessing counselling in addition to the group. This tended to be where the individual was struggling with their emotions to an extent that could not be resolved through the group work. The participants and agency staff indicated that working in a group was not suitable for or wanted by everyone and it was important that clients were given choices about the support they were offered. The group was accessed by five of the participants and delivered a mixture of education and experience sharing.

The mix of the men involved was commented upon by the participants, who indicated their surprise that businessmen sat alongside factory workers and the unemployed, joined together both in their experience of abuse and in their difficulty in talking about their feelings relating to DV. The initial attempts by the group leader to prompt some discussion led to long and awkward silences.

> Matthew: I think initially [counsellor] found it hard to get any information out of us [...] he'd throw a topic in and say 'discuss that amongst ourselves for a few minutes' [...] then we'd sit there looking at each other [...] like we couldn't talk about feelings or emotions or anything like that

Setting the task for each member of the group to tell their own story in turn worked better, as they each had the opportunity to say something about what happened to them. As Peter explains, this also presented a personal challenge as talking about his experiences was not just a difficulty he found within the group, but something he had struggled with before coming to the agency as well.

> Peter: I came here and I sat down and there were three or four other guys there and started talking and found it very, extremely difficult to kind of open up and to talk about myself. I don't know if it's a 'guy thing' or what, I just found it very hard

This experience of anxiety at having to talk about their experience was one related by each of the participants. However, once the group had begun to get used to sharing their experiences with one another, they appreciated the process they were undergoing.

> Andrew: it is easier, much easier to talk to an absolute stranger than to talk to a family member about what happened, and talking about it has been such a great part of the healing process

This description of the difficulties the participants faced mirrored the experience expressed previously by participants accessing one-to-one support, that is, of finding it hard initially to talk about their experiences in terms of their feelings or emotions and finding it easier to talk to someone removed from day-to-day life, than someone they might see regularly.

Facilitating disclosure has been suggested as one of the most difficult aspects of group work with men (Heppner, 1981). Heppner (1981) hypothesised that society has conditioned them to believe that they should not have problems and that it is 'unmanly' if they need assistance to deal with them, hence they are unlikely to want to share their difficulties. Nevertheless, men can view accepting help in different ways and they are more likely to seek help: if they believe they are not the only ones to struggle with a particular task; if they feel they have been able to make a conscious decision to seek help; if they feel they may be able to help others at the same time; and if the others involved are likely to be supportive and remote from normal life (Addis and Mahalik, 2003). In this study, these factors could be found within the group setting, as each had sought out the agency following a referral, the group provided evidence that they were not the only ones to suffer and the group members were remote from normal life. In addition, there were three areas that the participants believed were particularly helpful in the group work, and are described in more detail below. These were: hearing the other group members' stories; appreciating the camaraderie that developed; and finally the specific learning from each session. Thus the group also provided the opportunity to share knowledge and advice with each other and over time support through camaraderie developed. In effect, the dynamics generated by the group and valued by the participants in this study matched well with other research into male group work.

Hearing other group members' stories

As the participants remembered the stories that they had heard on the first night of the group, there were two common reactions. The first was that they were not alone and that what they thought could only happen to them was also happening to others in the group.

James: Well I know our stories were different, but they were all the same. They all had one underlying situation or whatever you want to call it.

The second was that they each felt that there were others in the group who had experienced a much worse situation than they had themselves.

Peter: Now, I don't know if this is just with me, but I came out of the first session thinking 'God, Jesus, I'm not that bad, like', you know, because some of the guys had worse stories than I had.

This feeling that there were others worse off than themselves was consistently reported and has been noted in previous research into group work with men (Heppner, 1981), at that time being described as early male competition. It is also possible that this feeling enabled each of them to see themselves in a more positive light, particularly given the range of men in the group, which could prompt feelings of hope rather than hopelessness (Larsen and Stege, 2012). However, it is also possible that perceiving someone else with more problems might increase the chance that the individual could be helpful within the group (Addis and Mahalik, 2003). Being helped has already been identified in this chapter as a specific valuable aspect of the one-to-one work and so it seems possible that the opportunity to give as well as receive help could be valued here. The participants acknowledged that there was value in listening to the stories as they emerged over the weeks, of things that the men had tried that had worked, things that had gone wrong, each providing ideas to others of what to try next to help to resolve their own situation.

Andrew: you were listening, but you were also learning from other people's stories [...] how they were handling it and that

It is also possible that with variations between the men in background and experiences, each may have had their own views about what was tolerable. What was tolerable for one may have been intolerable for another and hence there was no-one in the group who was consistently in the worst position. Having come into the group feeling that no-one had suffered as much as they had, finding someone that they perceived was in a worse position created hope. In this case, however, hope was not about taking action, but about believing they were in a better position than they had thought (Larsen et al., 2007).

The participants also felt that, from the stories they had heard in their respective groups, it was the psychological and emotional abuse that they had suffered which had affected them most.

> Matthew: my wife did attack me with a knife, she did throw things, she did break my finger with a knife an' all, but it was more just threats as such, she just was trying purely to get me to go. It was the mental, the mental bullying, or the mental torture, that was worse.

As Matthew notes here, he could understand where the physical violence came from, the frustration that had built up in his wife as she considered that he ought to leave the family home, as she had a new partner, and he refused to do so. However, he was not able to explain why she treated him so badly over the course of their relationship. This was a view shared by others.

> James: it showed me first of all the things that were said to me, because that was the game. I'd get up in the morning skipping and jumping and before I went out the door I would be in the doldrums, because my wife would have come down and got a load off.

It was easier to cope with physical violence as this was something they could defend themselves against. However, the psychological abuse built up over the years and was very difficult to manage.

This is consistent with other research into the male experience of DV, that is, being able to contain the physical attack but losing control of their lives as they tried to respond to emotional and psychological abuse (Cook, 2009). In a survey of male callers to a USA helpline (Hines et al., 2007), almost 95% of those surveyed indicated that they were being controlled by their partners with around three quarters indicating that this was through coercive behaviour or emotional abuse. In contrast, fewer than half of the callers indicated any form of physical violence. Whilst much of the focus for DV research has been around the perpetration of physical abuse and the resultant psychological harm, from a male perspective the presenting issue in counselling appears to have been more about the psychological harm resulting from perpetrated psychological abuse. DV is ultimately about power and control and it is possible that men may be more likely to try to control women through physical acts, whilst women may be more likely to try to control men through psychological and emotional means. However, either gender appears capable of using a variety of ways to do so.

Important learning

All of the participants had suffered a breakdown of their relation-ship. Four of them had left the family home and the fifth was now a single parent. Each found it difficult to come to terms with their new situation. For most of the participants, the loss of the relationship also brought the loss of their children as well as their home. At the time of the breakup, each was employed and relied to some extent on their part-ner at home. Now, they were living alone and struggling to cope. Each was having to undertake a new caring role, for self and/or for family, and needed to learn life skills to support their new roles.

> Andrew: The most helpful things were, I suppose, was that we could look after ourselves, first and foremost, and how to start the heal-ing process, and how to learn how to move on, and to, you know, like be eating properly and not dwell on stuff and not be on your own.

This topic, on self-care, was most appreciated by the participants. They had previously interpreted their role as working hard and bringing home money to feed the family: a traditional male view. This meant that they were not used to planning meals or cooking. The dominance issues in their relationship meant that they had little say in their home life and now being on their own brought with it a deficit of life skills that were not described by female participants. Whilst this seems like a very sensible aspect to include within the group work, it was also indica-tive of the position the men were in, that it was both included and valued.

In addition, the men noticed a difference in themselves. As they became more open in the group, they noticed that they were being more open elsewhere too.

> James: going back to being a man again, [...] I have learned to be very open. I don't care anymore. I've got nothing to hide.

This is an interesting point from James, in that DV often comes with a great deal of secrecy, including making excuses for their partner's behaviour. Here, James is indicating that the way he views this has changed, and that he is now prepared to be open about what happened. Whilst he previously had believed that being a man meant not say-ing anything against his partner and containing his emotions, he now believed that it was more important to be open and honest about what was happening. This reflection was one shared by other participants, and several disclosed the shedding of tears by themselves or others during the sessions.

For these participants, just as for others who have experienced DV, a key piece of learning was about how the abuse occurred.

> Matthew: 'I'll show you who your wife is, and who you are.' They showed us who we were, it didn't make us a better person but they showed us that our good points were more important than our bad points and that we could maybe improve on them.

Part of this learning was also about how they might have contributed to the escalation of events, so that they could be more aware of the impact they may have on others, and take steps to behave differently should they be in a similar situation in future. However, the focus on the strengths of the individual and understanding the relationship dynamics rather than accepting or allocating blame was helpful. This created an environment for the participants of being able to make choices which can assist with self-esteem and confidence.

Finally, the participants talked about the benefits of understanding the different forms of abuse.

> Andrew: different forms of abuse, yeah. It seemed to be like everyone went through such similar, and I was wondering, are they reading the same book.

There appeared to be patterns of abusive behaviour in their partners which were recognisable from the female literature (Craven and Fleming, 2008). This helped their sense of not being the only victim and not being wholly responsible, as well as seeing new ways to deal with her difficult behaviour. Once again the need for education about the processes and types of abuse is central to the learning. Finding out through the group that DV was independent of economic status, and that their experiences were not unusual for DV, all helped their image of themselves. However, for these participants, the additional learning about self-care, which included cooking, and the development of new communication skills was also very important. These factors helped the participants to become more independent and more resilient as they found it easier to articulate what they needed in a specific situation.

Camaraderie

Just as the participants accessing one-to-one support indicated their appreciation of having someone to care, so the group participants began to appreciate the interest and support of their fellow members as the group developed.

> James: at least once a week one of us had had a traumatic week and it was just priceless to let it flow out and get people's feedback.

The men's increased ability to share their experiences and feelings with other men showed their development in emotional intimacy (Garfield, 2010). There was a sense that the men were genuinely interested in what had happened to the others during the week, particularly if there had been a court date. They wanted good outcomes for each other, perhaps feeling that if one had a good day, the others might too. The success of others led to hope for their own situations as their perspective on what was possible changed (Larsen and Stege, 2012).

The group developed through shared experiences. This was a place where they could be completely open with each other about what had happened, because they knew that others would have experienced the same thing.

> Andrew: it was just like knowing that I'm not on my own, [...] I can't believe that I thought I was the only one [...] I thought I didn't fit in anywhere, that I was the only one going through this, which was totally wrong

As with one-to-one support, it was a sense of caring that seemed to be important. The experiences described by the men seemed to reflect the definition of compassion outlined earlier (Ricard et al., 2011): of feeling for individuals, understanding them and wanting to help. And finally, as the group developed to allow emotion to be expressed, the emotion that arrived was not only in the form of tears, but also laughter.

> Matthew: you can imagine with five or six men we did have our schoolboy moments there, you can imagine some of the answers to 'what do you think intimacy is?'

The importance of humour when working in a group made up of individuals with experiences such as DV has been noted before (Herman,

2011) and provides a way of connecting the group together and acknowledging shared difficulties. It has also been noted that laughter can help to release tension and facilitate movement at times when feeling stuck (Snyder, 1994). Both are equally valid interpretations and indicate the value of different emotions being present within the group environment.

Whilst the group sessions were regarded as hugely successful by the participants, there were some issues that arose from these which it is also appropriate to acknowledge.

Group issues

In keeping with the research data on DV, a number of the men who accessed support at the agency also had addiction issues: alcohol, drugs or gambling. Although the groups tried to accept and accommodate these members, this was sometimes quite difficult.

> Matthew: there was a few fellas who had addiction problems and it wasn't good: [...] you wouldn't know what way they would behave.

It was very important for the group leader to have very clear boundaries and to keep the respect of each of the group members in handling what could become a very difficult situation. Whilst the feedback was that this was handled well, it is clear that this is something that would need to be clearly addressed from the outset.

It has been shown that some male victims will suffer from addiction (Douglas and Hines, 2011) and yet the prevalence of addictive behaviours is much higher in those perpetrating abuse (Hines et al., 2007). In the UK, Respect have recently published some research conducted to determine whether those calling the victims help-line were perpetrators or victims (Debbonaire and Panteloudakis, 2013). In assessing the callers they used a multi-page assessment tool which identified that about half of the men who called were victims of DV; about a quarter could not be identified as being abused although they may have been in unhappy relationships; and about a sixth were described as perpetrators. Hence men have been shown to be accessing support appropriately.

The participants' agency did not assess whether those who called were perpetrators or not, and it is not clear whether there has been similar research conducted to determine the number of perpetrator/non-victim female callers to women's help-lines or agencies. Whilst it is possible that some of these more difficult group members could have been abusers or co-abusers in their relationship, they could equally have been victims. Whatever their background, they were able to benefit from the group programme through learning life skills, recognising relationship and behavioural dynamics and hearing from other men. The men were not judged as they came into the agency and were allowed the freedom to decide the reality of their situation, whilst the agency put in place appropriate procedures to ensure safety for all.

Another issue was that of the level of intervention and the selected topics. Whilst the participants were generally supportive of the content of the sessions they received, one session, which was mandated by the organisation providing funding, received criticism.

> Peter: one of the stipulations for the government funding was they had to do health education. It was funny because there was stuff like sex education and stuff that we were taught at school and there's men in their thirties and forties having to go through it again.

It was not clear from the interviews with the participants what the rationale was for this intervention, but Peter makes a reasonable point about the appropriateness of this particular session. The difficulty with this topic is not a new finding. Although Heppner (1981) suggested group work might be useful for those who have difficulty with intimate relations, 30 years later the application of group work in this area was still being developed (Garfield, 2010). This may have suggested that it is an area of work that required more development and yet it was an area that the funding organisation had specifically requested to be included. The men reported that the session was at a very basic level. In this context, there is an additional question about the perception of the funding organisation of the issues presented by male victims.

The final issue was a little more complicated as it related to the development of relationships within the group. This could lead to tensions as some group members wanted to keep the group separate to their lives outside, whereas others made friends and developed those friendships outside.

> Matthew: We often bump into each other [...] or we have each others 'phone numbers, and every few months I might say 'oh I'll give so and so a ring and see how he's getting on'.

There was a general acceptance amongst the participants that some members of their groups had much less support than others. Although the men recognised that not everyone would necessarily have their needs met, there was some sadness for those who wanted more companionship than they could access from the group.

> Andrew: he hadn't got very many family, and friends weren't that plentiful for him either like, but I could see he was having it tough enough. So I kind of feel for him, [...] you could tell that he wanted more out of it.

Although some individuals within the group built friendships and kept in touch through their own efforts, it is questionable whether, as a group, they had the skills necessary after a relatively short intervention to be able to set up their own group contact process without some facilitation. Although the participants valued the sense of connection in the group, there appeared to be no encouragement to make contact outside the group, but neither were there restrictions.

Other groups that have focused on developing men's emotional intimacy have encouraged participants to meet each other outside group sessions (Garfield, 2010) to get the members used to having normal friendships outside the agency. However, in structured therapy groups, contact outside sessions is generally discouraged (Yalom and Leszcz, 2005) to maintain the group process. In this study, the work of the group was part therapy, as individuals were encouraged to reflect on and share their experiences and feelings, and part support, as information was offered as part of the group process and support for members within the group environment encouraged. This left the development of relationships beyond the group up to the men themselves.

Surprisingly, perhaps, most of the participants relayed their sense of shock when the groups were over. They had been unaware, or did not acknowledge, that the last session was coming up.

> Andrew: It was parting that night from the lads, [...] it was a bit strange that, just how it all came to a stop.

As they reflected on their loss, it had a number of dimensions. Partly they had become used to going to the group on a specific night each week, partly they acknowledged they would miss the camaraderie. They had also become interested in and supportive of their fellow group members and were disappointed that they would not be able to hear the outcomes of their stories. In some ways the sudden ending and enforced separation could be seen to mirror the loss of their family, as most had been shocked at the ending of their relationship. Although Andrew was very clear that he did not want to bring the group into his private life, he nevertheless regretted the end of the group.

> Andrew: It would have been nice maybe just to cut it back, [...] maybe once a month for five or six months [...] just to keep following up on how things were progressing.

This particular aspect of group work is perhaps an area for development to ensure that all voices in the group are heard and that their needs to some extent are explored. As can be seen in Chapter 5, endings where the participants are in control of the decision to end appear to be more successful. In addition, there was a feeling that the group had just started to work well together when the ending came. Given the time required, potentially, for the group to learn how to discuss things together and to establish trust, it is possible that the length of the group programme was a little too short. Equally, it may have been possible for the group to have continued on in some form with some assistance in facilitation until it came to a natural end. These are issues that could be usefully discussed in other groups run by the agency once relationships between group members have established.

Despite these highlighted issues, the group programmes appeared very helpful to the men. The nature of group work for these participants seemed particularly useful for the issues that emerged through DV. This suggests that further consideration should be given to the development of the format and the inclusion of group support within a men's DV support service.

Summary

Whilst this is a very small study, it is interesting to note what the participants described they had gained through the two models of support. Although the one-to-one support offered a direct relationship and exploration in detail of the individual's specific issues, the group support offered a place of connection and shared experiences that allowed the men the opportunity to evaluate their own issues. However, there were some common themes across both models of support. Both talked about:

- the difficulties in talking at the beginning in both one-to-one support and the groups

- the benefits of being able to talk to people who were not involved in their family life
- working with people who believed their description of what had happened and did not judge them
- feeling cared for, by the counsellor, support worker or group
- understanding more about domestic violence, behaviours, dynamics
- understanding more about themselves and their role in their relationship
- finding coping mechanisms for the continued intrusions into their lives by their abusers
- the process being helpful to them in picking up the pieces of their lives and starting again

However, there were also differences. For the participants who engaged in group work:

- Recognising that there were others in the same situation irrespective of background was helpful.
- The sense that others were worse off than they were was very helpful.
- Workshops involving life-skills and self-care were useful in preparing them for their new lives, whether as single parents or living alone.
- Changes to their lives was primarily down to the individual and how much they contributed to or engaged with the others in the group or were prepared to try outside the group.

Those who had received one-to-one support:

- described being able to focus on and process the issues that they currently had
- identified ways of resolving their problem and either found a way through or accepted the reality of the situation
- could re-engage with the process, as more difficulties emerged, learning a bit more each time

For those who had received counselling, there was an additional factor: they had developed the confidence and skills to deal with issues that might come up in the future and had not needed to access emotional support from the agency again.

All of the interventions provided were perceived as helpful by participants, that is, moving them further along the road to recovery. The two methods of support were clearly valuable to the participants in different ways. For those men who needed more information and some support to begin the change process, the group worked very well. For those who needed a little bit more support and some facilitation to determine and prioritise specific issues, counselling and one-to-one support was helpful. For those who needed support to work through the events within their relationship, one-to-one counselling was most helpful. However, there was no assessment about the value or otherwise of the opportunity to explore past life events and this needs further research.

As with the female participants, there were underpinning concepts of trust, compassion and hope:

- Trust was seen to be either present or developed over time. Whilst each of the support models showed knowledge of the participants' situation and provided a framework that supported confidentiality, the final aspect of wanting the best for the individual took a little longer to establish in the group than in one-to-one support. Nevertheless, having established a supportive and trusting group environment, the loss of that at the end of the group work was keenly felt. Endings, and preferences about how these are conducted, are discussed in more detail in Chapter 5.
- Compassion also appeared, especially within one-to-one support, as the participants described the benefits of working with people who cared about them and what happened to them. Although the same core roots (described in Chapter 4) were present (being valued, accepted and understood), these participants appreciated interventions that they felt were helpful, such as reducing their degree of distress, increasing their understanding or enabling actions to be taken. The group work also encouraged caring and support for all of the group members and, through sharing experiences, help for and an understanding of their own experiences.
- Hope could also be seen to develop throughout both models of support. Whereas the group work helped by showing that DV is something that affects people from all walks of life and provided tools to be able to cope as well as social connection, one-to-one work built hope through developing the participants' ability to deal with difficult situations successfully and to begin to have a sense of control over their lives.

It is useful to note the differences in the models of support and the way the participants engaged with them. Clearly there are differences in what they gained from each one, and yet each has a role to play in recovery from abuse. Currently in the UK, most of the support for men is provided through telephone helplines. Although there are some local agencies that offer support specifically for male victims, most areas will offer support through agencies established to support women and children. It is unlikely that male victims of DV would be able to access the range of support described here locally and this is something that could perhaps be considered by funding organisations and those planning to set up services in the future.

Note

1. Siegel and Germer (2011) quote Hangartner in their text as he was the presenter of the conference paper, but the authors of the paper were Ricard, Kerzin and Hangartner (2011). The reference is provided in this book using all three authors' names.

5
Endings and Life after Counselling

This chapter describes how the counselling ended for the participants and how they then saw their lives subsequently. The research interview encouraged each participant to reflect on what had changed between the beginning and ending of counselling and whether that had been helpful to them in their lives subsequently.

What appeared from the limited data available was once more commonality between the female and male descriptions of ending. Perhaps this suggests that ending is more associated with the counselling process than the specific issues which brought the individual into counselling. The positive outcomes reported by the participants suggest that many of the presenting issues had been resolved and therefore there may be a commonality of ending. The descriptions of what the participants found both helpful and difficult about ending are explored below.

In addition, the value that the participants gained from the counselling is explored. The benefits as perceived by the participants are not necessarily the same as the measures often used when assessing the effectiveness or efficacy of a counselling service. However, it does show benefits to the well-being of the individual and, on the whole, appears to reduce the likelihood of requiring further support at a later date. Although this may be a little controversial, it seems appropriate to highlight the apparent discrepancies as a means to stimulate debate in the sector.

Endings

One of the specific aspects of counselling and psychotherapy that therapists try to manage appropriately is the ending to the work. This is quite different to the one to one support that some of the male participants received, as each ending was perceived as temporary and there was an expectation that they would return for further support at a later date. The group ending was discussed previously in Chapter 4. Hence the endings here are specifically associated with counselling.

One of the interesting findings in this study was that the participants went through a process of deciding to leave counselling prior to that being discussed with their counsellor. Some of the participants talked about feeling much better about themselves, which indicated to them that it was time to move on.

> Veronica: I felt happy with who I was, I didn't feel as though I was that person any more. So I think that was the end of it [. . .] because I'd finally got to where I needed to be.

For others it was more about feeling that they had done enough to be able to leave, without necessarily achieving the sort of level of change that Veronica described.

> Amanda: I just felt like actually I don't feel like I need counselling any more. I feel much better.
> Hugh: I knew coming in that night, I don't need much more of this and he actually said that he had that feeling coming in, [. . .] he could see by my attitude, I was bubbly, smiling.

For both male and female participants it was important, as Hugh describes above, that the counsellor agreed with their assessment that they did not need further therapy.

There were a number of factors, reported in the literature, that would have suggested these participants were more likely to have a positive ending: they had reported a positive therapeutic relationship and a discussion with their therapist about endings (Knox, Adrians, Everson et al., 2011); they had initially sought counselling due to feelings of hopelessness, rather than hope of improvement (Elliott and Williams, 2003); and the participants had mostly undertaken counselling before and were able to assess that they had had enough counselling for that time and were ready to leave (Manthei, 2007). Having an ending process that allowed the participant to make the decision to end and yet also allowed discussion and agreement from their counsellor, helped to maintain their positive outlook beyond counselling. With both in agreement that the future was something the participant could cope with alone, it was much more likely to be a good decision.

Once the two parties had agreed an ending was appropriate, some participants wanted to have a final ending with the counsellor.

> Lucy: I said 'I would like to say this is my last session and I don't need to come any more but I'm scared' [...] so she very kindly arranged a session a month later if I wanted it and I had the choice whether to come.

Part of the ending process for some participants included testing whether they were able to continue with the progress they had made without the support of counselling. This is not something that has been described before in client based studies, although it appears to follow the same principles as relapse prevention techniques in CBT (McLeod, 2003).

Others were happy to end on the day, having had the assurance that the counsellor was also relaxed about them finishing.

> Ailsa: I just felt I didn't need it any more. And [counsellor] thought I didn't, but if I ever did, I just had to get back in touch.
>
> Peter: towards the end it was fine and then I think it was around [month] of last year I said 'you know, I think I'm ok' and he said 'No, you are' he said 'now keep my number though, and if you do ever need to call, you call me.'

The descriptions of Ailsa and Peter also highlight one other important aspect of ending: the assurance from their counsellor that if they needed to, they could always come back again. The ending was made easier for the participants because they had been told they could re-access counselling again if they needed to, and whilst almost all had not had to do so, each had remembered they could. This has been described as creating an image of interrupted counselling rather than termination (Cummings, 2001; Etherington and Bridges, 2011) and was also found to be helpful in a general study on the process of counselling (Manthei, 2007). This suggests that this aspect of ending is not unique to DV and is more generally part of a positive ending to therapy.

Whilst there was strong agreement amongst the participants about how comforting it was to know they could go back if they wanted to, almost all were pleased to describe how they had been able to resolve issues that had come up themselves.

Hugh: I don't think I would need any more counselling, because I know I can handle, for what I'm after learning from then to now, I can handle things more, gentler, without being this stressed.

Samantha: I think it was, what helped that, was knowing that I could dip in again if I needed to [...] and I haven't.

There were still things which happened in their lives but, as Hugh describes, they now had ways of coping and were starting to believe they could manage on their own. The realisation that they now had the necessary skills themselves was critical and allowed the possibility of independence. The time to take the next step to end counselling depended on the participant, with some taking weeks to feel confident on their own, and others realising they were ready to leave within a single session.

Sanderson (2008) suggested that endings created anxiety for both therapist and client and therefore endings should be planned and discussed carefully between therapist and client as part of goal setting. However, the findings in this study suggested that clients were more likely to feel a sense of pride and accomplishment on ending (Fortune, Pearlingi and Rochelle, 1992). The role of the counsellor here was in confirming their decisions, reviewing successful outcomes and sharing their positive future expectations for the client, providing hope for the future (Larsen and Stege, 2012).

It has been suggested that the more effective the therapy has been, the more important it is to have a proper ending (Elliott and Williams, 2003) and this would appear to be the case here. Each of the participants who had discussed endings with their counsellor felt they had gained enormously from their experience and a part of their ending process was using their new found confidence to leave their counsellor.

Whilst these were stories of counselling ending at an appropriate time for the participant, there were a few examples where the ending was not quite so satisfactory.

Elizabeth: I don't think there was anything more she could have done for us, you know. [...] I hope I don't but I'll probably will relapse and get so low that I've got to come back, but I know that she's there, you know, if I need to see her.

Here Elizabeth had ended the counselling because she felt she was no longer making progress. She had not quite reached the stage of some of the other participants of knowing that they could deal with life on their own. Nevertheless, she kept the knowledge that she could go back as something that helped her to keep going, in keeping with the others. The difference was simply that she seemed to feel that a relapse was more likely than the others. Her hope was in not relapsing, rather than her belief in herself that she could carry on.

Needing a little more time can be indicative of a less substantive therapeutic relationship and poorer outcomes (Knox et al., 2011). For Elizabeth, there may have been a self-imposed need to disclose her situation early in the relationship and once that had happened, she made a number of decisions quite quickly which required significant action. It is possible that in her rush to disclose and take action, the foundations for the process were undermined.

One of the sad stories of endings came from Karen. Karen had worked with her counsellor for over a year and was getting to the point of feeling she might be confident enough to leave counselling soon.

> Karen: I got a phone call to say that she could no longer counsel me but somebody else could take over. [...] they've said that they'll keep the door open, and I can come back any time. I don't feel like I am in a place now where I could go back again to the beginning and explain to another person the ins and outs again.

The telephone call was from the agency. The lack of an ending clearly upset her and there was a sense of, perhaps, unfinished business. Since then, she had been able to continue growing and using everything she had learned. Whilst it was disappointing, it has been something she was able to move on from and she has not accessed the agency again for counselling. Whilst she, too, had indicated that a little bit more time was required, in this case she recognised that external, rather than therapist, factors were at play. The agency's ability to ensure the participant understood that the ending was related to organisational factors, and not to her progress in counselling or to her personally, helped to ensure a positive outcome.

The topic of endings was not explored as well as other aspects of the counselling, in part due to the time limit for the interview and in part due to the presentation of ending as a much less complex issue by the participants. The participants' descriptions seemed to reflect the situation reported in general counselling, that a planned and managed ending is easier to bear than a sudden and abrupt one (Knox et al., 2011). The ending process described by the clients is well supported by the literature, and reflected a positive outcome, encouraged by their counsellors.

It is interesting to note that the concept of hope followed through into the ending session. However, the main factor to be taken away from this section is the idea of incorporating a positive ending process into practice.

Life after counselling

Reflecting on their lives after ending therapy, the participants were in agreement that the counselling had made a positive impact on their lives. However, it would be wrong to suggest that their lives were now perfect as a result of attending therapy.

The participants were clear that there were still issues that needed to be addressed. For the women, those tended to be about their awareness of continuing to develop their independence and confidence.

> Fiona: We still don't answer the house 'phone. We let people leave a message and then we ring back [...] even though that's fine now.
> Paula: he'd been choosing my clothes if I went anywhere. I didn't have any choices myself and [counsellor] said 'you have got choices' and [...] it causes a lot of arguments actually with my husband at the moment, I say 'No, I don't want to do that' and [he says] 'Oh no, you've got choices!'

If Paula had been in a physically abusive relationship, her response could have resulted in another battering incident. This highlights the need to do a careful risk assessment with clients before embarking on counselling. In cases where there is a high risk of physical harm a referral to a local DV agency for advice on how to stay safe and prepare to leave an abusive partner would be more appropriate. For a list of organisations that can assist with this, see Appendix 1.

However, Paula's situation was different as her present relationship had begun after her most abusive relationship had ended and it was not violent. As she had gone through counselling and begun to see things differently, her relationship with her new partner had changed. She had been able to discuss with him her realisation that she needed different things now and they concluded that they both still wanted to make the relationship work. Although they were both committed to having a different relationship, this did not happen overnight, and this is an example of how difficult change can be, even with willing parties.

For the men, these issues tended to be linked to their ex-partner, usually relating to child access and the negative impact they felt she was having on their children.

> Andrew: She's still after doing something with the kids or that, she's still throwing emotional abuse and [...] she's still trying to be the bully.
> James: I find it very hard to see what my wife is doing to my children because you love your children [...] I would daily struggle with that.

This study showed, in line with other research (Hines et al., 2007), that female partners involved their children in their attempts to control their partners. Here the men often had to address these issues through the court systems. Although some of the issues were driven by the social and legal system in Eire and were not directly transferable to the UK, it is possible that some of the attitudinal difficulties reported within organisations may also be found in the UK (Debbonaire and Panteloudakis, 2013). Engaging with the courts appeared to require advocacy rather than emotional support. However, the stress of court appearances for individuals who had not been involved in legal systems before, showed that emotional support may also be needed initially (Cook, 2009; Douglas et al., 2012). Here the participants indicated that they were now able to deal with legal challenges and court appearances, although they each indicated a desire to find a different way to communicate with their ex-partner. Whilst this can also be an issue for women with children who have suffered DV, this was not a specific feature of this research study.

Despite these difficulties, there were many more positive indications of the value of the counselling they had received.

For some, feeling better and more capable to take action and resolve problems was important.

> Jackie: I just feel stronger and more able, more confident to do things.
> Peter: all the worries were still there, but I know I can deal with it now.

For others it was now being able to go beyond day to day activities that had been the focus of their lives for many years and to do things they felt they would enjoy.

Hugh: now I wake up in the morning and I say it's a lovely day out and I go and enjoy the day with the lady I've met, meeting up with her and having a coffee or whatever, and I love it.

Paula: It changed my life completely. And I look back and I think I could be like that now, I'd be, I felt like I was in prison. Now I can wake up in the morning and think 'what shall I do?'

They talked about changes they had made to the way they respond to people and situations, particularly where this may lead to difficult or abusive situations.

Andrew: I have a friend who is in a similar situation [...] and we just speak maybe every other day and rather than react or something like that, we just talk to each other, just say 'ignore it, just ignore it'.

Mary: Whereas before, I would have just gone along with it [...] but when you realise no, you don't have to put up with this, then you can get on with your life and do what you want to do, and move on.

They also noted that the way they behaved with other people had changed, showing increases in their confidence to speak out and their belief in the value of their contribution.

Lucy: I wasn't as suspicious of other people as I used to be [...] So that gives me a bit more self confidence into be able to voice my opinions when I have an opinion about something, rather than thinking 'I'd better keep quiet!'

Matthew: now I find [...] I don't shut up. Because I never used to talk, I never opened me mouth, I'd just sit there.

Some of the changes that occurred were significant enough to be noticed by others, which in turn has encouraged sustainability.

Ailsa: But everybody has noticed a difference. I can talk to more people.

Peter: And my family think I'm a nicer person [...] they say the old Peter's back.

However, there were also differences between men and women in the progress that the participants had made. The women, as expressed by Mary above and Ruth below, valued changes in their ability to maintain boundaries.

Ruth: You know invaluable in terms of the future and not allowing abusive people to get into my life again.

The men, as expressed by Peter, Andrew and Hugh above as well as James here, valued connection with people, renewing old family ties and making new friendships.

James: I speak to me mam now. I used to come down and I wouldn't see her from one end of the month to the other.

It is possible that this is a reflection of the counselling they had, as the male participants' counsellors seemed to focus more on relationship, whereas the female participants' counsellors seemed to focus more on establishing a sense of self. However, it is also possible that this reflects a difference in the needs of the two groups as a result of the way DV was experienced.

Overall, the participants felt that they had gained from counselling and indicated a change in the way they experienced their lives from the beginning of therapy to the end.

Andrew: It is great to be backed, like, to pick up the pieces, to start living again. And like that, there is life after abuse.

Jenny: In two words, my life. I didn't have a life before, I existed; and there's a big, big difference between living and existence.

Looking back to the descriptions that the participants gave in Chapter 2 of their situation prior to accessing counselling from the agencies, it is clear to see that there has been a change in their outlook and demeanour. From feelings of hopelessness, not knowing how to cope and, for some, thoughts of suicide, to a sense of having a life that can be lived and enjoyed, with hope for the future.

However, it is perhaps best to hear finally from Jenny. She had spent many years in abusive relationships, and was one of the oldest participants. Although she had tried to access counselling previously, she had not been able to work with the counsellors she had been allocated, as she had felt they did not understand her or her situation. Asked if she had any regrets about the counselling she had received this time, she was equally clear.

Jenny: my biggest regret is that it didn't happen years ago. You know, because I've missed out on a lot.

One wonders how many other people have tried to access counselling with a history of DV and concluded that counselling could not help them.

Measuring appropriate counselling outcomes

After leaving counselling, the participants felt that they continued to grow personally and to enjoy their lives more than they had done before. As this research was conducted some months after concluding counselling, it supports previous research (Nicholson and Berman, 1983) that the gains in therapy can be maintained for a three to six month period after ending. It would be interesting to conduct further research to see whether these benefits were maintained over a longer period of time. Although the male and female support processes were different, it appeared that there were similarities in the way participants described the benefits of counselling after the support ended.

There has only been substantive research conducted on the effects of counselling with female victims. Quantitative research assessing the efficacy of different counselling models have each used a different set of measurements (Howard et al., 2003; Kubany et al., 2004; Reed and Enright, 2006; McNamara et al., 2008). These include measures of empowerment, self-esteem and problem-solving, as well as depression, PTSD, shame, anxiety and life-coping skills. Although there are connections to each of these measures in the context of the presentation of issues particularly found after exposure to DV, there does not appear to be agreement over which of these are more important from a client perspective.

Although many therapists are asked to measure the degree of improvement in the client's presenting symptoms to show the value of their counselling, here the participants talked about what had made a difference to them in their lives. One participant mentioned that the changes to her depression and anxiety on her exit questionnaire from the agency suggested little improvement, but she wanted to take part in the research to share how much the counselling had meant to her, and how much her life had improved as a result. The changes she mentioned were aligned with those mentioned by other participants: she felt she had moved on a long way as an individual and the main benefit was how she was now engaging with life. It is perhaps appropriate to look in more detail at specifically highlighted factors for DV to see whether these participants had gained in the way recommended by experts in the field, namely self-esteem (Sanderson, 2008), empowerment (Walker, 1994) and life coping skills (Dutton, 1992; Lee, 2007).

In comparing self-esteem measures (Coopersmith, 1967; Rosenberg, Schooler and Schoenbach, 1989) with the outcomes reported by the participants, there was evidence that they felt more confidence in doing things and that they felt more valuable as individuals. However, many of the Rosenberg items are related to a sense that the individual feels equal to or better than others. There was little to suggest in the interviews with any of the participants that this was important to them. The description of counselling was more about prompting an improvement in their perception of themselves, rather than themselves relative to others. The Coopersmith items did investigate the person's perception of themselves, but not in the context of the way the individual behaves or responds to people. It is possible that increases in self-compassion could be a better indicator of long-term improvement rather than increases in self-esteem (Neff and Vonk, 2009) and Neff's self-compassion scale (Neff, 2003) appears to better reflect the changes the participants reported in terms of their outlook on life. The measure also focuses more on feelings than thoughts, which links the compassion offered by the counsellor to the compassion the participant could now feel for themselves.

Investigation of an empowerment scale which was specifically constructed to look at empowerment among mental health users (Rogers, Chamberlin, Ellison et al., 1997) also indicated some limitations. The five factors included in the assessment were: self-esteem/self-efficacy; power/powerlessness; community activism and autonomy; optimism and control over the future; and righteous anger. In considering the questions provided for each category with the answers from the participants, it is possible that there may have been an increase in optimism, self-efficacy and autonomy for some of them. However, there was little mentioned that could be related to power, community activism or righteous anger. Indeed, not feeling angry any longer, whether righteous or not, was more likely to be mentioned. From this limited comparison, it would seem that empowerment as defined by this particular measurement was not a significant outcome for these participants.

There was no data from the study to assess whether the participants' problem-solving ability (Heppner and Petersen, 1982) had improved, as this particular measurement primarily considered an analytical problem-solving process. In addition, another assessment which had been used by researchers, the Life Coping Inventory (McNamara et al., 2008), included issues such as finance and housing, which were not raised as issues for this group, and work, which was mentioned by only a few of the participants, as particular issues. The other factors were family and partner/spouse which were mentioned to some extent. As a group, the participants were individuals who generally had coped with the practicalities of life, and the need for counselling was an indication of their emotional distress rather than their particular economic situation.

More positively, a survey constructed specifically for DV (Bennett, Riger, Schewe et al., 2004) appeared more closely related to the counselling process developed in this study: investigating outcomes of knowing the abuse was not the client's fault; having coping strategies; and trusting the client's ability to solve problems and make decisions. However, this appears to track the expected deliverables of the counselling process rather than the benefits to the client of the counselling. The Outcome Assessment (Lambert, Okiishi, Finch et al., 1998) appears to be a good assessment tool for the beginning of counselling as it focuses on much of the emotional distress that was reported at the outset. However, this would then simply show an improvement in those symptoms over time, rather than reflecting the outcomes reported by the women. As such, none of the assessment methods used for outcomes appear to match those items valued by the participants very well. Although current quantitative measures may not match the views presented in this small qualitative study, it is worth noting that the measures in the other studies will have been developed for other purposes. It is not necessarily appropriate to compare and contrast different types of research or to draw firm conclusions from this, but it is interesting to note the potential discrepancies.

It is of course possible that these participants are in some way different and not representative of other counselling clients who have experienced DV. Looking at other qualitative studies may provide some indication of how different these participants are to others. Unfortunately, most qualitative studies appear to have been focused on the process of DV and gaining assistance (Stenius and Veysey, 2005; Hage, 2006; Social Policy & Research team, 2009; McLeod et al., 2010; Oswald et al., 2010) rather than the outcomes. However, one report on the outcome of group-work in DV (Allen and Wozniak, 2011) did report improved connections with family, more focus on things they enjoyed and their ability to make their own choices now as important factors. In a more recent European study (Farmer et al., 2013) findings from the UK suggested that the key outcomes for counselling clients were being able to perceive a future after previous suicidal thoughts, as well as being more positive and confident in themselves. In other parts of Europe responses also included improved family relationships. As such, there is some support from other recent qualitative research publications for the findings in this research.

The factors valued by the participants in completing counselling, such as improvements in relating to others, changes in the way they respond to things, feeling more in control again and appreciating life each day fit much better with the posttraumatic growth inventory (PTGI) (Tedeschi and Calhoun, 1996). Although there is a fifth spiritual dimension suggested, which includes having a stronger religious faith, this was not a factor mentioned by the participants in the present study. However, the development of hope throughout the counselling process and ultimately a belief that the future will be a positive experience, could potentially be seen as an increase in non-religious faith.

The PTGI is believed to be useful in determining how successfully individuals will reconstruct their perception of self, others and the meaning of events following trauma. In the case of this study, the participants had mostly left their relationships prior to the counselling and, despite this, had been unable to complete that reconstructive process on their own. This implies that working through and resolving their experiences in some way resulted in posttraumatic growth. The introduction of posttraumatic growth as a potential indicator of benefit from DV counselling is not necessarily a new concept as Sanderson (2008) mentioned it briefly as a potential benefit. However, taking it from being a potential benefit of counselling to being a measurable outcome will require further research and development.

This finding of posttraumatic growth is important, both in acknowledging the potential benefits to clients undertaking DV counselling and in assessing the value of the work to a client group who may struggle to engage initially. However, there may be some surprise that both male and female participants appear to have experienced some form of posttraumatic growth when many of the participants did not suffer significant physical harm. More recent studies on posttraumatic shame (Wilson, Droždek and Turkovic, 2006; Herman, 2011) suggest that the shame resulting from DV experiences may be sufficient to prompt PTSD. This can occur when the psychological vulnerabilities of the victim are exploited by the perpetrator (Wilson et al., 2006). In other words, for some individuals, feeling deeply shamed by their experiences may prompt the psychological issues presented here, independent of gender or physical threat.

It is possible that focusing on the measurement of symptom relief, such as depression, might underrate the benefits of the counselling, as highlighted by Jenny's final comments in the previous section. It is also possible that the focus of DV support on autonomy, decision making and understanding DV may not on its own be sufficient to resolve the trauma. The need for closeness, compassion and valuing of their own lives, as described by participants and also included within the PTGI, is important. As well as aligning well with the reported experiences of the participants, the PTGI shows links to the depth of the therapeutic relationship described by participants offering theoretical support for both the model and outcomes. This is particularly interesting when considering counselling outcome research that has recently emerged (Baldwin, Wampold and Imel, 2007). This showed that client outcomes were related specifically to the therapist's ability to build relationships rather than the client's. Further research showed that the degree of clients' improvement was related to the ability of the therapist rather than to their own starting position or issues, and some therapists had consistently better outcomes with clients than others (Del Re, Flückiger, Horvath et al., 2012).

This is of particular relevance to this study when considering the high level of counselling skill employed by the majority of the counsellors working with participants in this study. The therapists involved in this research were experienced and had been selected and trained by agencies that offer specialist DV support and counselling. All of the agencies had stories of the service being continued through funding shortages showing their commitment to the client base. In the light of this research, however, it has to be considered whether the client view of DV counselling being developed here is dependent upon the skill level of the therapist and if so, whether this is part of the personality of the counsellor or can be developed through training and experience. This will be explored further in Chapter 6.

Finally, it is worth reflecting that from a client perspective many of the things that these participants said were helpful in therapy have been previously reported (Bohart and Tallman, 1999; Paulson et al., 1999). Other research about unhelpful or hindering factors from a client perspective (Paulson et al., 2001) produced issues of client vulnerability also reflected in this research, as well as a number of factors such as counselling structure or barriers to feeling understood, which appear to have been managed out of the process by the way the agencies have been set up. This suggests that the quality of the therapeutic engagement, together with the backup provided through the agency approach may also positively influence outcomes.

Summary

The endings reported by the participants were in keeping with good therapeutic practice. The decision to end was, for the majority of participants, one that they took themselves when they were ready to leave. Each counsellor left the participant free to re-access if required, although most had not had to do so. This practice could be usefully included in therapeutic work more widely.

The reported benefits post-counselling are, however, intriguing. Although the results have some support from other qualitative studies, the factors valued by the participants do not clearly align with any previously defined assessment tool in DV research. Instead, there is some evidence to support the idea that some form of posttraumatic growth has been experienced. As such the posttraumatic growth index (PTGI) may be a better indicator of the potential value of counselling to clients. This finding requires further development and research however.

In summary, the key points from this chapter were:

- Participants began the decision process to end before discussing it with their counsellor, as they tried to assess whether they could deal with things without the therapist in future.
- Having the counsellor's agreement that they were making the right decision to leave was important.
- Each counsellor offered the participant the option to return at a later date should they need to do so and most participants thought about the offer but had not needed to return.
- Clear and managed endings provided a secure start to post-counselling life.
- Life after counselling was not always perfect and some of the female participants indicated that they were continuing to develop their confidence in some areas, whilst some of the male participants were still concerned about their ex-partners' behaviour with their children.
- More positively, participants indicated feeling able to cope with difficulties in life, enjoying new activities, implementing coping strategies to deal with their abusive ex-partners and being more confident in their interactions with others.
- However, whilst the female participants talked about being better at creating and maintaining appropriate boundaries with others, the male participants talked about reconnecting with family and friends.
- Overall, the participants felt that life had begun again, or in some cases for the first time, and that life was now for living.
- The outcomes described by the participants aligned well with outcomes described in other qualitative research, however, they did not appear to agree particularly well with items listed in existing quantitative measures used in DV research.

- The most appropriate measurement for the improvements reported in this study appears to be the posttraumatic growth inventory (PTGI) which suggests that the participants had experienced some form of posttraumatic growth as a result of their counselling experiences.

Although this is one of the shortest chapters in the book, the findings are interesting and could provide a platform for further discussion on the role and outcomes appropriate for this work. However, it is important to remember that it is a small qualitative study, and further research and development would be required to confirm and develop any new metrics in this area.

6
Working with Domestic Violence Clients

The previous chapters have introduced a number of ideas about what the participants felt was helpful in the counselling they received after experiencing domestic violence. The purpose of this chapter is to explore what the findings might mean in the context of counsellor work. It is important to highlight that this chapter does not represent the views of the participants, although it is informed by those views. It does include many of my personal views, gained largely from my research and practice experiences, together with my interpretation of what they might mean in the context of counsellor training.

After I published a short article in Therapy Today (Roddy, 2011a) about my journey from becoming a counsellor trainee to beginning to specialise in domestic violence counselling, two letters were published relating to domestic violence as a specialism. One felt that it was not a specialism because it was something any counsellor could learn to do (Jones, 2011), although acknowledging the advantages in multi-agency working. The other felt that it was a specialism, and one that was already embraced by the third sector (Hayes, 2011), in particular women's domestic violence organisations. Nevertheless, both authors agreed that the provision of counselling services was restricted by funding issues and that much more could be done with additional resources.

As I have presented and discussed my findings up and down the UK and in Europe, I have talked to many individuals passionate about the work being done within the domestic violence field. I have also sensed a lot of disappointment and frustration that the knowledge, skill and resourcefulness of the people involved is largely unrewarded and unrecognised, and delivered with ever fewer resources. There is no doubt in my mind that the training provided in many agencies to employees and volunteers, prior to starting work, ensures that everyone understands how to respond to domestic violence victims. I also believe that working with domestic violence regularly helps to embed that knowledge and that staff can become specialists in the area very quickly. Given that the participants valued the counsellor's knowledge of domestic violence, it would make sense that such counselling services continue to be provided by third sector specialist agencies. It makes no sense to stop counselling provided in this way and yet funding cuts are continuing to reduce the number of counselling services available (Farmer et al., 2013).

The issue which I believe requires further discussion, however, is not whether a knowledge of domestic violence is key: the answer to this is clearly yes. The issue instead is whether providing existing counsellors in general counselling practice with some knowledge of domestic violence in order to work with clients is sufficient, or whether the experience of domestic violence is so complex that it requires a specialist environment where experience can be built up quickly. Looking back through the preceding chapters, many of the things valued by the participants, beyond knowledge of domestic violence, could be provided by highly competent, professional counsellors. Clearly, with the funding issues so clearly identified, finding a way to extend the capability of the counselling profession to provide good counselling for these clients could be beneficial to all.

At this stage I am introducing this as a topic to open the debate and to prompt practitioner views, rather than reaching a firm conclusion. Taking this approach means that I can explore both sides of this argument. I consider my own experience of counselling in an agency as making it easier for me to work with clients who have suffered domestic violence and therefore I can see the potential for this work to be a specialism. However, I am also aware of a number of gifted general practitioners who could work well with this client group if they understood more about the presenting issues and models of abuse. Either model could work, although it may be logistically easier to train a few people to a high standard. Given the prevalence of domestic violence within the UK and the potential for mental health issues to continue even after leaving the abusive relationship, it is likely that the presenting issues could form a part of many counselling conversations up and down the country, both inside and outside the third sector.

Therefore, those considering, or already offering, a domestic violence counselling service may want to think about the following areas as they shape their practice: the issue of gender; the characteristics and aptitude of the counsellor; the training required; and the capability of the organisation to deliver the service required by the client. Each of those areas will be discussed in this chapter. Ideas about how a counsellor can be properly equipped to work with clients of either gender who have experienced domestic violence, or not, will be introduced. Ultimately, it is up to each practitioner and each agency to make up their own mind about their position on this, and I hope that this chapter helps them to do so.

Organisational considerations

From the findings of the research, it is perhaps not surprising that meeting the needs of these counselling clients goes beyond the counselling room and into staff training and support, referral networks and marketing. My previous work roles have involved organisational development, marketing and strategy and so to me, this is an important aspect of the research study. What follows below are some suggestions to consider if seeking to improve a counselling service. It is not an exhaustive list, but one which has been prompted by specific comments from the participants. There will be other helpful approaches which are not mentioned here.

Initially, the participants indicated how important the first telephone contact and then the first meeting (counselling or assessment) was to their decision to engage initially with counselling. For agencies which are fortunate enough to have funding for administrative staff, points for consideration may include agency policies on how telephones are answered, the level of domestic violence training given to reception or administrative staff to allow initial calls to be handled appropriately, and how diary time can be allocated to allow an initial appointment for assessment or counselling to be made at the time of the call. Of course, there will often be waiting lists, and in those circumstances, it may be helpful to keep in touch with the client to show that the agency is still keeping the client in mind and that progress is being made towards beginning counselling.

It may be appropriate to assess whether there is the potential for secondary traumatic stress to develop in agency staff as a result of, for example, answering telephone calls and whether supervision or debriefing opportunities can be offered more widely in the organisation. Whilst admittedly, this potentially adds costs to the organisation, it seems appropriate to raise this with funders as many of them will have procurement guidelines which are sympathetic to the health and safety requirements of staff members. The involvement of all staff in the support of each other will also provide the opportunity for building strong teams with trust in, and respect for, the roles and responsibilities of the others. Not only does this have the potential to provide a strong protective element for the organisation to withstand the difficulties such work can present, it also provides a cohesive face for the outside world which can have a beneficial impact on the client base accessing support. It would seem that the positive provision of training and support has benefits to the agency service and organisation as well as to the individuals working there.

Building a cohesive organisation also has important benefits for interaction with external organisations too. Having a consistent approach from all staff can help to build trust with other organisations that may have common objectives or wish to collaborate in the provision of care for those who have experienced domestic violence. What was highlighted in participants' stories was the importance of the referral pathway and the confidence and trust of the person making that referral in the agency. It is possible that if an agency did not live up to expectations, the individual might feel let down by both the agency and the person making the referral. Hence it is important that both the agency and those making referrals are clear about the service that is being offered and have confidence in the agency's ability to deliver the service.

The participants described how trusted individuals, such as friends and colleagues who had also used the service, played an important role in helping them to find help. Agencies who have worked successfully with a number of clients in the past could have an important asset base for reaching other clients in the future. It may be appropriate to consider how the agency can ethically keep in touch with individuals (with their permission) such as including, within any ending session or formal discharge process, a request for further referrals to be made should they encounter someone in similar circumstances. Whilst this may not be required because the client group actively support the agency anyway, sometimes knowing that such action is encouraged can make the difference between saying something to someone in distress and not doing so when given the opportunity.

It is also of note that referrals came through professional services such as the police and sometimes from GPs, where the service was seen to offer a relevant specialist service. The agencies involved in this study were all funded and could offer counselling free at the point of use. This could have been why these professional groups were willing to refer on to the service. The relationships that the counselling services have with other professional bodies will have an effect on their ability to provide a much needed service. This suggests that regular meetings with professional groups or their liaison officer, together with events where the agency can show their work, and information leaflets which allow the quick assimilation of information about the service, can all help.

Perhaps a more difficult issue to address is that of marketing. This is difficult because of the need to maintain a level of safety for staff and clients at the organisation and so information such as the address and postcode of the organisation may not be provided. Websites and telephone numbers can be helpful, as marketing from a counselling perspective is likely to be more about helping an individual to recognise that a service is available to meet their needs and can be accessed remotely. As discussed throughout this book, the need for trust is implicit in all activities. The marketing that was specifically referred to by participants was available publicly and showed that the agency could help with people who had experienced certain situations or who could identify with the symptoms of psychological abuse presented. In that sense, the agency was displaying its competency with the issues the participant was experiencing very clearly. It is worth noting that many of the participants did not recognise their experience as one of domestic violence even at the point of access. They were surprised to be told that it was, as well as relieved to finally understand what had been going on.

Marketing also has additional problems in the way that counselling and domestic violence services are funded. As things currently stand, there are many waiting lists for counselling, both within the public and third sectors. There appears to be a very strong case to suggest that there is no need for additional marketing, as that would only increase the pressure on services which are already stretched. However, this approach can hide the underlying issue. If individuals are unaware that their distress is caused by the impact of their relationship and they continue to cope whatever their circumstances, then they have become a hidden population. If we could increase marketing to prompt them to seek appropriate assistance based on their own assessment of their need, we would have a much better idea of the scale of the problem and the resources needed to address it. Whilst this may seem like an impossible dream to some, it is important to remember that there are costs associated with mental illness when not treated. Future relationships, the environment children experience growing up, and longer term health issues which can develop as a result of years of stress, anxiety and depression are all future-based costs. It seems appropriate to consider marketing as a way to identify the need for services and to build the case for spending now to reduce the cost of interventions in the future.

Presuming that a case can be made and funding made available, decisions about what the money could be spent on will need to be made. Whilst there is always a case for public relations, such as press releases and local radio and television appearances, these opportunities tend to be more easily identified for physical violence, where the press is already well briefed. The damage from psychological violence is less understood and acknowledged and therefore may not be as attractive to the media. Instead, posters positioned in places that are accessible to women and men, leaflets that can be handed over by professionals, websites that talk about symptoms, behaviours and recovery are all options for organisations. It is important to remember that men and women can lead very different lives. Whilst the male participants made references to driving, hearing things on the radio or seeing adverts on buses around the town, some women referred to seeing things whilst they were out shopping or in cafés. The presumption that one set of advertising would help both male and female victims may be flawed, and consideration needs to be given not only to the type of resources available, but also to the positioning of those resources.

It may be that domestic violence agencies who currently offer counselling are already undertaking all of these things. However, not all domestic violence agencies offer counselling, and not all counselling agencies offer to work specifically with domestic violence. This section may provide some ideas of where to start and some of the things that may need to be put in place to begin such a service. For those who do offer counselling, it may provide a useful checklist for things to include in providing counselling. The purpose of this section is not to provide an extensive checklist for marketing a domestic violence counselling service, but more to highlight the need for an active process to ensure that people in need can find their way to the resources that can best help them.

Characteristics and aptitude of the counsellor

It is perhaps not surprising that much of the support for the findings of this research has come from the 'common factors' approach, that is, researchers and therapists who believe that there are beneficial aspects of counselling which occur irrespective of the philosophy or modality employed. Such research has consistently shown the importance of a counsellor's empathy, as well as the contribution of positive regard and congruence in developing the counselling relationship and facilitating positive outcomes for clients (Cooper, 2008; Laska, Gurman and Wampold, 2014). Indeed, there has been evidence for many years suggesting that the focus on technique has been misplaced (Asay and Lambert, 1999) since technique and the model of counselling used accounted for only 15% of the change seen in a client. However, as Cooper (2008) notes, a problem with the common factors approach could be the assumption that clients with similar diagnoses require similar things.

This suggestion of common factors which help the client to change being present in all types of psychotherapy, has been around for a number of years (Duncan, Miller, Wampold et al., 2010) and formed part of the outcomes from a Task Force set up by the American Psychological Association and the North American Society for Psychotherapy Research (Castonguay and Beutler, 2006). This group suggested that the required therapist skills were as follows:

1. strong working alliance established at the outset and maintained throughout
2. high degree of collaboration
3. being able to relate to client in an empathic way
4. having an attitude of caring, warmth and acceptance
5. adopting an attitude of congruence or authenticity
6. using relational interpretations sparingly and only when reasonably sure of accuracy

This description of what is required of therapists does agree to some extent with the participants' views, although they were not simply looking for an empathic counsellor, that is one who could relate and paraphrase what they were saying, but for one who could infer accurately what was meant from only a small amount of disclosure. In addition, the therapist was not described as having an attitude of caring or authenticity, but of being caring and authentic with the client. Interestingly, the participants did not specifically note relational interpretations, but did welcome accurate interpretations of their experiences in the context of a domestic violence model, as they did not have the resources themselves to make sense of things. As such, it would appear that, to an extent, the participants agreed that the common factors approach might meet their needs. However, it is important to note that the expression of most of those factors was at a higher level than that implied in Castonguay and Beutler's (2006) description above.

Another way of looking at this is to consider the 14 qualities and actions of effective therapists which were identified (Wampold, 2011) and are currently being used in training by the American Psychological Association. This research highlighted that therapists needed a range of high-level interpersonal skills, plus the ability to understand and build trust with the client, as well as engender a feeling that both they and the therapy can help the client. In addition, being able to provide an explanation for the client's distress which resonates with the client and linking what happens in therapy to that explanation is seen to be helpful. Wampold (2011) also recommends checking in with the client and being flexible in adjusting what is happening in session with how the client is responding. He believes that therapists should be open and willing to discuss difficult material and communicate hope and optimism to their clients. In addition, he suggests that therapists should be aware of the client situation, of strengths and weaknesses and also their own psychological process so that this does not impinge on the client work. All of these factors could be seen in the descriptions of counselling provided by the participants. This raises the question of whether the model identified within this study simply reflects the best practice of therapists, or whether it describes a model of practice that is particularly helpful for this client group.

Certainly there are aspects of this work which reflect good clinical practice, for example being open and willing to discuss difficulties and to check in regularly with the client to see how things are progressing for them (McLeod, 2009). Working with hope and optimism for the client in the process is also something that is not unique to domestic violence (Cutcliffe, 2004). However, as highlighted in the preceding chapters, it appears to be the ability of the counsellor to properly understand domestic violence that facilitates understanding, trust and hope to develop. It is also this knowledge that helps the therapist to provide an explanation for the client's distress and suggest different ways to help them. So it would appear that counsellors providing therapy for the participants in this study were effective therapists in a wider context, although their effectiveness with domestic violence issues specifically was explained to some extent by their knowledge and experience of the sort of client issues that were being presented.

It has also been suggested that therapists who may have preconceived ideas about particular client groups are less able to connect and work effectively with them (Cooper, 2008). It is possible that therapists who make assumptions about domestic violence or have not been exposed to the sort of experiences or consequences of DV that clients may describe will be less effective. Admittedly, there is a difference between the intellectual understanding of the different types of abuses and hearing the stories of those abuses from someone who has suffered as a result. Not everyone can listen to stories of domestic violence without tuning out when particularly traumatic or demeaning stories are shared (Richards, 2011). Those who feel shocked by the client's story may find it difficult to continue to connect psychologically with the client during the session, as they struggle to process the information (Dutton, 1992; Sanderson, 2008). For individuals who have no experience of this kind of situation, it can be hard to understand how such a thing could ever have happened. Meanwhile the client may experience the silence which can result from such a response as a sign that the counsellor cannot cope with the material or that they are being judged. Either way, it could result in a decision by the client to limit the amount of disclosure in future or not to return.

Experiencing domestic violence can also bring with it feelings of shame (Dutton, 1992; Wilson et al., 2006; Sanderson, 2008). If the therapist then responds sympathetically, the client may feel pitied, which can exacerbate such feelings. Providing support, validation of the experience and an empathic response showing understanding is more likely to facilitate a therapeutic connection (Tangney and Dearing, 2011). Hence, the aptitude for domestic violence work must include the ability to empathise with stories of abuse, to walk with and understand the client in their experience, rather than to respond sympathetically. For this reason, it is sometimes thought that the best people to work with domestic violence clients are those who have previously experienced domestic violence themselves. This is because they are likely to be more aware of what might happen in abusive relationships and find it easier to understand and empathise with the client situation (Sanderson, 2008). However, it is also possible that such therapists could bring pre-conceived ideas with them.

> Jackie: I think you've got to have the empathy to go into [this kind of work]. Not the empathy because you've done it.

This is an important point. It may be tempting to assume that having personal experience of domestic violence will make it easier for someone to be empathic. However, as Jackie notes, there is always the risk that client experiences are interpreted through the therapist's understanding, rather than the client's. Personal therapy would help to ensure that was not the case, but the focus must always be on assessing the counsellor's capability to work in the client's frame of reference, rather than whether or not they have a relevant personal history.

Another aspect of previously experiencing abuse is whether or not the counsellor should disclose their experience to the client. In general, it is considered that if a disclosure is made, it should be on an occasional basis only (Knight, 2012). Counsellors who have been trained to carefully explore their own reactions to material in therapy will usually reflect carefully on whether disclosing their own story is helpful to the client or not, before doing so. It is important that this is done in a considered way and with a specific objective that is in the best interests of the client (Cooper, 2008).

> Paula: She was somebody who, she said she'd been through something similar herself and obviously she didn't tell me more, and she made me feel relaxed.

Here, Paula's therapist correctly judged that it would help the counselling if she let her client know that she had some knowledge of what might have happened, without going into detail, and only on that occasion.

As with all counselling, the therapist must separate out their own experiences from those of the client, and work with the client's perspective and identified difficulties. It is important not to make assumptions based on one's own experience and knowledge. In fact, Wampold (2011) also notes that effective therapists are aware of their own psychological process so that they can identify whether their felt response during a counselling session is related to their own issues or those of the client. For any counsellors working in this field, having a good sense of self and a high level of self-awareness is important. If the therapist has had their own history of abusive experiences, it is particularly important that they have been able to work through those in their own counselling to be able to separate out their own feelings from those of the client (Dutton, 1992).

As highlighted in the earlier chapters, building trust is not only about understanding domestic violence, but also about genuinely wanting the best for the client and having integrity. These factors are generally covered in most counselling training and are part of counselling and psychotherapy ethical frameworks (British Association for Counselling and Psychotherapy, 2010). However, as a counsellor, it is also important to be aware of policies within your agency on issues such as self-harm, suicidal intent, disclosure of historic child-abuse and so on. If the policies do not align with your own personal values or beliefs about the appropriate course of action, it can be difficult to adhere to guidelines as this will not form part of your natural process. Because of the nature of domestic violence and the potential for difficult issues to emerge in the course of counselling, being able to deal with such issues as they arise confidently, competently and with the client's best interests in mind will help to minimise any resultant rupture to the therapeutic relationship.

Another factor that emerged from the study was the importance of building and holding hope for both the client and the counselling. In order to do so, it is important that as a counsellor you feel that therapy could be helpful to the client and that you are generally positive in your expectations of the outcome for the work (O'Hara and O'Hara, 2012). Whilst it is true that many therapists will feel moments of self-doubt, and there may be times when interactions between therapist and client do not go as well as they could have, believing that ultimately things will work out despite the difficulties is helpful to both parties. As the relationship strengthens, it is not unusual for the client to also begin to experience hope for the outcome of the counselling as they start to see what may be possible. In terms of the characteristics required of a counsellor working with this client group, they are perhaps those of a quiet confidence in their ability to help their clients and a belief in the value of the work done.

Finally, the study identified compassion as something valued by participants. Compassion is certainly linked to the high level of empathic skills already noted and, as shown earlier, it is also bound up in trust as it shows the therapist wanting the best for the client. It requires a skill level high enough to keep both parties safe whatever disclosure is made as well as being seen as helpful to the client in resolving their difficulties. However, compassion is also about being able and willing to genuinely care about the client's welfare, not only during the therapy hour but in their life outside counselling as well. Compassion for the other may well be borne of receiving compassion from others and generating compassion for one's self (Vivino et al., 2009). Counsellors who are capable of compassion for themselves and others may be particularly helpful to this client group. However, as will be shown in the next section, having self-compassion as a therapist may not only facilitate the client but also reduce the psychological risk to the counsellor.

Potential risks to the counsellor

It will be clear from this section so far that a key characteristic of therapists is engaging with the client's story. However, it is not just hearing the story that is important. Another factor highlighted by the participants was how much they valued working with a counsellor who cared about what happened to them. Therefore the role of the counsellor included connecting with the client at a fairly deep level (Mearns and Cooper, 2005), requiring advanced empathy and the provision of a compassionate presence. Interestingly, the roots of the word compassion suggest a meaning of suffering together. Hence, in connecting with someone who is suffering emotionally there is a risk of that suffering being transferred to and accepted by the counsellor.

Experiencing suffering as a counsellor, which endures beyond the client sessions undertaken, has been highlighted many times in the literature as the risk of vicarious trauma (Dutton, 1992), compassion fatigue, secondary traumatic stress or burnout (Sanderson, 2008). Although historically these labels have been used interchangeably, each of these conditions has now been separately described (Bush, 2009), although recognising that one could lead to another. Equally, this is not only a risk for counsellors working with domestic violence, but may also present in those who work in end of life care or in supporting victims of disasters (Berzoff and Kita, 2010). However, the critical factor for anyone in this situation is that not responding to the symptoms presenting can result in the individual being unable to continue work in their chosen field.

Compassion fatigue has been well documented in the nursing literature and shows that being continually exposed to difficult and traumatic experiences can result in the individual losing the ability to care for their patients or clients (Bush, 2009). Bush (2009) describes this as a loss of self, and the individual may feel stressed, detached and/or angry and that perhaps there is nowhere for them to recharge. As counsellors listen to their clients and empathise with their experiences, they are exposed to the pain and suffering of their client. Many therapists will be able to leave their work behind at the end of each day, but for some, this becomes increasingly difficult and the feelings generated from listening to the trauma increase but with nowhere to go. It has been suggested that counsellors who have their own history of abuse are more likely to be at risk than those who have not (Baird and Kracen, 2006). As time goes on, the counsellor feels more and more tired and stressed and begins to disconnect from the work as a way to protect themselves. Symptoms might include becoming blasé about the level of abuse encountered or being dismissive of a client who is not judged to have suffered as much as others. This change of world view may have a negative impact not only on the quality of their client work but also on their quality of life as this potentially results in the loss of the humanity that brought them into counselling initially.

Compassion fatigue can be avoided by ensuring the counsellor adopts appropriate levels of self-care and by providing opportunities for debriefing or offloading within the workplace (Berzoff and Kita, 2010). Having a life outside of work which is both interesting and enjoyable is believed to reduce the likelihood of compassion fatigue. Recent work has suggested that building self-compassion is more effective than building self-esteem in creating a sense of self-worth (Neff and Vonk, 2009) which can also be a protecting factor. Developing self-compassion involves becoming kind and understanding towards oneself rather than self-critical; feeling connected to others through suffering rather than isolated by it; and keeping difficult thoughts in mind without over-identifying with them (Neff, 2003). An on-line assessment is available for those wishing to test their own levels of self-compassion (Neff, 2009). As well as taking care of oneself, it has been suggested that it can be helpful to have a supportive work environment, where colleagues can acknowledge and assist each other when dealing with particularly difficult and disturbing client stories (Iliffe and Steed, 2000). For individuals wishing to work within domestic violence, it would seem that having high levels of self-compassion as well as the ability to provide and receive compassionate support, would be helpful and self-protective attributes.

Consideration also needs to be given to vicarious trauma. Here, the counsellor begins to recognise changes in the way they perceive the world. Although initially coming into domestic violence work to make a difference, over time they begin to lose their sense of purpose and feelings of safety in the world, perhaps feeling hopelessness (Baird and Kracen, 2006; Bush, 2009). This could be seen as transference of some of the feelings of this client group onto the therapist, although there is evidence to suggest that, once again, having a personal history of trauma may increase the risk of this occurring (Baird and Kracen, 2006). There is also evidence to suggest that having a particularly high load of trauma type work may increase the risk of vicarious trauma and a number of commentators have suggested that therapists should try to balance their trauma-based workload with more general counselling (Iliffe and Steed, 2000; Sanderson, 2008). This variation in workload plus good supervision, to ensure a balanced view of both work and life beyond work, are considered to be good protective factors (Baird and Kracen, 2006). Of course, for those who have experienced trauma before, it may be that the work is triggering unresolved issues from the past, and seeking counselling to address the changes in beliefs is also likely to be helpful. Whilst I was working as a domestic violence counsellor, I split my time between the DV agency and other agencies and found it helpful to have a reminder that there were different problems of varying severity at the other organisations. On the other hand, whilst completing my PhD and being immersed in the world of domestic violence and constantly reviewing the trauma and abuse that had been described in my own research and had been written about in the research literature, I found it necessary to debrief with my supervisors on a regular basis. It would appear that part of the aptitude for working with domestic violence in the longer term is the ability to balance the counselling workload with other activities both at work and at home.

Secondary traumatic stress is a slightly different response to working with domestic violence. In this case, the symptoms are much closer to those for posttraumatic stress disorder even without personally experiencing the event. This can include irritability, distressing dreams or intrusive memories (Bush, 2009). In this case, the symptoms may be prompted by a specific incident described by a client but which stays with the counsellor after that session and subsequent sessions have ended (Canfield, 2005). For example, as the client is describing an incident, the therapist may be building up a mental image of what is happening and it is this mental image which comes back into dreams and memories. In this way, the posttraumatic stress being experienced by the client is transferred to the counsellor. Canfield (2005) suggests that the memory or event can be re-integrated by the therapist over time. The provision of peer debriefing and supervision by an organisation to allow early discussion of the material may help that process (McCann and Pearlman, 1990). However, if the work to integrate the experience changes into developing coping mechanisms to deal with the continued intrusion, it would make sense for the counsellor to access professional therapy. Secondary traumatic stress is also believed to be more likely with a higher trauma caseload (Baird and Kracen, 2006).

Preventative factors include the ability to be able to create distance from the affective part of the memory, such as having particular routines at the end of sessions to be able to leave the client material at work, and having access to good supervision (Dutton, 1992). When I was training to be a counsellor, my tutors explained that when working at therapeutic depth it was important that the therapist maintained an anchor point with the outside world at the same time. In this way, the therapist could return to the real world at any point and bring the client back too, if necessary. If both the client and therapist were engrossed in the content, imagery and feelings of the client world, then no-one was managing the session. Perhaps it is this concept that is important in working with traumatic imagery. Whilst a particular memory may trigger something in the counsellor which is unexpected, for most client work it is important to be able to work at depth with the client but not to become immersed in the material. Having the ability to maintain a link with the here and now during therapeutic work is perhaps also a necessary characteristic for working effectively with domestic violence.

Finally, there is a risk of burnout, or emotional exhaustion. This experience is not restricted to working with domestic violence but has been noted in a range of job roles and specifically related to the work environment (Canfield, 2005). Organisations are less likely to see burnout in their staff where: meaningful, valued work with a sustainable workload is provided; staff have some choice and control in what is attempted; there is some recognition and reward; and where there is a sense of community with respect and fairness for staff (Leiter and Maslach, 2009), although workload appears to be the most significant factor.

Many third sector organisations would expect to provide a supportive environment, particularly in the context of volunteers. However, the current economic climate has resulted in increased pressure on the third sector, with more referrals being made and increasing numbers of clients on waiting lists for counselling. At the same time, many funding sources have been reduced or removed, resulting in some staff working for reduced or no salaries whilst additional funding is found, or the closure of services (Farmer et al., 2013). Even when funding is found, the organisation may have to change the delivery of services to achieve specific outcomes which may not fully align with the service they feel needs to be delivered. These factors could have a detrimental effect on staff, as changes in the organisation and service delivery could increase the risk of compassion fatigue and vicarious trauma. However, taken in the context of the characteristics required for counsellors, it would seem that the ability to create, maintain and balance work-load boundaries, as well as facilitating good relationships with other staff members, would be vital.

Gender

As I have talked to people about domestic violence counselling, I have been aware of their passion for supporting their specific client groups and representing their best interests. One of the questions that I have struggled with, as a researcher who consciously included female and male victims in the study, is that of gender. I have had discussions with women working with female victims who were unhappy that I had included men in the study. I have talked to individuals who believed that it is only women who really suffer from domestic violence and that any men I interviewed will have been perpetrators of some kind. I have had many more discussions with people who have been really interested in the difficulties of male victims and were keen to learn more about how they could be helped. I have not yet had a discussion with anyone who has suggested that the biggest problem is female abuser to male victim, but I have had several with people who believe that male victims are not being heard or provided with the support that they need.

Both my research and my own life experiences have led me to believe that psychologically abusive behaviour can be present in both men and women. My understanding of the impact of such abuse is that on a regular and systematic basis, it causes psychological harm to the victim. I do not feel the need to determine whether that victim has suffered more or less than another, simply that the relief of psychological distress is an aim for any counsellor or psychotherapist. Heterosexual and homosexual relationships have the capability to be abusive and there is no perfect relationship. Those of you with partners may recognise that we all fall somewhere on the continuum between a completely loving and completely abusive relationship. The degree of support or harm experienced will vary on a daily basis by frequency, nature and individual. However, those in relationships which only vary in the degree of abuse endured are those we most need to support.

My concern about gender is therefore not related to the individual who has experienced domestic violence. It is in the nature of counselling support. I am aware that many of the stories told about difficult counselling experiences from a female perspective involved a male counsellor. When male participants indicated that they felt their male counsellor would know what it was to be a man, I had to conclude that I had no idea how that might feel. But then, as a Scot, I do not know what it is like to be English or American or French or Japanese. Equally, I am aware that as a woman, I do not always immediately understand all of the issues presented by female clients. All I can do is to try to keep an open mind and help clients to explore what is important for them.

In fact, there is little agreement in the literature about whether gender is an important aspect of client-counsellor relationships. Hence, in keeping with other counsellors, the gender of my client is not necessarily of concern to me. However, I have to be aware that it may be very important to my client. As noted in Chapter 1, there appears to a slight tendency for those experiencing domestic violence to be in more traditionally male or female occupations, which may make it easier for them to relate to counsellors of the same gender. Hence, I feel that DV clients, both male and female, should be free to choose the gender of their counsellor. Given the need for trust to be built up over a period of time, it seems appropriate that the client should be given the opportunity to create an environment that feels most comfortable for them and is most conducive to the establishment of trust. Whilst this can be part of the decision process for someone seeking private counselling, it is important that individuals accessing funded services are afforded the same choice.

Another concern, speaking specifically from my own experiences in research and practice, is the effect of receiving domestic violence training in, and working from, a male perpetrator/female victim perspective on my ability to hear the story of male victims. I was very aware in the first interviews I conducted with male victims that the stories I was hearing sounded familiar, both in the way the stories were told and in the dynamics that were being described. I could see the male-female dynamic I knew about being played out as a female-male dynamic. I felt shocked to realise that my response to that was to feel that there must have been something else going on. I had been able to hear the women's stories empathically, but as I heard the men's stories, I was somehow sitting in judgement. Having become aware of this, I was able to put it to one side for the purposes of the interview, but it took me much longer (several weeks) to process my reaction to the content and to reach a philosophical position that allowed the experiences of both men and women. I am sharing this experience because I felt, as I went into the research, that I was sympathetic to the male experience of abuse. Yet, reflecting on that experience now, I do not believe that I could, at that time, have been able to work appropriately with male victims. When we consider the current practice of including men as part of the service we offer to women, I now wonder whether that is really serving the needs of the male victims or whether it is serving the needs of funding bodies. If we truly want to offer services to female and male victims together, then we must also embrace the rhetoric associated with both.

Finally, it seems from this research that there could be differences in the gendered experience of domestic violence. Whilst the model of abuse may be recognisable for both client groups, the impact of suffering that abuse is different, and therefore the issues that may need to be addressed and the way they are addressed through counselling may also be different. Trying to use a tried and trusted female model of support with a male client or vice-versa may not meet the needs of either. Hence, if we want to offer services to both, we need counsellors who are aware of the issues and concerns of both, and can adapt their practice to suit. If this is too great a task, for example, where the person has worked specifically with one group of clients over an extended period of time, then practitioners may need to choose whether to specialise in working with male or female clients.

Appropriate preparation and training

Many of the textbooks on working with domestic violence have been written for social workers or support workers who spend time working with individuals still in abusive relationships. A lot of their work is on safety assessment, both for the abused partner and their children (Stanley and Humphreys, 2014) and many of these books discuss how domestic violence takes place, the warning signs, risk factors, and difficulties of staying in the relationship or leaving and so on. There are also many training courses available to raise awareness of the issues or to assist employees to facilitate domestic violence disclosures, and to help to provide appropriate support to the individual following disclosure. However, these are not the issues that the men and women in this study faced. For almost all of them, the decision to end the relationship had already been made and, due to the referral process, the initial disclosure had also been made. Hence the focus in this section is not about the training necessary to work with individuals who are currently in domestically violent relationships, but on the sort of counselling training that would support a therapist to undertake this work with someone who has already left the abusive relationship.

This study suggests that having a fairly broad-based counselling education and a relationally-based approach to the work would be helpful. Note that there does not appear to be a requirement for the counsellor to have come from a specifically CBT, psychodynamic or person-centred core-training. Instead, it is more about openness to incorporating aspects of each of these therapies into practice whilst holding the construction of a deep and meaningful therapeutic relationship as an integral part of the work. My own career in personal development began initially by training first as a corporate coach, which was very solution-focused, and then as a counsellor based on a person-centred approach. Ultimately, like many counsellors, I moved towards an integrative model, which also included some psychodynamic features. Hence I can see value and benefit in both relational and task focused models. As I looked at the findings of the research, I was therefore not necessarily looking for one model of practice to adhere to, rather I was interested in the process for the participants.

Rogers' theories and recommended approaches (Rogers, 1957; 1958; 1959; 1964) appear to fit with some of the issues which can result from domestic violence and the feedback from the participants. The relationship with the counsellor was an important aspect of the work, and the findings in this study have shown that both men and women valued having a counsellor who cared for them. What was perhaps more surprising was that the participants did not appear to value the deeply caring aspect of the therapy initially. Instead, what they appreciated was the ability of the counsellor to help them to understand the situation they had been in and to help them to change the situation they were now in. Acknowledging the value of feeling cared for took a little longer.

This type of initial relationship, one of collaboration and sharing information, would be fairly easy to establish when working from a cognitive-behavioural base (Castonguay et al., 2010). However, a therapist working from a person-centred perspective could miss the client need for information in their desire to facilitate client autonomy and exploration (Watson and Kalogerakos, 2010). It would therefore appear that having some training in both therapies would be helpful, to allow the therapist to choose an appropriate approach dependent on the presenting issues.

As the counselling continued, there appears to be a much stronger case for developing the counselling to meet relational needs, including the effect of past life experiences. This may suggest a strong case for psychodynamic therapy, which provides insight into the past as well as a relational based therapy (Messer and Wolitzky, 2010). This, in conjunction with knowledge of domestic violence, could provide a platform for successfully exploring issues that need to be explored. It is possible that therapists initially trained in this way would be able to work successfully with the client. However, once again there is a continuum of practice, from those trying to work with transference exclusively, to those prepared to show at least part of themselves within the therapeutic relationship. Too strong a focus on what was going on in the room may miss some of the issues currently occurring outside the room which require attention.

It would seem that domestic violence counselling may not work too well with counsellors adopting a highly purist approach. The need for a real, collaborative, warm, highly empathic, consistent, insight based therapy which also allows flexibility for the client does suggest that an integrative approach may be preferred. In addition, it would be useful for counsellors to have received particular training in issues such as anxiety (Donohoe and Ricketts, 2006) and working with suicidal ideation (Reeves, 2012), remembering that anxieties regarding personal safety and previous or current partners may be real rather than imaginary. For many domestic violence clients, perceived threats come through highly developed senses which have protected them thus far. Even clients who have left their relationship and may not experience danger on a daily basis may still be at risk (Women's Aid, 2015). Research has shown that this client group are, in general, quite astute at managing their own safety (Bell, Cattaneo, Goodman et al., 2008) and any concerns raised about changes to their safety should be taken seriously.

It is also appropriate to make an additional point about the risk to counsellors in working with this client group. For those individuals still in touch with their abuser, even after they have left the relationship, there is the possibility that their movements could be monitored. If movements are monitored, then the abuser may observe the client's attendance at an agency or, if working in private practice, the counsellor's home. There have been incidents noted in the past of attacks on domestic violence agencies because the client's partner is unhappy with the changes to their relationship. There are reasons for the secrecy surrounding the addresses of refuges and the security systems present in domestic violence agencies to allow screening of individuals prior to entry. Whilst these issues can always be a risk in working as a therapist, it is important to note these may be higher in these cases. Whilst it should not prevent counsellors from working with clients, it is a timely reminder to ensure that there are systems in place, wherever you work, such that an unexpected incident can be managed and support can be requested and received quickly in an emergency.

As well as basic counselling training, there are two other areas of additional training. The first is in working with trauma. From this study, what seemed to be most important was that the therapist was comfortable with and could facilitate exploration of difficult and painful memories for the client, with appropriately informed consent. As the counsellor was comfortable in the session, so the client was able to explore and confront their own issues. It would be helpful for therapists working in this area to have a good knowledge of how trauma presents, in the psyche and body, and to be trained in a trauma technique that felt appropriate to their philosophical and skills base. Currently, there are a range of therapies which can be considered (Marzillier, 2014) which include bodywork, EMDR and imagery. Being trained in an approach that is interesting, and that the counsellor believes will work well, will increase confidence and effectiveness.

The second is the requirement for domestic violence knowledge. The need for appropriate training and knowledge of domestic violence has been highlighted throughout this book and has also been highlighted in the recently updated NICE guidance (National Institute for Health and Clinical Excellence, 2014). There are many training programmes available through the third sector, public sector and private sector. Each will have their own particular emphasis, but will cover the essential aspects. As a minimum, it would seem appropriate for counsellors to know about the cycle of violence (Walker, 1979), as well as the abusive behaviours and strategies that have been identified in domestic violence perpetrators (Craven and Fleming, 2008; Domestic Abuse Intervention Programs, 2012). Whilst these models are written as examples of male perpetrator behaviour, it would seem that these behaviours can also be seen in women. For example, it is not only men who can take control over the home environment, women can do so too. There are also text books which cover the psychology of domestic violence in more detail, and reading one or more would be a good way to gain background information on the issues most likely to present (Dutton, 1992; Walker, 1994; Sanderson, 2008; Nicolson, 2010).

Although this sort of background information is helpful, it is not just learning about the models but determining how they can be implemented within counselling that is valuable. As a trainee counsellor, one of the most useful aspects of the training I received at a DV agency was case study role play. Here, the trainer had provided us with details of a role play which we had to develop in the counselling scenario. This provided two benefits. Firstly, it helped us to get used to hearing the sorts of stories we would need to work with and try out appropriate responses. Secondly, it provided the opportunity for us to pretend to be a client which provided additional insight into their situation. Having the opportunity to experience both positions in the counselling was valuable when finally working with clients.

Of course, scenarios in a training session are different to those in real life. It is unlikely that a trainee will be able to act out with the same levels of emotion as present in a client. Nevertheless, using scenarios which accurately reflect the type of situation that occurs within domestic violence allows the counsellor to hear such stories in the context of therapeutic work. Having to present such a story helps the trainee to understand the difficulties the client might have in doing so and also to see how such a situation could occur despite the client's best endeavours to prevent it. If therapists have the opportunity to participate in domestic violence counselling training with such an experiential component, it would be worth considering.

As well as preparing professionally as a counsellor, through extending knowledge and skills, it is worth considering what personal preparation may also be required. It may be appropriate to consider how you will exercise, what your boundaries regarding work might be, what programmes you can watch or books you can read that will take you away from work issues, and how relationships with colleagues can be developed to allow debriefing when required (Bush, 2009). In addition, it is important to have a good relationship with your supervisor and consider what level of supervision you require depending on your caseload and client issues. If you have previously experienced violence or abuse yourself, you may want to find a local counsellor that you can call upon should you need to do so. It is so much easier to call someone you have already met when issues arise than to begin a selection process. Equally, accessing training to learn about different relaxation techniques could be useful not only in client work, but in your own self-care too.

Finally, and perhaps most importantly, counsellors do need to be aware of the client's safety from the outset. One of the interesting points from this study was that participants were only referred to counselling when they were either out of their abusive relationship, or the relationship was psychologically, rather than physically abusive. This means that the need for a safety assessment or for adopting safety measures to ensure the physical safety of the participants was not something that was highlighted as part of counselling. Whilst this is entirely appropriate for the situation these participants were in, it is equally important to recognise that this will not always be the case. Some men and women will try to access counselling whilst in physically abusive relationships and at risk of serious harm. In these situations, it is important to refer the client to someone who has been trained in conducting domestic violence safety assessments, through a local domestic violence agency. This will ensure that appropriate advice is given as well as access to any specific resources required at that time. It is possible that a counsellor, even with some domestic violence training, could misunderstand or fail to enquire about some of the subtleties of a complex and violent relationship, which could have significant and potentially fatal consequences for the client. If a counsellor is in any doubt at all about the safety of their client, the best course of action is to make contact with the nearest local agency. A list of contact numbers for domestic violence support is given in Appendix 1 in this book, but anyone working regularly with domestic violence clients should be aware of, and in contact with, the nearest agency in their area.

This section may initially appear daunting to trainee counsellors and it is not my intention to dissuade individuals from seeking work in this area of counselling, more to make them aware of the risks and challenges which may occur and to be clear about what they need to do to prepare themselves physically and psychologically. It is always appropriate to remember the importance of care of self as well as care of the other. Working with clients who have experienced domestic violence can be both heart-warming and uplifting, through witnessing the profound changes that can take place during counselling as each reclaims their life. We owe it to our clients to take care of ourselves so that we can witness that transformation.

Summary

This section is extraordinarily brief considering the amount of information that could have been included. Indeed, it is possible that with further research, this section could be extended into a book in its own right. It provides signposting of some relevant points rather than providing a detailed description of how counsellors might work with clients. It seemed important to take the information from participants and to present at least some interpretation of what their views might mean in the context of counselling practice.

One of the surprising factors to come out of the study was the role of the organisation in the counselling process. The key points from this section include:

- the important role that the administrative team play in the first contact with clients
- the need to include all team members in assessing the potential for secondary traumatic stress
- the value of a consistent organisational view across the team
- identifying ways to connect with and keep in touch with those who will refer to the organisation
- using marketing messages associated with symptoms and behaviours that can be recognised by clients
- ensuring that marketing information is appropriately placed according to the interests of the clients groups

I appreciate that this chapter covers only a small part of what could be covered under organisational role and relied heavily on my personal interpretation, but I felt it important to introduce the topic as one that counsellors in general may wish to contemplate further. Here, it seems that the organisation and the way it integrates into the professional community may have significant implications for its success in delivering funding, recruiting clients and maintaining the health and well-being of its employees.

In addition, I have introduced the difficult topic of counsellor aptitude. The key points from this section include:

- the relevance of the common factors research literature to the findings from this study
- the agreement between the therapist characteristics described by participants and the literature on the characteristics of effective therapists
- the need for counsellors to be robust enough to hear the client's story and sensitive enough to understand it from the client's perspective
- understanding that a therapist with a previous history of abuse may find additional challenges in working with this client group
- the importance of a counsellor being aware of their own processes so that they can appropriately respond to what is happening in session
- the protective factors of hope and self-compassion for therapists

I am mindful of discussions with some counsellors who have indicated that there is little new in my findings. The link to common factors in counselling would support that stance. I hope that I have been able to show that it is not just about meeting the basic requirements in counselling, but in having the personal qualities, interest and desire to do the work. If funding can be found to address the unmet need for DV counselling, these factors will become increasingly important. Much more could be written about this, but all I wanted to do was introduce the topic and provide a simple explanation of my own understanding of the issues to prompt further discussion.

Although this may be a slightly controversial topic, I thought it important to introduce the concept of gender within counselling. The key points from this section include:

- The issue is not related to the gender of the abusive partner or of the client, but the gender preference of the client for the counsellor offering support.
- Although counsellors may feel able to work with clients of either gender, clients may feel differently.

- Offering the client a choice about the gender of the counsellor they work with may help in establishing the therapeutic relationship.

Whilst I am aware that there are many people who have studied this particular issue at length, I hope that I have been able to explain why I do not believe the issue of gender is not simply about the model of male perpetrator and female victim, but also about the issues associated with gender in terms of counsellor training and client preferences.

Finally, I have made some suggestions about appropriate training and preparation for working with domestic violence clients. The key points from this section include:

- working from an integrative counselling base which includes aspects of CBT, psychodynamic and person-centred ideas
- being aware of the need to confirm the safety of the client and to refer to specialist services for a safety assessment if there are any doubts
- undertaking specific training in areas such as working with anxiety or trauma
- undergoing training in working with domestic violence
- ensuring that the workplace is secure
- beginning self-care strategies before beginning work in this area

Whilst many textbooks on domestic violence counselling have opted to use one or two chapters to provide the theory, I made a decision not to do so, as it has already been covered very well by other authors. Instead, I wanted to talk more about the training required as a counsellor, the philosophical position, specialist knowledge and again some of the personal characteristics. Here it also seemed important to link the home life with work life to show that preparation for work in this area, when done well, is more than simply delivering counselling sessions.

Despite the brevity in introducing a range of different concepts and ideas, I hope this provokes some constructive thoughts from others as we seek to improve our provision of counselling for this client group.

7
Conclusions

This research study was completed to enable counselling clients to make their views about appropriate counselling following domestic violence known. This final chapter has been written to pull together the many different aspects of the study and to draw some conclusions from what has been presented. Although there are a number of different ideas and concepts emerging from the study, it is important to remember that this was a small piece of qualitative research and hence much of what is described below necessarily indicates that further work is required to substantiate the work. Nevertheless, the study has produced some interesting ideas which warrant further consideration.

At the start of this book, the mental health issues associated with experiencing domestic violence were highlighted, with depression, suicidal ideation and PTSD specifically highlighted from previous research. Although there were no diagnoses available for the participants within this study, the level of emotional distress described by the participants was high and suicidal ideation was mentioned by some of them. This suggests some agreement between the experience of the participants and the research data presented, that is, the development or maintenance of mental health issues during domestic violence can continue beyond the termination of the relationship.

It is possible that leaving the abusive relationship inspires hope that all will now be well, until the realisation that some of the emotional and psychological factors have remained unchanged. As a group, the participants described themselves as people who coped with things and tried their best to make things right. This realisation that all was not well may have taken some time to emerge, but once there, led to feelings of hopelessness, which carry an existential burden. It is possible that just as clients instinctively seek help when at risk of death through physical violence, so there is an equal help-seeking desire when there is a threat to life through psychological harm.

Much of the existing research on domestic violence and mental health for women has been related to leaving their relationship to seek safety from physical harm. In general the average age of the women involved is late twenties to early thirties. In this study, where the main issue was mental health, the average age for female participants was 45 years. The agencies confirmed that this was representative of their counselling clients. Male participants, on the other hand, also had an average age of 45 but this was in keeping with other studies with male victims. Further work is required to see whether this age profile is reflective of a need for mental health support later on in the recovery from domestic violence or whether the harm from psychological abuse takes longer to establish. Either way, this may reflect a slightly different domestic violence population which might benefit from further study.

The engagement with professionals and colleagues rather than friends and family as referral sources highlighted issues of trust in, as well as isolation from, friends and family. This, however, may not be wholly related to the quality of the relationships. It may also reflect the individual's lack of confidence in not only disclosing what has happened, but also in being understood and supported with the issues of abuse associated with their mental distress. The model of trust put forward, initially in Chapter 1, suggested that expertise in the topic as well as wanting the best for the individual may both be required to generate sufficient trust to talk about what happened. This may not always be possible with friends and family.

However, the delay in accessing mental health services until well after the relationship is over, or a new relationship has begun, may be part of the reason why many of the participants had previously accessed general counselling. The time delay may make it harder to see the link between the experience of abuse and emotional distress. Hence the referral process into domestic violence counselling for individuals who have not previously had professional support for their relationship issues or did not recognise the abusive nature of their relationship may be problematic.

The situation for individuals in these circumstances may be additionally complicated through their reluctance or inability to talk about or explain their situation, together with the general suspiciousness described by some of the female participants. For such individuals, it may be hard to settle within a 6-session model of counselling, as it takes time to begin to talk openly and having a time constraint can be seen to present additional difficulties. What was clear from the interviews with participants was the relief that the participants described once the link between their experience of distress and their experiences in their relationships had been made. This study indicated that the counsellor having a knowledge of domestic violence and the ability to prompt experiences and emotions was helpful in establishing trust and helping the participant to express and understand their situation. However, it is equally possible that working with someone who does not understand the nature of the issues experienced might stop the counselling process, as it could potentially undermine trust in both the therapist and the process. Hence, these factors may present a reasonable explanation for the participants' previously poor counselling experiences which would require further exploration.

In considering what might be a good approach to working with domestic violence, most therapeutic models for working with women appear to be based to some extent on Herman's (1992) model (described in Chapter 1) and this study confirms this as an underlying philosophy and approach. However, the intertwining of hope-based strategies throughout the participant experience suggests that Lee's (2007) model of a strengths and competency based approach could also be integrated. The factors highlighted in Chapter 3 can also be adopted. However, the study also raised the importance of working with clients who have suffered previous traumas at a pace the client can tolerate. This can reduce the difficulties that can occur between sessions when a process of remembering too much too quickly can be problematic for the individual. It also highlighted the importance of appropriate preparation of clients by the counsellor where this is a possibility, so that they are aware of what might happen and have already identified coping mechanisms if needed. Nevertheless, it would seem that there is a reasonably robust process model for working with women already in the literature, which could be accessed by counsellors with appropriate training.

However, the situation for men appears a little more complex, as very few of the participants had the opportunity to explore their issues in the same depth as was available to the women. Nevertheless, there were some signs that a similar process of establishing a relationship through a common understanding of their experience and an approach that helped to solve day to day problems initially would help. There is some evidence that some of the men might have benefited from a more in-depth approach addressing other issues, but investigating this remains a research objective for future work. Clearly the value that the male participants gained from reconnecting socially with others shows that the third step of Herman's model is valid. However, further work with men who have experienced domestic violence, within an environment that could respond flexibly to their needs, would be helpful. This would help to determine the value of, and need for, more in-depth work, as well as assessing the most appropriate services and how best to deliver them.

This is an important consideration, as there were both similarities and differences in the approaches valued by the female and male participants. Whilst women were clear about valuing their new found confidence in establishing boundaries for themselves, the men valued reconnecting and connecting with friends and family after the end of their relationship. The different social situations of each also created different support needs, and it is possible that the two groups valued different aspects of the service offered. For example, Chapters 3 and 4, highlighted possible differences in the way that compassion was experienced. This indicated an interesting difference in emphasis and approach in terms of counselling. Clearly this research was conducted with a small number of participants, and needs more work to confirm the findings, but it is an interesting concept.

At the end of the study, the participants indicated a significant change in their perception of their lives, both in terms of their motivation day to day and their desire to plan for the future. It is worth considering whether we do measure the value of counselling to this client group appropriately and whether the PTGI would be worth developing in this context. Once again, further work would be required to produce an appropriate and reliable measure for counselling.

Looking back at the information on counselling provided by the participants prompted consideration of what was needed to work with domestic violence counselling clients, in the context of the organisation and the counsellor. As well as highlighting the need for staff in this area of work to look after their own wellbeing, particularly those with a previous history of abuse, specific aspects of counsellor working were highlighted. The model of working identified could be adapted from any initial training, although there are a number of helpful therapist characteristics identified. This may include the issue of counsellor gender, as there were indications from the study that it could be important from both a male and female client perspective.

What is not yet clear from the study is whether counsellors working with DV clients can gain sufficient insight from undergoing a short domestic violence awareness training course, or whether an in-depth training to understand the experience of clients who have experienced domestic violence is required. Another area for discussion and debate is whether it would make sense to develop training programmes for counsellors working either privately or in general counselling services to enable them to work appropriately with this client group. There may be many individuals accessing general counselling who are in less abusive relationships, and yet still find there are psychological problems arising as a result. Given the level of skill highlighted for counsellors in this study, a more defined training programme could be beneficial to encourage the development of specific skills as well as to embed knowledge, but this too will require further testing and development. It would seem, from this small study, that there is the potential to widen the capability of counsellors in the UK to work effectively with domestic violence clients, provided appropriate training and experience can be provided.

Finally, this brings us to the debate surrounding advocacy and counselling, introduced in Chapter 1. Whilst there is undoubtedly value in providing support to an individual as they leave their abusive relationship, it is not as clear that the support should include counselling at that time. For many individuals, leaving the relationship and starting again, sometimes as a single parent, has a number of demands relating to their new lifestyle which need to be addressed. It is often a hectic time, requiring a lot of energy to deal with new and different challenges. Given the value placed by the participants on reflection and understanding of their relationship in counselling, trying to engage with such a process whilst leaving the relationship has the potential to increase, rather than decrease, stress levels.

The current policy of offering advocacy support with legal issues, which can also include support work more generally, seems to be an appropriate solution. As the individual develops into their new life, many will need less support as they develop their own new networks of friends and family. However, for those who continue to struggle some months after leaving, a referral to counselling to explore the nature of the relationship and the impact of that on the individual, could be highly beneficial. In other words, it is not a debate about whether counselling or advocacy is preferable, it is about the right support, at the right time, for the individual.

Providing those who seem to struggle initially with details of a counselling service, which could be accessed in the future should it be required, would be very helpful and could become part of a new referral pathway. This would allow the decision to be taken by the individual, whilst recognising that it may take some time for the individual to recognise the need to do so. Health workers, legal teams and support workers could form part of that referral process. Existing referral pathways through previous clients and the police will also be beneficial. However, there is also a need to ensure that there are appropriate counselling services available to which those referrals can be made.

As things stand currently in the UK, domestic violence counselling is a specialist service provided by some organisations in the third sector. With limited resources available to both counsellors and clients, this may continue to be the case for some time. However, it is my hope that some of this research may be used as a basis for other work to support or disprove the findings from this study. Then as our knowledge in this area grows, the aspirations of the participants in this study to improve counselling support for those who have suffered domestic violence are more likely to be fulfilled.

Appendix 1: Contact Details for Domestic Violence Support

This list of domestic violence support helplines is not intended to be exhaustive, but to provide a first point of contact for someone experiencing domestic violence or who knows of a person experiencing domestic violence. These agencies can help to identify an appropriate local service and/or provide a referral. The contact details provided here were accurate on the 17 February 2015.

UK

Women

24-hour National Domestic Violence Freephone Helpline

This helpline is run in partnership between Women's Aid and Refuge for women who are experiencing domestic violence.

Tel: 0808-2000-247
Website: http://www.nationaldomesticviolencehelpline.org.uk/

Men

ManKind Initiative

This is an organisation which works with male victims of domestic violence. Currently the telephone lines are open Monday–Friday 10am–4pm and 7pm–9pm. At the time of writing an urgent call for funding was being made to enable the helpline to continue.

Tel: 01823-334244
Website: http://www.mankind.org.uk/

Men's Advice Line

This service is for men experiencing domestic violence from their partner and is provided by Respect. The telephone lines are currently open Monday–Friday 9am–5pm.

Tel: 0808-801-0327
Website: http://www.mensadviceline.org.uk/mens_advice.php.html

Perpetrators

Respect

For anyone who is perpetrating domestic violence, or is working with someone who is doing so, the main support agency in the UK is Respect. Respect specialise in working with men, women and young people who perpetrate domestic violence. Telephone lines are currently open Monday–Friday 9am–5pm.

Tel: 0808-802-4040
Website: http://www.respectphoneline.org.uk/pages/male-domestic-vio
lence-perpetrators.html

In addition, for all victims and perpetrators of domestic violence in Northern Ireland

Indirect

This is a government body offering a 24-hour domestic violence helpline.

Tel: 0800-917-1414
Website: http://www.dhsspsni.gov.uk/freephone-helpline

Eire

Women

Women's Aid

Women's Aid for Ireland offer help and support for women experiencing domestic violence. The Freephone helpline is currently open 10am–10pm, 7 days per week.

Tel: 1800-341-900
Website: http://www.womensaid.ie/

Men

AMEN

AMEN is an organisation offering a helpline and support service for men who have experienced domestic violence. The helpline is currently open Monday–Friday 9am–5pm.

Tel: 046 9023 718
Website: http://www.amen.ie/

USA

Women

The National Domestic Violence Hotline

This is main helpline number within the USA and is presented as a gender-neutral website for survivors. However, many of the resources appear to be more relevant to female victims. The hotline is open 24 hours per day, 7 days per week.

Tel: 1-800-799-SAFE (7233) or 1-800-787-3224 (TTY)
Website: http://www.thehotline.org/

Men

Domestic Abuse Helpline for Men and Women

This is also a gender-neutral website for survivors, but with resources focused on male victims. The helpline is open 24 hours per day, 7 days per week, although the service was off-line on the day accessed due to funding shortages.

Tel: 1-888-7HELPLINE or 1-888-743-5754
Website: http://www.dahmw.org/

Canada

Women and Men

National Domestic Violence Hotline (Canada)

This telephone service is bi-lingual (French and English) and is available 24 hours per day, 7 days per week.

Tel: 1-800-363-9010

Public Health Agency of Canada

Domestic violence services in Canada are determined and delivered primarily by each province. The details of what is available for each area can be found by accessing the Public Health Agency Website.

Website: http://www.phac-aspc.gc.ca/sfv-avf/index-eng.php

Australia

Women

1800RESPECT

This is the main domestic violence helpline in Australia and can provide both information and referrals. The telephone lines are available 24 hours per day, 7 days per week.

Tel: 1800-737-732
Website: https://www.1800respect.org.au/

Men

MensLine

This is a general support and information service for men with family or relationship concerns, including a specific service for men experiencing domestic violence. The service is available 24 hours per day, 7 days per week.

Tel: 1300-78-99-78
Website: http://www.mensline.org.au/improving-relationships/are-you-experiencing-violence-or-abuse-in-your-relationship

International

Women

Hot Peaches

This is a website which contains a database of organisations that can provide information and support on domestic violence for women and children across the world. The information is available in 110 languages.

Website: http://www.hotpeachpages.net/

Men

At the time of writing, no resources specifically for male victims internationally were identified. However, the Hot Peaches website above also shows some links to general victim support services which may be able to identify appropriate local support.

Appendix 2: Research Methodology Summary

The decision to put the methodology section in an appendix was not one that was taken lightly. As this book is predominantly about the findings from a PhD research study, a chapter on methodology would have been appropriate and acceptable to most readers. However, this book was always intended as a resource for practitioners, and it has tried to focus on what might be helpful to know in working with DV clients, rather than the research process. Priority has been given to describing the experience of DV counselling through the participants' words, rather than the process of obtaining those words, acknowledging that the methodology has already been scrutinised through the PhD examination process.

However, it is important in terms of transparency that a description of the way the research was conducted is available for those who wish to make their own judgements about the applicability of the research to their work or who are contemplating a similar project in the future. For this reason, a summary of the key points from the methodology is given below. For those who are interested in more detail, such as the interview questions used or the documentation associated with ethical approval, the published thesis will soon be available electronically (Roddy, 2014). Otherwise, if there are further questions, please write to Jeannette Roddy at the publisher's address.

The research question

The research question developed for this study was:

> What was significant, in going through counselling, for those who suffered DV?

This specific question was selected for a number of reasons:

- The word 'significant' was used in the context of the clients' experiences and allowed flexibility to determine what was of significance to them during counselling, either positively or negatively, without the constraints of counselling theory and could include incidents, process or outcomes.
- The past tense indicated the decision to work with clients after counselling had ended.
- A focus on 'going through counselling' to explore the client process from beginning to end, including any differences in need emerging as the process evolved.
- Using the word 'those' to include anyone who may have encountered DV, rather than a specifically defined client group.

The word 'suffered' within the context of DV, rather than victim, survivor, perpetrator or co-abuser, was used to identify those who felt harmed as a result of their experience, without judgement. This allowed a lot of flexibility in working with participants who wanted to take part in the research.

Ethics and the research process

The research process was really an example of team work between the agencies and the university. Four agencies participated in the research, three working with women in the north east of England, and one working with men in Eire. The ethical review outlining the detail of the research process was signed off by the university, and was also signed off by each agency prior to the research beginning. This ensured clarity about our respective commitments. Personal contact details of clients were held by the agency and so interviews were arranged by the agency. Question and answer sheets outlining the purpose, risks and protocol for the research were sent to the participants prior to the interview by the agency. These were then reviewed with and signed by participants prior to beginning the interview to ensure fully informed consent.

Ethical considerations were an important part of the research design (Roddy, 2011c). As can be seen from Chapter 1, the degree of mental distress for clients seeking treatment was potentially high as was the possibility of a client also suffering trauma. This led to an early decision to work only with clients who had completed their counselling at least three months previously. This helped to ensure that participants had resolved the issues that had brought them into counselling, as well as providing time and space following counselling to reflect on the whole experience.

However, the issue of trauma meant that, however carefully I worked during the research interview, there was a risk that an unresolved aspect of the experience might emerge resulting in re-traumatisation of the participant. For this reason, all of the agencies involved in the research agreed to provide additional counselling to any participants who required support as a result of the interview. The participants were not asked to and did not review their transcripts as a further way to reduce any risk to them of revisiting material. As it happened, the interviews went well and no-one needed to access further support from the agency. Indeed, the feedback from participants indicated that the interviews had been a positive experience. The interview process also had the potential to be an intense experience for me as the researcher. In order to deal with my sometimes significant emotional response to the material presented in the interviews by participants, at times I accessed research supervision, professional supervision and private therapy.

Equally, my interaction with the research material meant there was potential for bias in interpreting what emerged not only as a researcher, but also as a counsellor with experience of working with DV, and as an individual with my own experiences of counselling. I recorded my own views of the counselling process prior to beginning the research and then reviewed those two years later at the end of the research process to check for unintended bias. Careful interview preparation and review helped me to reduce any bias in the way the interview was conducted and four (one in six) of the transcripts were reviewed by my research supervisors, both for construct and analysis. Four of the female participants and two of the male participants also reviewed the emerging models of practice to check that they fitted with the experiences they had shared. In addition, I wrote about whatever I was currently exploring for each PhD supervision session which allowed further exploration of particular issues. I wrote two articles for publication and presented at three or four conferences per year to gain feedback and comment from fellow professionals. The combination of these activities assured me that what has been presented here is a good reflection of the views of the participants.

Finally, permission to reproduce limited sections of their transcripts was given by each of the participants prior to the initial interview. All of the names presented in the written output and conference presentations associated with this research are pseudonyms and personal details have been removed or changed to protect the identities of each of the participants.

Participants

Each of the agencies was provided with criteria for selecting candidates for the research. Each candidate had to have completed counselling at least three months previously and no longer than 18 months ago, to allow separation from the counsellor and agency, but to still be able to recall some details of the experience. In addition, the participants were seen by a range of counsellors at the agencies with different backgrounds to ensure that the practice described was generally experienced and not a description of the way one practitioner worked. These constraints were often sufficient, but where more than one client may have been suitable and willing, clients outside the age range 40–55 or of non-white ethnicity were prioritised. The agencies confirmed that the majority of their clients were aged 30–60 as younger clients tended not to engage as well with the counselling process. Despite several attempts by the agencies, I was unable to interview anyone under the age of 30. All of the participants were white and of either British or Irish descent and reflected the demographics of the north of England and Eire where the agencies were based. A summary of the characteristics of the participants is given in Table A.1.

Age range

The average age of the participants for both men and women was 45 years old and their ages ranged from 33 to 64. The women's ages were evenly split between their thirties, forties and fifties, but the men were

Table A.1 Demographics of the participants

	Female	Male
Number of participants	14	6
Age range (average)	33–64 (45)	33–64 (45)
Number of participants who were employed/self-employed	11	3
Number of participants in a relationship	6	2
Highest level of educational qualification	Postgraduate degree	Honours degree
Number of participants who had previously attended counselling elsewhere	11	4

predominantly in their forties. Although this is similar to some DV research for women (Walker, 2009) where the age range was 18–69 (average 42.5) many other studies conducted with women indicated average ages of participants in their thirties (Henning and Klesges, 2002; Stenius and Veysey, 2005; Hage, 2006; Moe, 2007; Allen and Wozniak, 2011). However, this was different for the men. Here the participants were only slightly older than in other research with males (Carrado et al., 1996; Coker et al., 2002; Hines and Douglas, 2010a).

Employment

Eleven of the 14 women were in employment at the time of the interview, compared to three of the six men. One of the participants was registered as disabled. Many of the women had opted for a traditionally female career choice, such as working as a carer or teacher or more generally within the public sector, but it is worth noting that two were self-employed, a higher proportion than normal within the UK (Institute for Small Business and Entrepreneurship, 2014). It is hard to compare these data with other studies involving women, as the employment status of the participants is rarely presented. This may be due to many studies being conducted within a refuge environment where the individual may have had to leave employment when they left home. However, as a generally older group of women, with fewer childcare responsibilities, it is reasonable that there would be a higher percentage of the participants in employment than in studies where employment figures are given, for example Allen and Wozniak (2011).

The men had generally opted for traditionally male careers such as engineering and technology, which was in line with other studies of men who had experienced DV (Hines et al., 2007). The men chose to disclose that at the time of their relationship break-down, they all worked full-time: three were employed and three self-employed. However, at the time of the research interview, only three of the men were still in fulltime employment.

Relationship status

This question was not specifically asked, but data was supplied by participants during the interview. Six of the 14 women were in a relationship, three of whom had significantly improved the relationship with their abusive partner following counselling and three of whom were in new relationships. Two of the six men were in new relationships following the break-up of their marriages. Nineteen of the participants were heterosexual. One of the participants had been abused by their child. The remaining participants had been abused by their partner.

Education

The women had had a variety of educational experiences, ranging from leaving school at 15 to attaining post-graduate qualifications. Just over half of the participants had achieved GCSE, A-level equivalent qualifications or further education qualifications; four had achieved higher education qualifications; and the rest had left school without qualifications. This broadly matched other research conducted in the field (Hage, 2006; Allen and Wozniak, 2011) but is at a higher level than some (Walker, 2009). Similarly the men's educational attainment ranged from leaving school at 15 without qualifications to attaining higher education qualifications, and was in keeping with other published research (Douglas and Hines, 2011).

Past and present counselling experience

The women had spent between two months and 21 months in one-to-one counselling. Nearly 80% of the women had accessed some counselling before. Only one reported having a single, very positive counselling experience previously which had resolved her issues, but this was for an issue unrelated to DV.

The men also reported counselling ranging from two months to 21 months. Two-thirds of the men had accessed counselling before, with two reporting unsatisfactory experiences and two reporting a referral process to the agency once the issues presented became clearer. It is important to note that the men included telephone and one-to-one support, as well as group counselling in their assessment of counselling and this cannot be directly compared with the level of support provided to female participants over the same time period.

It would be wrong to draw generalised conclusions about counselling from such a small sample, however, the number of reported previously unsatisfactory counselling experiences is notable. It was estimated that on average, the participants received 20 sessions of satisfactory counselling from the participating agencies.

Data analysis

The interviews were transcribed within a few weeks of being recorded. Over 250,000 words of data were collected over the research period. The data was analysed using adapted grounded theory, which was a form of grounded theory based on the original description of the technique (Glaser and Strauss, 1967) but with a reflexive position taken regarding data analysis (Charmaz, 2006).

In keeping with this methodology, the grounded theory was under construction throughout the data collection period, and specific issues that emerged were explored with participants as the opportunity presented. Whilst conventional grounded theory would encourage participants to be selected on the basis of the information required to test the emerging model (Glaser and Strauss, 1967), this was not possible here as there were limited numbers of clients who were prepared to be interviewed about their experiences. Instead, exploration of specific issues occurred as they were introduced into the interview by the participant.

Although the data was originally going to be analysed using an NVIVO package, technical difficulties surrounding the size of data files and integrity of the system resulted in a different process being developed. This involved a stage-wise process of transcription, coding and mind-mapping using text documents, paper and coloured pens. This resulted in a model for each individual. These models were then combined, using the same processes, to generate separate theories for male and female participants. These theories were generated sequentially as new interviews became available. A final check was completed by rearranging all the data alphabetically according to the pseudonym and re-analysing the data. This concluded that the process was robust.

However, when I stepped back from the model generated, I became aware that there were some significant aspects of the stories that I had heard that were not coming out in this analysis. These were primarily aspects with a high emotional content. I drew the model out on a large piece of paper, and then drew each participant's journey through the model. This highlighted specific issues which needed to be included but had been missed earlier. This was mainly because they had been described in different ways by the participants and the analytical technique had not noted the underlying similarities because of this. This is perhaps a good example of one of the limitations of grounded theory as a technique.

The final models presented in the thesis showed the structure of grounded theory and the relative weight of each factor making up elements of the final theory. This structure has not been repeated in the book as it is too detailed for a book of this size. In addition, I have rearranged the material associated with the decision to access agency services (Chapter 2) and the benefits of doing so (Chapter 5) to show the overlap of experiences of male and female participants. The models of specific support have, however, been maintained on a gendered basis, as shown in Chapter 3 for women and Chapter 4 for men as the two were very different. The main points from the thesis have been presented in a more descriptive way, which was intended to be more accessible.

Conclusions

The methodology described above produced interesting and detailed findings. It is possible that it could be used again for future research projects in this area.

References

Abrahams, H. (2007). *Supporting women after domestic violence: Loss, trauma and recovery.* London; Philadelphia: Jessica Kingsley Publishers.

Addis, M. E. (2008). 'Gender and depression in men'. *Clinical Psychology – Science and Practice*, 15 (3), 153–168.

Addis, M. E. & Mahalik, J. R. (2003). 'Men, masculinity, and the contexts of help seeking'. *American Psychologist*, 58 (1), 5–14.

Adkins, K. S. & Kamp Dush, C. M. (2010). 'Implications of violent and controlling unions for mothers mental health and leaving'. *Social Science Research*, 39 (6), 925–937.

Afifi, T. O., Macmillan, H., Cox, B. J., Asmundson, G. J. G., Stein, M. B. & Sareen, J. (2009). 'Mental health correlates of intimate partner violence in marital relationships in a nationally representative sample of males and females'. *Journal of Interpersonal Violence*, 24 (8), 1398–1417.

Agnew Davies, R. (2013). *Counselling masterclass series: Domestic violence.* York: York St. John University.

Ainsworth, M. D., Blehar, M. C., Waters, E. & Wall, S. (1978). *Patterns of attachment: Assessed in the strange situation and at home.* Hillsdale, NJ: Lawrence Erlbaum.

Allen, J. G. (2005). *Coping with trauma: Hope through understanding.* Washington, DC: American Psychiatric Press.

Allen, K. N. & Wozniak, D. F. (2011). 'The language of healing: Women's voices in healing and recovering from domestic violence'. *Social Work in Mental Health*, 9 (1), 37–55.

Ansara, D. L. & Hindin, M. J. (2010). 'Formal and informal help-seeking associated with women's and men's experiences of intimate partner violence in Canada'. *Social Science & Medicine*, 70 (7), 1011–1018.

Araszkiewicz, A. & Dabkowska, M. (2010). 'Women's mental health: P02–372 – Social and demographic factors and severity of symptoms of posttraumatic stress disorder in victims of intimate partner violence'. *European Psychiatry*, 25 (Supplement 1), 1388.

Asay, T. P. & Lambert, M. J. (1999). 'The empirical case for the common factors in therapy: Quantitative findings'. In: Hubble, M. A., Duncan, B. L. & Miller, S. D. (eds.) *The Heart and Soul of Change: What Works in Therapy* (pp. 23–55). Washington, DC: American Psychological Association.

Bachmann, R. (2001). 'Trust, power and control in trans-organizational relations'. *Organization Studies (Walter de Gruyter GmbH & Co. KG.)*, 22 (2), 337–365.

Baird, K. & Kracen, A. C. (2006). 'Vicarious traumatization and secondary traumatic stress: A research synthesis'. *Counselling Psychology Quarterly*, 19 (2), 181–188.

Baldwin, S. A., Wampold, B. E. & Imel, Z. E. (2007). 'Untangling the alliance-outcome correlation: Exploring the relative importance of therapist and patient variability in the alliance'. *Journal of Consulting and Clinical Psychology*, 75 (6), 842–852.

Bandura, A. (1982). 'Self-efficacy mechanism in human agency'. *American Psychologist*, 37 (2), 122–147.

Barber, J. P., Khalsa, S.-R. & Sharpless, B. A. (2010). 'The validity of the alliance as a predictor of psychotherapy outcome'. In: Muran, J. C. & Barber, J. P. (eds.) *The Therapeutic Alliance: An Evidence-Based Guide to Practice* (pp. 29–43). New York, NY: Guilford Press.

Barcus, R. (1997). 'Partners of survivors of abuse: A men's therapy group'. *Psychotherapy: Theory, Research, Practice, Training*, 34 (3), 316–323.

Bargai, N., Ben-Shakhar, G. & Shalev, A. Y. (2007). 'Posttraumatic stress disorder and depression in battered women: The mediating role of learned helplessness'. *Journal of Family Violence*, 22 (5), 267–275.

Barnard, L. K. & Curry, J. F. (2011). 'Self-compassion: Conceptualizations, correlates, & interventions'. *Review of General Psychology*, 15 (4), 289–303.

Bartholomew, K. & Horowitz, L. M. (1991). 'Attachment styles among young adults: A test of a four-category model'. *Journal of Personality & Social Psychology*, 61 (2), 226–244.

Battaglia, T. A., Finley, E. & Liebschutz, J. M. (2003). 'Survivors of intimate partner violence speak out: Trust in the patient-provider relationship'. *Journal of General Internal Medicine*, 18 (8), 617–623.

Beaulaurier, R. L., Seff, L. R. & Newman, F. L. (2008). 'Barriers to help-seeking for older women who experience intimate partner violence: A descriptive model'. *Journal of Women & Aging*, 20 (3–4), 231–248.

Beck, A. T. & Steer, R. A. (1971). *Beck depression inventory, revised edition (BDI)*. San Antonio, TX: The Psychological Corporation.

Beck, A. T., Weissman, A., Lester, D. & Trexler, L. (1974). 'The measurement of pessimism: The hopelessness scale'. *Journal of Consulting and Clinical Psychology*, 42 (6), 861–865.

Beck, J. G., Mcniff, J., Clapp, J. D., Olsen, S. A., Avery, M. L. & Hagewood, J. H. (2011). 'Exploring negative emotion in women experiencing intimate partner violence: Shame, guilt, and PTSD'. *Behavior Therapy*, 42 (4), 740–750.

Belcher, M. & Jones, L. K. (2009). 'Graduate nurses experiences of developing trust in the nurse-patient relationship'. *Contemporary Nurse*, 31 (2), 142–152.

Bell, M., Cattaneo, L., Goodman, L. & Dutton, M. (2008). 'Assessing the risk of future psychological abuse: Predicting the accuracy of battered women's predictions'. *Journal of Family Violence*, 23 (2), 69–80.

Bennett, M. I. & Bennett, M. B. (1984). 'The uses of hopelessness'. *The American Journal of Psychiatry*, 141 (4), 559–562.

Bennett, L., Riger, S., Schewe, P., Howard, A. & Wasco, S. (2004). 'Effectiveness of hotline, advocacy, counseling, and shelter services for victims of domestic violence'. *Journal of Interpersonal Violence*, 19 (7), 815–829.

Berzoff, J. & Kita, E. (2010). 'Compassion fatigue and counter transference: Two different concepts'. *Clinical Social Work Journal*, 38, 341–349.

Betz, N. E. & Fitzgerald, L. F. (1993). 'Individuality and diversity: Theory and research in counseling psychology'. *Annual Review of Psychology*, 44 (1), 343–381.

Blasco-Ros, C., Sánchez-Lorente, S. & Martinez, M. (2010). 'Recovery from depressive symptoms, state anxiety and post-traumatic stress disorder in women exposed to physical and psychological, but not to psychological intimate partner violence alone: A longitudinal study'. *BMC Psychiatry*, 10, 98.

Bloom, A. D. & Lyle, R. (2001). 'Vicariously traumatised: Male partners of sexual abuse survivors'. In: Brothers, B. J. (ed.) *The Abuse of Men: Trauma Begets Trauma*. New York: The Haworth Press, Inc.

Bohart, A. C. & Tallman, K. (1999). *How clients make therapy work: The process of active self-healing*. Washington, DC: American Psychological Association.

Bond, T. (2011). 'Professional ethics: Building trust in counselling practice and research'. *Remaining Inspired – Counselling and Psychotherapy Research Conference*. Newport: Newport Centre for Counselling Research.

Bostock, J., Plumpton, M. & Pratt, R. (2009). 'Domestic violence against women: Understanding social processes and women's experiences'. *Journal of Community and Applied Social Psychology*, 19 (2), 95–110.

Breger, L. (2012). *Psychotherapy lives intersecting*. Piscataway, NJ: Transaction Publishers.

Briere, J. (2002). 'Treating adult survivors of severe childhood abuse and neglect: Further development of an integrative model'. *In:* Myers, J. E. B., Berliner, L., Briere, J., Hendrix, C. T., Jenny, C. & Reid, T. A. (eds.) *The APSAC handbook on child maltreatment (2nd ed.)* (pp. 175–203). Thousand Oaks, CA US: Sage Publications, Inc.

Briere, J. (2012). 'Working with trauma: Mindfulness and compassion'. In: Germer, C. K. & Siegel, R. D. (eds.) *Wisdom and Compassion in Psychotherapy: Deepening Mindfulness in Clinical Practice* (pp. 265–279). New York, NY: Guilford Press.

British Association for Counselling and Psychotherapy (2010). *Ethical framework for good practice in counselling and psychotherapy*. Rugby: BACP.

British Association for Counselling and Psychotherapy (2013). *Evidence for counselling and psychotherapy*. Lutterworth: BACP.

Bstan Dzin Rgya, M. (2010). *Towards the true kinship of faiths: How the world's religions can come together*. London: Abacus.

Bush, N. J. (2009). 'Compassion fatigue: Are you at risk?' *Oncology Nursing Forum*, 36 (1), 24–28.

Calder, J., Mcvean, A. & Yang, W. (2010). 'History of abuse and current suicidal ideation: Results from a population based survey'. *Journal of Family Violence*, 25 (2), 205–214.

Caldwell, J. E., Swan, S. C. & Woodbrown, V. D. (2012). 'Gender differences in intimate partner violence outcomes'. *Psychology of Violence*, 2 (1), 42–57.

Calnan, M. & Rowe, R. (2008). 'Trust relations in a changing health service'. *Journal of Health Services Research & Policy*, 13 (Supplement 3), 97–103.

Campbell, R., Sullivan, C. M. & Davidson, W. S. (1995). 'Women who use domestic violence shelters: Changes in depression over time'. *Psychology of Women Quarterly*, 19 (2), 237–255.

Canfield, J. (2005). 'Secondary traumatization, burnout, and vicarious traumatization: A review of the literature as it relates to therapists who treat trauma'. *Smith College Studies in Social Work (Haworth)*, 75 (2), 81–101.

Carrado, M., George, M. J., Loxam, E. & Jones, L. (1996). 'Aggression in British heterosexual relationships: A descriptive analysis'. *Aggressive Behavior*, 22 (6), 401–415.

Cascardi, M., O'leary, K. D. & Schlee, K. A. (1999). 'Co-occurrence and correlates of posttraumatic stress disorder and major depression in physically abused women'. *Journal of Family Violence*, 14 (3), 227–249.

Castonguay, L. G. & Beutler, L. E. (2006). *Principles of therapeutic change that work*. Oxford: Oxford University Press.

Castonguay, L. G., Constantino, M. J., Mcaleavey, A. A. & Goldfried, M. R. (2010). 'The therapeutic alliance in cognitive-behavioral therapy'. In: Muran, J. C. & Barber, J. P. (eds.) *The Therapeutic Alliance: An Evidence-Based Guide to Practice* (pp. 150–171). New York: Guilford Press.

Chalk, R., King, P. A., National Research Council/Institute of Medicine & National Research Council (U.S.). Committee on the Assessment of Family Violence Interventions (1998). *Violence in Families: Assessing Prevention and Treatment Programs*.

Charmaz, K. (2006). *Constructing grounded theory: A practical guide through qualitative analysis*. London; Thousand Oaks, CA: Sage Publications.

Claiborn, C. D. (1979). 'Counselor verbal intervention, nonverbal behavior, and social power'. *Journal of Counseling Psychology*, 26 (5), 378–383.

Clements, C. M., Sabourin, C. M. & Spiby, L. (2004). 'Dysphoria and hopelessness following battering: The role of perceived control, coping, and self-esteem'. *Journal of Family Violence*, 19 (1), 25–36.

Clements, C. M. & Sawhney, D. K. (2000). 'Coping with domestic violence: Control attributions, dysphoria, and hopelessness'. *Journal of Traumatic Stress*, 13 (2), 219.

Cloitre, M., Stovall-Mcclough, K. C., Miranda, R. & Chemtob, C. M. (2004). 'Therapeutic alliance, negative mood regulation, and treatment outcome in child abuse-related posttraumatic stress disorder'. *Journal of Consulting and Clinical Psychology*, 72 (3), 411–416.

Coates, D. & Winston, T. (1983). 'Counteracting the deviance of depression: Peer support groups for victims'. *Journal of Social Issues*, 39 (2), 169–194.

Cochran, S. V. & Rabinowitz, F. E. (2003). 'Gender-sensitive recommendations for assessment and treatment of depression in men'. *Professional Psychology: Research and Practice*, 34 (2), 132–140.

Coker, A. L., Davis, K. E., Arias, I., Desai, S., Sanderson, M., Brandt, H. M. & Smith, P. H. (2002). 'Physical and mental health effects of intimate partner violence for men and women'. *American Journal of Preventive Medicine*, 23 (4), 260.

Coker, A. L., Weston, R., Creson, D. L., Justice, B. & Blakeney, P. (2005). 'PTSD symptoms among men and women survivors of intimate partner violence: The role of risk and protective factors'. *Violence And Victims*, 20 (6), 625–643.

Cook, P. W. (2009). *Abused men: The hidden side of domestic violence*. Westport, CT: Praeger.

Cooper, M. (2008). *Essential research findings in counselling and psychotherapy: The facts are friendly*. Los Angeles; London: SAGE.

Coopersmith, S. (1967). *Self-Esteem Inventory (SEI)*. Palo Alto, CA: Consulting Psychologists Press.

Craven, P. & Fleming, J. (2008). *Living with the dominator: A book about the freedom programme*. Gardners Books.

Crits-Christoph, P., Crits-Christoph, K. & Gibbons, M. B. C. (2010). 'Training in alliance-fostering techniques'. In: Muran, J. C. & Barber, J. P. (eds.) *The Therapeutic Alliance: An Evidence-Based Guide to Practice*. New York, NY: Guilford Press.

Cummings, N. A. (2001). 'Interruption, not termination: The model from focused, intermittent psychotherapy throughout the life cycle'. *Journal of Psychotherapy in Independent Practice*, 2 (3), 3–17.

Cutcliffe, J. R. (2004). *The inspiration of hope in bereavement counselling.* London; Philadelphia, PA: J. Kingsley Publishers.

Davis, K. & Taylor, B. (2006). 'Stories of resistance and healing in the process of leaving abusive relationships'. *Contemporary Nurse,* 21 (2), 199–208.

Day, A., Chung, D., O'leary, P., Justo, D., Moore, S., Carson, E. & Gerace, A. (2010). 'Integrated responses to domestic violence: Legally mandated intervention programs for male perpetrators. (cover story)'. *Trends & Issues in Crime & Criminal Justice,* (404), 1–8.

Day, R. (2009). 'Counseling victims of intimate partner violence: Listening to the voices of clients – Excerpts from a qualitative study'. *Trauma Psychology Newsletter* [Online], 4 (Fall 2009), 5–6. Available: http://www.apatraumadivision.org/newsletter/newsletter_2009_fall.pdf [Accessed 13th May 2011].

Day, R. Y. (2008). *Counseling victims of intimate partner violence: Listening to the voices of clients.* PhD thesis. Texas A&M University.

Debbonaire, T. & Panteloudakis, I. (2013). *Respect Toolkit for work with male victims of domestic violence.* 2nd edition. London: Respect.

Del Re, A. C., Flückiger, C., Horvath, A. O., Symonds, D. & Wampold, B. E. (2012). 'Therapist effects in the therapeutic alliance-outcome relationship: A restricted-maximum likelihood meta-analysis'. *Clinical Psychology Review,* 32 (7), 642–649.

Department of Health (2005). *Responding to domestic abuse: A handbook for health professionals.* London: Department of Health.

Department of Health (2011). *No health without mental health: A cross-government mental health outcomes strategy for people of all ages.* London: HM Government.

Dienemann, J., Campbell, J., Landenburger, K. & Curry, M. A. (2002). 'The domestic violence survivor assessment: A tool for counseling women in intimate partner violence relationships'. *Patient Education and Counseling,* 46 (3), 221–228.

Dietz, G. (2011). 'Going back to the source: Why do people trust each other?'. *Journal of Trust Research,* 1 (2), 215–222.

Dobash, R. E. & Dobash, R. P. (1980). *Violence against wives: A case against the patriarchy.* Shepton Mallet: Open Books Publishing Limited.

Domestic Abuse Intervention Programs. (2012). *Home of the Duluth model: Social change to end violence against women* [Online]. Duluth: Domestic Abuse Intervention Programs. Available: http://www.theduluthmodel.org/about/index.html [Accessed 7th September 2012].

Donohoe, G. & Ricketts, T. (2006). 'Anxiety and panic'. In: Feltham, C. & Horton, I. (eds.) *The Sage Handbook of Counselling and Psychotherapy.* 2nd edition. London: Sage Publishing Ltd.

Donovan, C. (2014). 'Living in a homo/bi/transphobic society: Implications for DVA in LGB and/or T relationships'. *The Coral Project: Exploring Abusive Behaviours in LGB and/or T Relationships.* Sunderland: University of Sunderland.

Douglas, E. & Hines, D. (2011). 'The helpseeking experiences of men who sustain intimate partner violence: An overlooked population and implications for practice'. *Journal of Family Violence,* 26 (6), 473–485.

Douglas, E. M., Hines, D. A. & Mccarthy, S. C. (2012). 'Men who sustain female-to-male partner violence: Factors associated with where they seek help and how they rate those resources'. *Violence & Victims,* 27 (6), 871–894.

Duell, M. (2014). ' "No one wanted England to win more than women": How domestic violence rises by a third when England exit World Cup'. *Daily Mail* (London), 27th June 2014.

Duncan, B. L., Miller, S. D., Wampold, B. E. & Hubble, M. A. (2010). *The heart and soul of change: Delivering what works in therapy (2nd ed.)*. Washington, DC: American Psychological Association.

Dutton, D. G. (1995). 'Trauma symptoms and PTSD-like profiles in perpetrators of intimate abuse'. *Journal of Traumatic Stress*, 8 (2), 299–316.

Dutton, D. G. (2006). *Rethinking domestic violence*. Vancouver: UBC Press.

Dutton, D. G. (2012). 'The case against the role of gender in intimate partner violence'. *Aggression and Violent Behavior*, 17 (1), 99–104.

Dutton, M. A. (1992). *Empowering and healing the battered woman: A model for assessment and intervention*. New York: Springer Pub. Co.

Ehrensaft, M. K., Moffitt, T. E. & Caspi, A. (2006). 'Is domestic violence followed by an increased risk of psychiatric disorders among women but not among men? A longitudinal cohort study'. *The American Journal of Psychiatry*, 163 (5), 885–892.

Elliott, M. & Williams, D. (2003). 'The client experience of counselling and psychotherapy'. *Counselling Psychology Review*, 18 (1), 34–38.

Erikson, E. H. (1966). 'Eight ages of man'. *International Journal of Psychiatry*, 2 (3), 281–307.

Etherington, K. (2003). *Trauma, the body and transformation: A narrative inquiry*. London, New York: Jessica Kingsley Publishers.

Etherington, K. & Bridges, N. (2011). 'Narrative case study research: On endings and six session reviews'. *Counselling & Psychotherapy Research*, 11 (1), 11–22.

Eubanks-Carter, C., Muran, J. C. & Safran, J. D. (2010). 'Alliance ruptures and resolution'. In: Muran, J. C. & Barber, J. P. (eds.) *The Therapeutic Alliance: An Evidence-Based Guide to Practice* (pp. 74–94). New York: Guilford Press.

Farmer, K., Morgan, A., Bohne, S., Silva, M. J., Calvaresi, G., Dilba, J., Naloop, R., Ruke, I. & Venelinova, R. (2013). 'Report 1 comparative analysis of perceptions of domestic violence counselling: Counsellors and clients'. *EU Comparative: Counselling Survivors of Domestic Violence*. Wolverhampton: The Haven.

Figley, C. R. (1995). 'Compassion fatigue as secondary traumatic stress disorder: An overview'. In: Figley, C. R. (ed.) *Compassion Fatigue: Coping with Secondary Traumatic Stress Disorder in those Who Treat the Traumatized*. Philadelphia: Brunner/Mazel.

Foa, E. B., Hembree, E. A., Riggs, D., Rauch, S. & Franklin, M. (2001). 'Common reactions to trauma'. *Nursing News*, 25 (4), 6.

Follette, V., Palm, K. M. & Pearson, A. N. (2006). 'Mindfulness and trauma: Implications for treatment'. *Journal of Rational-Emotive & Cognitive-Behavior Therapy*, 24 (1), 45–61.

Follingstad, D. R. (2007). 'Rethinking current approaches to psychological abuse: Conceptual and methodological issues'. *Aggression and Violent Behavior*, 12, 439–458.

Fong, M. L. & Cox, B. G. (1983). 'Trust as an underlying dynamic in the counseling process: How clients test trust'. *Personnel & Guidance Journal*, 62 (3), 163.

Fortune, A. E., Pearlingi, B. & Rochelle, C. D. (1992). 'Reactions to termination of individual treatment'. *Social Work*, 37 (2), 171–178.

Frank, J. D. (1963). *Persuasion and healing*. Oxford: Schocken.

Frank, J. D. & Frank, J. B. (1991). *Persuasion and healing: A comparative study of psychotherapy (3rd ed.)*. Baltimore: Johns Hopkins University Press.

Frost, M. (1999). *Clinical issues in domestic violence*. London: NT Books.

Garfield, R. (2010). 'Male emotional intimacy: How therapeutic men's groups can enhance couples therapy'. *Family Process*, 49 (1), 109–122.

Gilbert, A. R., Morrissey, J. P. & Domino, M. E. (2011). 'Service utilization patterns as predictors of response to trauma-informed integrated treatment for women with co-occurring disorders'. *Journal of Dual Diagnosis*, 7 (3), 117–129.

Gilbert, P. (2005a). 'Compassion and cruelty: A biopsychosocial approach'. In: Gilbert, P. (ed.) *Compassion: Conceptualisations, Research and Use in Psychotherapy* (pp. 9–74). New York, NY: Routledge.

Gilbert, P. (2005b). *Compassion: Conceptualisations, Research and Use in Psychotherapy*. New York, NY: Routledge.

Gilbert, P. (2006). 'Depression'. In: Feltham, C. & Horton, I. (eds.) *The Sage Handbook of Counselling and Psychotherapy* (pp. 389–393). 2nd edition. London: Sage Publications.

Gilbert, P. (2009). 'Introducing compassion-focused therapy'. *Advances in Psychiatric Treatment*, 15 (3), 199–208.

Gilbert, P., Mcewan, K., Matos, M. & Rivis, A. (2011). 'Fears of compassion: Development of three self-report measures'. *Psychology and Psychotherapy*, 84 (3), 239–255.

Glaser, B. G. & Strauss, A. L. (1967). *The discovery of grounded theory: Strategies for qualitative research*. Hawthorne, NY: Aldine de Gruyter.

Golding, J. M. (1999). 'Intimate partner violence as a risk factor for mental disorders: A meta-analysis'. *Journal of Family Violence*, 14 (2), 99–132.

Gormley, B. (2005). 'An adult attachment theoretical perspective of gender symmetry in intimate partner violence'. *Sex Roles*, 52 (11/12), 785–795.

Grealy, C., Humphreys, C., Milward, K. & Power, J. (2008). *Practice guidelines: Women and children's family violence counselling and support program*. Victoria: Children, Youth and Families Division, Victorian Government, 50 Lonsdale Street, Melbourne

Greenley, J. R. & Mechanic, D. (1976). 'Social selection in seeking help for psychological problems'. *Journal of Health & Social Behavior*, 17 (3), 249–262.

Grigsby, N. & Hartman, B. R. (1997). 'The barriers model: An integrated strategy for intervention with battered women'. *Psychotherapy: Theory, Research, Practice, Training*, 34 (4), 485–497.

Grimm, S., Beck, J., Schuepbach, D., Hell, D., Boesiger, P., Bermpohl, F., Niehaus, L., Boeker, H. & Northoff, G. (2008). 'Imbalance between left and right dorsolateral prefrontal cortex in major depression is linked to negative emotional judgment: An fMRI study in severe major depressive disorder'. *Biological Psychiatry*, 63 (4), 369–376.

Hage, S. M. (2006). 'Profiles of women survivors: The development of agency in abusive relationships'. *Journal of Counseling and Development*, 84 (1), 83–94.

Hammer, J. H. & Vogel, D. L. (2013). 'Assessing the utility of the willingness/prototype model in predicting help-seeking decisions'. *Journal of Counseling Psychology*, 60 (1), 83–97.

Hampton-Robb, S., Qualls, R. C. & Compton, W. C. (2003). 'Predicting first-session attendance: The influence of referral source and client income'. *Psychotherapy Research*, 13 (2), 223–233.

Harman, R. & Lee, D. (2010). 'The role of shame and self-critical thinking in the development and maintenance of current threat in post-traumatic stress disorder'. *Clinical Psychology & Psychotherapy*, 17 (1), 13–24.

Hattendorf, J. & Tollerud, T. R. (1997). 'Domestic violence: Counseling strategies that minimize the impact of secondary victimization'. *Perspectives in Psychiatric Care*, 33 (1), 14–23.

Hayes, H. (2011). 'Voluntary sector services'. *Therapy Today*, 22 (8), 39–40.

Hazler, R. J. & Barwick, N. (2001). 'Therapeutic environments: A comparative review'. In: Hazler, R. J. & Barwick, N. (eds.) *The Therapeutic Environment*. Buckingham: Open University Press.

Hegarty, K., Gunn, J., Chondros, P. & Small, R. (2004). 'Association between depression and abuse by partners of women attending general practice: Descriptive, cross sectional survey'. *British Medical Journal (International Edition)*, 328 (7440), 621–624.

Henderson, A. J. Z., Bartholomew, K. & Dutton, D. G. (1997). 'He loves me; He loves me not: Attachment and separation resolution of abused women'. *Journal of Family Violence*, 12 (2), 169–191.

Henderson, A. J. Z., Bartholomew, K., Trinke, S. J. & Kwong, M. J. (2005). 'When loving means hurting: An exploration of attachment and intimate abuse in a community sample'. *Journal of Family Violence*, 20 (4), 219–230.

Henning, K. R. & Klesges, L. M. (2002). 'Utilization of counseling and supportive services by female victims of domestic abuse'. *Violence and Victims*, 17 (5), 623–636.

Heppner, P. P. (1981). 'Counseling men in groups'. *Personnel & Guidance Journal*, 60 (4), 249.

Heppner, P. P. & Petersen, C. H. (1982). 'The development and implications of a personal problem-solving inventory'. *Journal of Counseling Psychology*, 29 (1), 66–75.

Herman, J. L. (1992). *Trauma and recovery*. London: Pandora.

Herman, J. L. (2011). 'Posttraumatic stress disorder as a shame disorder'. In: Dearing, R. L. & Tangney, J. P. (eds.) *Shame in the Therapy Hour*. Washington, DC: American Psychological Association.

Herrington, J. D., Mohanty, A., Koven, N. S., Fisher, J. E., Stewart, J. L., Banich, M. T., Webb, A. G., Miller, G. A. & Heller, W. (2005). 'Emotion-modulated performance and activity in left dorsolateral prefrontal cortex'. *Emotion (Washington, D.C.)*, 5 (2), 200–207.

Hick, K. (2008). *Moving beyond power and control: A qualitative analysis of adult attachment and intimate partner violence*. Thesis. Alliant International University.

Hines, D., Brown, J. & Dunning, E. (2007). 'Characteristics of callers to the domestic abuse helpline for men [corrected] [published erratum appears in J FAM VIOLENCE Nov; 22(8):773]'. *Journal of Family Violence*, 22 (2), 63–72.

Hines, D. A. (2007). 'Posttraumatic stress symptoms among men who sustain partner violence: An international multisite study of university students'. *Psychology of Men & Masculinity*, 8 (4), 225–239.

Hines, D. A. & Douglas, E. M. (2009). 'Women's use of intimate partner violence against men: Prevalence, implications, and consequences'. *Journal of Aggression, Maltreatment & Trauma*, 18 (6), 572–586.

Hines, D. A. & Douglas, E. M. (2010a). 'A closer look at men who sustain intimate terrorism by women'. *Partner Abuse*, 1 (3), 286–312.

Hines, D. A. & Douglas, E. M. (2010b). 'Intimate terrorism by women towards men: Does it exist?' *Journal of Aggression, Conflict and Peace Research*, 2 (3), 36–56.

Hines, D. A. & Douglas, E. M. (2011). 'Symptoms of posttraumatic stress disorder in men who sustain intimate partner violence: A study of helpseeking and community samples'. *Psychology of Men & Masculinity*, 12 (2), 112–127.

Hines, D. A. & Douglas, E. M. (2015). 'Health problems of partner violence victims: Comparing help-seeking men to a population-based sample'. *American Journal of Preventive Medicine*, 48 (2), 136–144.

Hogan, K. F., Hegarty, J. R., Ward, T. & Dodd, L. J. (2012). 'Counsellors' experiences of working with male victims of female-perpetrated domestic abuse'. *Counselling & Psychotherapy Research*, 12 (1), 44–52.

Holly, J. A. (2013). 'Complicated matters: Addressing domestic and sexual violence, mental ill-health and problematic substance abuse'. *Domestic Violence and Mental Health: Empowering Women and Professionals*. University of Turin: Associazione Italiana di Psicologia.

Home Office. (2011). *Call to end violence against women and girls*. London: Cabinet Office,

Home Office. (2012). *New definition of domestic violence* [Online]. Available: http://www.homeoffice.gov.uk/media-centre/news/domestic-violence-definition [Accessed 27th November 2012].

Home Office. (2014). *Government to create new domestic abuse offence* [Online]. London: Home Office. Available: https://www.gov.uk/government/news/government-to-create-new-domestic-abuse-offence [Accessed 4th January 2015].

Howard, A., Riger, S., Campbell, R. & Wasco, S. (2003). 'Counseling services for battered women: A comparison of outcomes for physical and sexual assault survivors'. *Journal of Interpersonal Violence*, 18 (7), 717–734.

Humphreys, C. & Joseph, S. (2004). 'Domestic violence and the politics of trauma'. *Women's Studies International Forum*, 27 (5/6), 559–570.

Humphreys, C. & Thiara, R. (2003). 'Mental health and domestic violence: "I call it symptoms of abuse"'. *British Journal of Social Work*, 33 (2), 209–226.

Iliffe, G. & Steed, L. G. (2000). 'Exploring the counselor's experience of working with perpetrators and survivors of domestic violence'. *Journal of Interpersonal Violence*, 15 (4), 393–412.

Institute for Small Business and Entrepreneurship. (2014). *Women's Enterprise – Some facts and figures* [Online]. London: ISBE Registered Charity. Available: http://www.isbe.org.uk/facts [Accessed 17th June 2014].

Johnson, H. (1996). *Dangerous domains: Violence against women in Canada*. Scarborough, Ontario: International Thomas Publishing.

Johnson, M. P. (2011). 'Gender and types of intimate partner violence: A response to an anti-feminist literature review'. *Aggression and Violent Behavior*, 16 (4), 289–296.

Johnson, M. P. & Ferraro, K. J. (2000). 'Research on domestic violence in the 1990s: Making distinctions'. *Journal of Marriage & Family*, 62 (4), 948–963.

Jones, C. (2011). 'Domestic violence is not a specialism'. *Therapy Today*, 22 (8), 38–39.

Judd, F., Komiti, A. & Jackson, H. (2008). 'How does being female assist help-seeking for mental health problems?' *Australian & New Zealand Journal of Psychiatry*, 42 (1), 24–29.

Kahn, M. (1996). *Between therapist and client: The new relationship*. New York: Holt & Co.

Kamimura, A., Parekh, A. & Olson, L. M. (2013). 'Health indicators, social support, and intimate partner violence among women utilizing services at a community organization'. *Women's Health Issues*, 23 (3), e179–e185.

Keeling, J. & Van Wormer, K. (2012). 'Social worker interventions in situations of domestic violence: What we can learn from survivors' personal narratives?' *British Journal of Social Work*, 42 (7), 1354–1370.

Keller, S. M., Zoellner, L. A. & Feeny, N. C. (2010). 'Understanding factors associated with early therapeutic alliance in PTSD treatment: Adherence, childhood sexual abuse history, and social support'. *Journal of Consulting and Clinical Psychology*, 78 (6), 974–979.

Kepner, J. I. (1996). *Healing tasks psychotherapy with adult survivors of childhood abuse*. New York: Routledge.

Kessler, R. C., Brown, R. L. & Broman, C. L. (1981). 'Sex differences in psychiatric help-seeking: Evidence from four large-scale surveys'. *Journal of Health & Social Behavior*, 22 (1), 49–64.

Kirouac, S. & Mcbride, D. L. (2009). 'The impact of childhood trauma on brain development: A literature review and supporting handouts'. Available: http://www.eric.ed.gov/contentdelivery/servlet/ERICServlet?accno=ED512316 [Accessed 3rd June 2013].

Knight, C. C. (2012). 'Therapeutic use of self: Theoretical and evidence-based considerations for clinical practice and supervision'. *Clinical Supervisor*, 31 (1), 1–24.

Knox, S., Adrians, N., Everson, E., Hess, S., Hill, C. & Crook-Lyon, R. (2011). 'Clients' perspectives on therapy termination'. *Psychotherapy Research*, 21 (2), 154–167.

Krause, E. D., Kaltman, S., Goodman, L. A. & Dutton, M. A. (2008). 'Avoidant coping and PTSD symptoms related to domestic violence exposure: A longitudinal study'. *Journal of Traumatic Stress*, 21 (1), 83–90.

Kubany, E. S., Hill, E. E., Owens, J. A., Iannce-Spencer, C., Mccaig, M. A., Tremayne, K. J. & Williams, P. L. (2004). 'Cognitive trauma therapy for battered women with PTSD (CTT-BW)'. *Journal of Consulting and Clinical Psychology*, 72 (1), 3–18.

Lambert, M. J., Okiishi, J. C., Finch, A. E. & Johnson, L. D. (1998). 'Outcome assessment: From conceptualization to implementation'. *Professional Psychology: Research and Practice*, 29 (1), 63–70.

Lambert, P. (2007). 'Client perspectives on counselling: Before, during and after'. *Counselling & Psychotherapy Research*, 7 (2), 106–113.

Langhinrichsen-Rohling, J. (2010). 'Controversies involving gender and intimate partner violence in the United States'. *Sex Roles*, 62 (3/4), 179–193.

Larsen, D., Edey, W. & Lemay, L. (2007). 'Understanding the role of hope in counselling: Exploring the intentional uses of hope'. *Counselling Psychology Quarterly*, 20 (4), 401–416.

Larsen, D. J. & Stege, R. (2010). 'Hope-focused practices during early psychotherapy sessions: Part I: Implicit approaches'. *Journal of Psychotherapy Integration*, 20 (3), 271–292.

Larsen, D. J. & Stege, R. (2012). 'Client accounts of hope in early counseling sessions: A qualitative study'. *Journal of Counseling & Development*, 90 (1), 45–54.

Laska, K. M., Gurman, A. S. & Wampold, B. E. (2014). 'Expanding the lens of evidence-based practice in psychotherapy: A common factors perspective'. *Psychotherapy*, 51 (4), 467–481.

Lee, D. Y., Uhlemann, M. R. & Haase, R. F. (1985). 'Counselor verbal and nonverbal responses and perceived expertness, trustworthiness, and attractiveness'. *Journal of Counseling Psychology*, 32 (2), 181–187.

Lee, M.-Y. (2007). 'Discovering strengths and competencies in female domestic violence survivors: An application of Roberts' Continuum of the Duration and Severity of Woman Battering'. *Brief Treatment and Crisis Intervention*, 7 (2), 102–114.

Leiter, M. P. & Maslach, C. (2009). 'Nurse turnover: The mediating role of burnout'. *Journal of Nursing Management*, 17 (3), 331–339.

Levitt, H., Butler, M. & Hill, T. (2006). 'What clients find helpful in psychotherapy: Developing principles for facilitating moment-to-moment change'. *Journal of Counseling Psychology*, 53 (3), 314–324.

Lloyd, S. (1998). 'What happens now? Issues of good practice in working with domestic abuse'. In: Bear, Z. (ed.) *Good Practice in Counselling People Who Have Been Abused*. London: Jessica Kingsley Publishers.

Lombard, N. (2013). ' "What about the men?" Understanding men's experiences of domestic abuse within a gender-based model of violence'. In: Lombard, N. & Mcmillan, L. (eds.) *Violence Against Women* (pp. 177–193). London: Jessica Kingsley.

Lutz, A., Brefczynski-Lewis, J., Johnstone, T. & Davidson, R. J. (2008). 'Regulation of the neural circuitry of emotion by compassion meditation: Effects of meditative expertise'. *Plos One*, 3 (3), e1897–e1897.

Main, M. & Solomon, J. (1986). 'Discovery of an insecure-disorganized/disoriented attachment pattern'. In: Brazelton, T. B. & Yogman, M. W. (eds.) *Affective Development in Infancy* (pp. 95–124). Westport, CT: Ablex Publishing.

Manthei, R. J. (2007). 'Clients talk about their experience of the process of counselling'. *Counselling Psychology Quarterly*, 20 (1), 1–26.

Martin, D. J., Garske, J. P. & Davis, M. K. (2000). 'Relation of the therapeutic alliance with outcome and other variables: A meta-analytic review'. *Journal of Consulting and Clinical Psychology*, 68 (3), 438–450.

Marzillier, J. (2014). *The trauma therapies*. Oxford: Oxford University Press.

Matlow, R. B. & Deprince, A. P. (2012). 'The influence of victimization history on PTSD symptom expression in women exposed to intimate partner violence'. *Psychological Trauma: Theory, Research, Practice, and Policy*, 5 (3), 241–250.

Matsakis, A. (2001). 'The impact of the abuse of males on intimate relationships'. In: Brothers, B. J. (ed.) *The Abuse of Men: Trauma Begets Trauma*. New York: The Haworth Press, Inc.

Mayer, R. C., Davis, J. H. & Schoorman, F. D. (1995). 'An integrative model of organizational trust'. *Academy of Management Review*, 20 (3), 709–734.

Mccann, I. L. & Pearlman, L. A. (1990). 'Vicarious traumatization: A framework for understanding the psychological effects of working with victims'. *Journal of Traumatic Stress*, 3 (1), 131–149.

Mclaughlin, J., O'carroll, R. E. & O'connor, R. C. (2012). 'Intimate partner abuse and suicidality: A systematic review'. *Clinical Psychology Review*, 32 (8), 677–689.

Mcleod, A. L., Hays, D. G. & Chang, C. Y. (2010). 'Female intimate partner violence survivors' experiences with accessing resources'. *Journal of Counseling & Development*, 88 (3), 303–310.

Mcleod, J. (2003). *An introduction to counselling*. Buckingham: Open University Press.

Mcleod, J. (2009). *An introduction to counselling*. London: Open University Press.

Mcnamara, J. R., Tamanini, K. & Pelletier-Walker, S. (2008). 'The impact of short-term counseling at a domestic violence shelter'. *Research on Social Work Practice*, 18 (2), 132–136.

Mearns, D. & Cooper, M. (2005). *Working at relational depth in counselling and psychotherapy*. London; Thousand Oaks: SAGE.

Mearns, D. & Thorne, B. (1999). *Person-centred counselling in action*. London: Sage.

Menninger, K. (1959). 'The academic lecture: Hope'. *The American Journal of Psychiatry*, 116, 481–491.

Mertin, P. & Mohr, P. B. (2001). 'A follow-up study of posttraumatic stress disorder, anxiety, and depression in Australian victims of domestic violence'. *Violence and Victims*, 16 (6), 645–654.

Messer, S. B. & Wolitzky, D. L. (2010). 'A psychodynamic perspective on the therapeutic alliance: Theory, research, and practice'. In: Muran, J. C. & Barber, J. P. (eds.) *The Therapeutic Alliance: An Evidence-Based Guide to Practice* (pp. 97–122). New York, NY: Guilford Press.

Migliaccio, T. A. (2002). 'Abused husbands: A narrative analysis'. *Journal of Family Issues*, 23 (1), 26–52.

Moe, A. M. (2007). 'Silenced voices and structured survival: Battered women's help seeking'. *Violence Against Women*, 13 (7), 676–699.

Morgan, D. R. (1998). *Domestic violence: A health care issue?* London: British Medical Association.

Morgan, K. & Björkert, S. T. (2006). ' "I'd rather you'd lay me on the floor and start kicking me": Understanding symbolic violence in everyday life'. *Women's Studies International Forum*, 29 (5), 441–452.

Morrell, J. S. & Rubin, L. J. (2001). 'The Minnesota Multiphasic Personality Inventory-2, posttraumatic stress disorder, and women domestic violence survivors'. *Professional Psychology: Research and Practice*, 32 (2), 151–156.

Morrison, A. (2014). *Domestic violence: One month's death toll* [Online]. London: British Broadcasting Corporation. Available: http://www.bbc.co.uk/news/uk-22610534 [Accessed 3rd February 2015].

Morrissey, J. P., Jackson, E. W., Ellis, A. R., Amaro, H., Brown, V. B. & Najavits, L. M. (2005). 'Twelve-month outcomes of trauma-informed interventions for women with co-occurring disorders'. *Psychiatric Services*, 56 (10), 1213–1222.

Muller, R. T. (2009). 'Trauma and dismissing (avoidant) attachment: Intervention strategies in individual psychotherapy'. *Psychotherapy: Theory, Research, Practice, Training*, 46 (1), 68–81.

Muran, J. C., Safran, J. D. & Eubanks-Carter, C. (2010). 'Developing therapist abilities to negotiate alliance ruptures'. In: Muran, J. C. & Barber, J. P. (eds.) *The Therapeutic Alliance: An Evidence-Based Guide to Practice*. New York, NY: Guilford Press.

National Collaborating Centre for Mental Health (2005). *Post-traumatic stress disorder The management of PTSD in adults and children in primary and secondary care*. London: Gaskell and the British Psychological Society.

National Collaborating Centre for Mental Health (2009). *Depression The Treatment and Management of Depression in Adults (Updated Edition) National Clinical Practice Guideline 90*. London: The British Psychological Society and The Royal College of Psychiatrists.

National Institute for Health and Clinical Excellence. (2014). 'PH50 Domestic violence and abuse – how services can respond effectively: Supporting evidence'. Available: http://guidance.nice.org.uk/PH50/SupportingEvidence [Accessed 28th February 2014].

Neff, K. D. (2003). 'The development and validation of a scale to measure self-compassion'. *Self and Identity*, 2 (3), 223–250.

Neff, K. D. (2009). *Test how self-compassionate you are* [Online]. Austin: Self compassion, Kristin Neff. Available: http://www.self-compassion.org/test-your-self-compassion-level.html [Accessed 18th January 2015].

Neff, K. D. & Vonk, R. (2009). 'Self-compassion versus global self-esteem: Two different ways of relating to oneself'. *Journal of Personality*, 77 (1), 23–50.

Nicholson, R. A. & Berman, J. S. (1983). 'Is follow-up necessary in evaluating psychotherapy?' *Psychological Bulletin*, 93 (2), 261–278.

Nicolson, P. (2010). *Domestic violence and psychology: A critical perspective*. London, New York: Routledge.

Nixon, R. D. V., Resick, P. A. & Nishith, P. (2004). 'An exploration of comorbid depression among female victims of intimate partner violence with posttraumatic stress disorder'. *Journal of Affective Disorders*, 82 (2), 315–320.

Norwood, A. & Murphy, C. (2012). 'What forms of abuse correlate with PTSD symptoms in partners of men being treated for intimate partner violence?' *Psychological Trauma: Theory, Research, Practice, and Policy*, 4 (6), 596–604.

OECD (2011). *OECD factbook 2011–2012: Economic, environmental and social statistics*. Paris: OECD Publishing.

O'Hara, D. J. (2011). 'Psychotherapy and the dialectics of hope and despair'. *Counselling Psychology Quarterly*, 24 (4), 323–329.

O'Hara, D. J. & O'Hara, E. F. (2012). 'Towards a grounded theory of therapist hope'. *Counselling Psychology Review*, 27 (4), 42–55.

O'Neil, J. M. (2008). 'Summarizing 25 years of research on men's gender role conflict using the gender role conflict scale: New research paradigms and clinical implications'. *The Counseling Psychologist*, 36 (3), 358–445.

Oswald, R. F., Fonseca, C. A. & Hardesty, J. L. (2010). 'Lesbian mothers' counseling experiences in the context of intimate partner violence'. *Psychology of Women Quarterly*, 34 (3), 286–296.

Overstreet, N. M. & Quinn, D. M. (2013). 'The intimate partner violence stigmatization model and barriers to help seeking'. *Basic & Applied Social Psychology*, 35 (1), 109–122.

Oxforddictionaries.Com. (2012). *Hope* [Online]. Oxford: Oxford University Press. Available: http://oxforddictionaries.com/definition/hope [Accessed 23rd May 2012].

Paivio, S. C. & Patterson, L. A. (1999). 'Alliance development in therapy for resolving child abuse issues'. *Psychotherapy*, 36, 343–354.

Paulson, B. L., Everall, R. D. & Stuart, J. (2001). 'Client perceptions of hindering experiences in counselling'. *Counselling & Psychotherapy Research*, 1 (1), 53–61.

Paulson, B. L., Truscott, D. & Stuart, J. (1999). 'Clients' perceptions of helpful experiences in counseling'. *Journal of Counseling Psychology*, 46 (3), 317–324.

Payne, A., Liebling-Kalifani, H. & Joseph, S. (2007). 'Client-centred group therapy for survivors of interpersonal trauma: A pilot investigation'. *Counselling & Psychotherapy Research*, 7 (2), 100–105.

Pence, E. & Paymar, M. (1993). *Education groups for men who batter: The Duluth model*. New York, NY: Springer Publishing Co.

Pico-Alfonso, M. A., Garcia-Linares, M. I., Celda-Navarro, N., Blasco-Ros, C., Echeburúa, E. & Martinez, M. (2006). 'The impact of physical, psychological, and sexual intimate male partner violence on women's mental health: Depressive symptoms, posttraumatic stress disorder, state anxiety, and suicide'. *Journal of Women's Health (15409996)*, 15 (5), 599–611.

Pidd, H. (2013). Christmas spike in domestic violence keeps courts busy on New Year's Eve. *The Guardian* (London).

Quintana, J. G. (1974). 'Counseling center receptionist: Where client contact begins'. *Journal of College Student Personnel*, 15 (6), 439–441.

Ramsay, J., Rivas, C. & Feder, G. (2005). *Interventions to reduce violence and promote the physical and psychosocial well-being of women who experience partner violence: A systematic review of controlled evaluations*. London: Queen Mary's School of Medicine and Dentistry.

Reed, G. L. & Enright, R. D. (2006). 'The effects of forgiveness therapy on depression, anxiety, and posttraumatic stress for women after spousal emotional abuse'. *Journal of Consulting and Clinical Psychology*, 74 (5), 920–929.

Reeves, A. (2012). 'Working with suicide and self-harm in counselling and psychotherapy'. In: Feltham, C. & Horton, I. (eds.) *The Sage Handbook of Counselling and Psychotherapy*. 3rd edition. London: Sage Publications Ltd.

Reid, R. J., Bonomi, A. E., Rivara, F. P., Anderson, M. L., Fishman, P. A., Carrell, D. S. & Thompson, R. S. (2008). 'Intimate partner violence among men. Prevalence, chronicity, and health effects'. *American Journal of Preventive Medicine*, 34 (6), 478–485.

Rennie, D. L. (2001). 'The client as a self-aware agent in counselling and psychotherapy'. *Counselling & Psychotherapy Research*, 1 (2), 82–89.

Rennie, D. L. (2011). *RE: Discussion at BACP Annual Research Conference during the poster presentation*. 6th May 2011. Liverpool.

Ricard, M., Kerzin, B. & Hangartner, D. (2011). 'Cultivating compassion from a Buddhist perspective'. *How to Train Compassion Conference*. Max-Planck Institute, Berlin.

Richards, C. (2011). 'Alliance ruptures: Etiology and resolution'. *Counselling Psychology Review*, 26 (3), 56–62.

Roddy, J. (2011a). 'From trainee to specialist: Learning about domestic violence counselling'. *Therapy Today*, 22 (6), 16–19.

Roddy, J. (2011b). 'Stories of domestic violence counselling: The importance of understanding'. *Value and Virtue in Practice-Based Research Conference*. York: York St. John University.

Roddy, J. (2011c). 'Working ethically and the impact on research design'. *Research Methodologies Conference*. York: York St. John University.

Roddy, J. (2012). 'Hope, belief and compassion: Values for the therapist, researcher and client'. *2012 Value and Virtue in Practice-Based Research Conference*. York St. John University.

Roddy, J. (2013). 'Client perspectives: The therapeutic challenge of domestic violence counselling – A pilot study'. *Counselling & Psychotherapy Research*, 13 (1) (1), 53–60.

Roddy, J. (2014). *A client informed view of domestic violence counselling*. PhD thesis. University of Leeds.

Rogers, C. R. (1957). 'The necessary and sufficient conditions of therapeutic personality change'. *Journal of Consulting Psychology*, 21 (2), 95–103.

Rogers, C. R. (1958). 'The characteristics of a helping relationship'. *Personnel & Guidance Journal*, 37 (1), 6–16.

Rogers, C. R. (1959). 'The theory of therapy, personality, and interpersonal relationships, as developed in the client-centred framework'. In: Koch, S. (ed.) *Psychology: A Study of a Science*. New York: McGraw-Hill.

Rogers, C. R. (1964). 'Toward a modern approach to values: The valuing process in the mature person'. *Journal of Abnormal & Social Psychology*, 68 (2), 160–167.

Rogers, E. S., Chamberlin, J., Ellison, M. L. & Crean, T. (1997). 'A consumer-constructed scale to measure empowerment among users of mental health services'. *Psychiatric Services*, 48 (8), 1042–1047.

Romito, P., Turan, J. M. & De Marchi, M. (2005). 'The impact of current and past interpersonal violence on women's mental health'. *Social Science & Medicine*, 60 (8), 1717–1727.

Rose, D., Trevillion, K., Woodall, A., Morgan, C., Feder, G. & Howard, L. (2011). 'Barriers and facilitators of disclosures of domestic violence by mental health service users: Qualitative study'. *The British Journal of Psychiatry*, 198 (3), 189–194.

Rosenberg, M., Schooler, C. & Schoenbach, C. (1989). 'Self-esteem and adolescent problems: Modeling reciprocal effects'. *American Sociological Review*, 54 (6), 1004–1018.

Ross, J. M. & Babcock, J. C. (2009). 'Gender differences in partner violence in context: Deconstructing Johnson's (2001) control-based typology of violent couples'. *Journal of Aggression, Maltreatment & Trauma*, 18 (6), 604–622.

Rothmeier, R. C. & Dixon, D. N. (1980). 'Trustworthiness and influence: A reexamination in an extended counseling analogue'. *Journal of Counseling Psychology*, 27 (4), 315–319.

Rothschild, B. (2000). *The body remembers: The psychophysiology of trauma and trauma treatment/Babette Rothschild*. New York, NY; London: Norton, 2000.

Royle, E. & Kerr, C. 7th June 2013 (2013). *RE: Counselling Masterclass Series: EMDR*. 7th June 2013. York.

Rushlow, L. (2009). *Childhood history of abuse association with adult interpersonal violence victimization*. Thesis. Adler School of Professional Psychology.

Sanderson, C. (2008). *Counselling survivors of domestic abuse*. London, Philadelphia: Jessica Kingsley.

Saypol, E. & Farber, B. A. (2010). 'Attachment style and patient disclosure in psychotherapy'. *Psychotherapy Research*, 20 (4), 462–471.

Scheffer Lindgren, M. & Renck, B. (2008). ' "It is still so deep-seated, the fear": Psychological stress reactions as consequences of intimate partner violence'. *Journal of Psychiatric & Mental Health Nursing*, 15 (3), 219–228.

Scheier, M. F. & Carver, C. S. (1985). 'Optimism, coping, and health: Assessment and implications of generalized outcome expectancies'. *Health Psychology*, 4 (3), 219–247.

Schoorman, F. D., Mayer, R. C. & Davis, J. H. (2007). 'An integrative model of organizational trust: Past, present, and future'. *Academy of Management Review*, 32 (2), 344–354.

Schwecke, L. H. (2009). 'Guest editorial: Childhood sexual abuse, PTSD, and borderline personality disorder: Understanding the connections'. *Journal of Psychosocial Nursing & Mental Health Services*, 47 (7), 4–6.

Scowcroft, E. (2014). *Samaritans suicide statistics report 2014: Including data from 2010–2012*. Ewell, Surrey: Samaritans.

Seedat, S., Stein, M. B. & Forde, D. R. (2005). 'Association between physical partner violence, posttraumatic stress, childhood trauma, and suicide attempts in a community sample of women'. *Violence & Victims*, 20 (1), 87–98.

Seeley, J. & Plunkett, C. (2002). *Women and domestic violence: Standards for counselling practice*. St. Kilda, Victoria, Australia: The Salvation Army Crisis Service.

Seligman, M. E. P. (1975). *Helplessness: On depression, development, and death*. New York, NY: W.H. Freeman/Times Books/Henry Holt & Co.

Sexton, L. (1999). 'Vicarious traumatisation of counsellors and effects on their workplaces'. *British Journal of Guidance & Counselling*, 27 (3), 393–403.

Siegel, R. D. & Germer, C. K. (2012). 'Wisdom and compassion: Two wings of a bird'. In: Germer, C. K. & Siegel, R. D. (eds.) *Wisdom and Compassion in Psychotherapy: Deepening Mindfulness in Clinical Practice* (pp. 7–34). New York: The Guilford Press.

Smith, K., Osborne, S., Lau, I. & Britton, A. (2012). *Homicides, firearm offences and intimate violence 2010/11: Supplementary volume 2 to crime in England and wales 2010/11*. London: Home Office

Snyder, C. R. (1994). *The psychology of hope: You can get there from here*. New York, NY: Free Press.

Snyder, C. R. (1995). 'Conceptualizing, measuring, and nurturing hope'. *Journal of Counseling & Development*, 73 (3), 355–360

Snyder, C. R., Harris, C., Anderson, J. R., Holleran, S. A., Irving, L. M., Sigmon, S. T., Yoshinobu, L., Gibb, J., Langelle, C. & Harney, P. (1991). 'The will and the ways: Development and validation of an individual-differences measure of hope'. *Journal of Personality and Social Psychology*, 60 (4), 570–585.

Snyder, C. R. & Lopez, S. J. (eds.) (2005). *Handbook of positive psychology*, New York; Oxford: Oxford University Press.

Snyder, C. R., Michael, S. T. & Cheavens, J. S. (1999). 'Hope as a psychotherapeutic foundation of common factors, placebos, and expectancies'. In: Hubble, M. A., Duncan, B. L. & Miller, S. D. (eds.) *The Heart and Soul of Change: What Works in Therapy* (pp. 179–200). Washington, DC: American Psychological Association.

Social Policy & Research Team (2009). *Moving forward women's journeys after leaving an abusive relationship*. Paddington, NSW: The Benevolent Society.

Sohal, A., Feder, G. & Johnson, M. (2012). 'Domestic Violence and Abuse'. *InnovAiT: The RCGP Journal for Associates in Training* [Online], 2012 (5), 750–756. Available: http://ino.sagepub.com/content/5/12/750 [Accessed 18th February 2013].

Stanley, N. & Humphreys, C. (2014). 'Multi-agency risk assessment and management for children and families experiencing domestic violence'. *Children and Youth Services Review*, 47 (Part 1), 78–85.

Stenius, V. M. K. & Veysey, B. M. (2005). ' "It's the little things": Women, trauma, and strategies for healing'. *Journal of Interpersonal Violence*, 20 (10), 1155–1174.

Stewart, R. M. & Jessell, J. C. (1986). 'Written versus videotaped precounseling training of clients for counseling'. *Counselor Education and Supervision*, 25 (3), 197–209.

Stiles, W. B. (2006). 'The client-therapist relationship'. In: Feltham, C. & Horton, I. (eds.) *The Sage Handbook of Counselling and Psychotherapy* (pp. 64–72). 2nd edition. London: Sage Publications.

Stiles, W. B. & Goldsmith, J. Z. (2010). 'The alliance over time'. In: Muran, J. C. & Barber, J. P. (eds.) *The therapeutic alliance: An evidence-based guide to practice* (pp. 44–62). New York, NY: Guilford Press.

Stith, S. M., Mccollum, E. E., Amanor-Boadu, Y. & Smith, D. (2012). 'Systemic perspectives on intimate partner violence treatment'. *Journal of Marital & Family Therapy*, 38 (1), 220–240.

Stotland, E. (1969). *The psychology of hope.* San Francisco: Jossey-Bass.

Straus, M. A. (2007). 'Processes explaining the concealment and distortion of evidence on gender symmetry in partner violence'. *European Journal on Criminal Policy & Research*, 13 (3/4), 227–232.

Straus, M. A. (2009). 'Why the overwhelming evidence on partner physical violence by women has not been perceived and is often denied'. *Journal of Aggression, Maltreatment & Trauma*, 18 (6), 552–571.

Straus, M. A., Gelles, R. J. & Steinmetz, S. K. (1980). *Behind closed doors: Violence in the American family*, Garden City, N.Y.: Anchor Press/Doubleday.

Straus, M. A., Hamby, S. L., Boney-Mccoy, S. & Sugarman, D. B. (1996). 'The revised conflict tactics scales (CTS2): Development and preliminary psychometric data'. *Journal of Family Issues*, 17 (3), 283–316.

Strauss, B. M., Mestel, R. & Kirchmann, H. A. (2011). 'Changes of attachment status among women with personality disorders undergoing inpatient treatment'. *Counselling & Psychotherapy Research*, 11 (4), 275–283.

Strong, S. R. (1968). 'Counseling: An interpersonal influence process'. *Journal of Counseling Psychology*, 15 (3), 215–224.

Sweet, D. (2010). *Towards gender equality: Exploratory evidence of the attitudes towards and the needs of male victims of domestic violence and abuse in Northern Ireland with recommendations for change.* Belfast: Mens Advisory Project.

Syme, G. (2012). 'Beareavement'. In: Feltham, C. & Horton, I. (eds.) *The SAGE Handbook of Counselling and Psychotherapy.* London: Sage Publications Ltd.

Tangney, J. P. & Dearing, R. L. (2011). 'Working with shame in the therapy hour: Summary and integration'. In: Tangney, J. P. & Dearing, R. L. (eds.) *Shame in the Therapy Hour* (pp. 375–404). Washington, DC: American Psychological Association.

Taskforce on the Health Aspects of Violence against Women and Children (2010). *Responding to violence against women and children – The role of the NHS: The report of the taskforce on the health aspects of violence against women and children*. London: Department of Health,

Tedeschi, R. G. & Calhoun, L. G. (1996). 'The posttraumatic growth inventory: Measuring the positive legacy of trauma'. *Journal of Traumatic Stress*, 9 (3), 455–471.

Torres, A., Garcia-Esteve, L., Navarro, P., Tarragona, M. J., Imaz, M. L., Gutiérrez, F., Santos, C., Ascaso, C., Martin-Santos, R. & Subirà, S. (2010). 'Women's mental health: P02–397 – Personality profile or postraumatic stress disorder? personality characteristics in women victim of chronic intimate partner violence'. *European Psychiatry*, 25 (Supplement 1), 1413.

Trevillion, K., Oram, S., Feder, G. & Howard, L. M. (2012). 'Experiences of domestic violence and mental disorders: A systematic review and meta-analysis'. *Plos One*, 7 (12), e51740.

Vivian, D. & Langhinrichsen-Rohling, J. (1994). 'Are bi-directionally violent couples mutually victimised? A gender-sensitive comparison'. *Violence & Victims*, 9 (2), 107–124.

Vivino, B. L., Thompson, B. J., Hill, C. E. & Ladany, N. (2009). 'Compassion in psychotherapy: The perspective of therapists nominated as compassionate'. *Psychotherapy Research*, 19 (2), 157–171.

Vogel, D. L., Wester, S. R. & Larson, L. M. (2007). 'Avoidance of counseling: Psychological factors that inhibit seeking help'. *Journal of Counseling & Development*, 85 (4), 410–422.

Walby, S. (2004). *The cost of domestic violence*. London: Department of Trade and Industry.

Walby, S. (2009). 'Cost of domestic violence: Up-date 2009'. *Project of the UNESCO Chair in Gender Research*, Lancaster University [Online]. Available: http://webcache.googleusercontent.com/search?q=cache:http://www.lancaster.ac.uk/fass/doc_library/sociology/Cost_of_domestic_violence_update.doc [Accessed 13th December 2013].

Walker, L. E. (1977). 'Battered women and learned helplessness'. *Victimology*, 2 (3–4), 525–534.

Walker, L. E. (1979). *The battered woman*. New York: Harper & Row.

Walker, L. E. (1994). *Abused women and survivor therapy: A practical guide for the psychotherapist*. Washington, DC: American Psychological Association.

Walker, L. E. (2000). *The battered woman syndrome*. New York: Springer Publishing.

Walker, L. E. A. (2009). *The battered woman syndrome*. New York, NY: Springer Publishing Co.

Wampold, B. E. (2011). 'Qualities and actions of effective therapists'. *Continuing Education in Psychology* [Online], 1–7. Available: http://www.apa.org/education/ce/effective-therapists.pdf [Accessed 17th January 2015].

Wang, S. (2005). 'A conceptual framework for integrating research related to the physiology of compassion and the wisdom of Buddhist teachings'. In: Gilbert, P. (ed.) *Compassion: Conceptualisations, Research and Use in Psychotherapy* (pp. 75–120). New York, NY: Routledge.

Wathan, C. N. & Macmillan, H. L. (2003). 'Interventions for violence against women scientific review'. *Journal of the American Medical Association*, 289 (5), 589–600.

Watson, J. C. & Kalogerakos, F. (2010). 'The therapeutic alliance in humanistic psychotherapy'. In: Muran, J. C. & Barber, J. P. (eds.) *The Therapeutic Alliance: An Evidence-Based Buide to Practice* (pp. 191–209). New York, NY: Guilford Press.

Webster, W. T. (2015). *Taking Lives – Liability for Suicide* [Online]. London: Refuge. Available: http://www.refuge.org.uk/what-we-do/campaigns/takinglives/ [Accessed 2nd January 2015].

Williams, S. L. & Mickelson, K. D. (2008). 'A paradox of support seeking and rejection among the stigmatized'. *Personal Relationships*, 15 (4), 493–509.

Wilson, J. P., Droždek, B. & Turkovic, S. (2006). 'Posttraumatic shame and guilt'. *Trauma, Violence, & Abuse*, 7 (2), 122–141.

Winnicott, D. W. (1953). 'Transitional objects and transitional phenomena; A study of the first not-me possession'. *The International Journal of Psychoanalysis*, 34, 89–97.

Women's Aid. (2007). *Statistics: Domestic Violence* [Online]. Women's Aid. Available: http://www.womensaid.org.uk/core/core_picker/download.asp?id=1636 [Accessed 6th January 2011].

Women's Aid. (2015). *Why doesn't she leave?* [Online]. Bristol: Women's Aid. [Accessed 10th February 2015].

Woods, S. J. (2000). 'Prevalence and patterns of posttraumatic stress disorder in abused and postabused women'. *Issues in Mental Health Nursing*, 21 (3), 309–324.

Wyllie, C., Platt, S., Browlie, J., Chandler, A., Connolly, S., Evans, R., Kennelly, B., Kirtley, O., Moore, G., O'Connor, R. & Scourfield, J. (2012). *Men, suicide and society: Why disadvantaged men in mid-life die from suicide*. Ewell, Surry: Samaritans.

Yalom, I. D. & Leszcz, M. (2005). *The theory and practice of group psychotherapy/Irvin D. Yalom with Molyn Leszcz*. New York: Basic Books.

Index

Lightning Source UK Ltd.
Milton Keynes UK
UKHW021900271021
392944UK00009B/76